STRATEGIC INTERVIEWING

Skills and Tactics
for Savvy Executives

JOAN C. CURTIS

QUORUM BOOKS
Westport, Connecticut • London

Library of Congress Cataloging-in-Publication Data

Curtis, Joan C., 1950–
    Strategic interviewing : skills and tactics for savvy executives / Joan C. Curtis.
      p.   cm.
    Includes bibliographical references and index.
    ISBN 1–56720–358–2 (alk. paper)
    1. Employment interviewing.   I. Title: Skills and tactics for savvy executives.
II. Title.
    HF5549.5.I6 C867   2000
    658.3'1124—dc21   99–462241

British Library Cataloguing in Publication Data is available.

Library of Congress Catalog Card Number: 99–462241
ISBN: 1–56720–358–2

First published in 2000

Quorum Books, 88 Post Road West, Westport, CT 06881
An imprint of Greenwood Publishing Group, Inc.
www.quorumbooks.com

Printed in the United States of America

The paper used in this book complies with the
Permanent Paper Standard issued by the National
Information Standards Organization (Z39.48–1984).

10 9 8 7 6 5 4 3 2 1

Contents

Acknowledgments

My thanks go to my husband who diligently read each chapter and the revisions. As a psychiatrist, he added important insights, particularly to Chapter 14.

I particularly thank the many people who attended my seminars. Their comments and experiences inspired many of the practical examples that appear in this book.

1

Introduction

WHY READ THIS BOOK?

Recent data from the Bureau of Labor Statistics report over 39,000,000 people working in managerial and professional jobs. Most of these people face hiring decisions multiple times in their careers. Usually these people face these decisions with the aid of the human resources manager in the organization. Human resources managers struggle to discover that magic formula that brings the right people into the organization. Bradford Smart tells us that major corporations estimate the cost for mistaken hires as two to four times the person's salary. He says these mistakes lead to an annual cost of $100 billion.[1] If cost isn't enough incentive to put more energy into hiring, think of the anguish to the individuals as well as the havoc poor hiring makes on company morale. The responsibility to hire falls on the human resources manager. Even when your boss and his or her boss make that final decision, if someone doesn't work out, you bear the burden. Conversely, hiring successes give you feathers in your cap. Your goal is to help managers understand the importance of making quality decisions while at the same time implementing interviewing processes that make those decisions possible.

Hiring in today's world poses even more difficulties than perhaps ten years ago. Companies fear providing reference information that might damage a person's character or chances for getting another job due to the possibility of legal action. References are almost becoming a luxury of the past. Ten years ago human resources managers picked up the telephone, talked to other managers, and learned more about a person's ability to do the job. References gave all sorts of information regarding reliability, likelihood for promotion, initiative, and rehire potential. Today when human resource managers call former bosses or companies, they learn the dates of an individual's employment and nothing more. That crucial question we might have asked ten years ago—"Would you recommend this person for rehire?"—no longer gets answered. Losing reference information places the interview in a more powerful position than ever before as far as hiring is concerned.

You, as human resource managers, know the challenges of interviewing. In your job, you face pressure from the top to hire the best possible candidates. When hiring decisions fail and when turnover increases, your boss turns to you. Yet, often hiring decisions in organizations involve more than the human resources manager. Not only must you constantly improve your interviewing skills, but you must also teach others. Sometimes the people you're teaching are your bosses and their bosses. Just because a person is high on the corporate organizational ladder doesn't necessarily mean that person knows how to interview.

The purpose of this book is to help managers become more efficient interviewers and to provide human resources managers with a tool they can share with the managers in their organization.

This book will not only provide tactics for strategic interviewing, but it will also provide exercises to enable you or others in your organization to practice the skills. In addition the sample résumés and the suggested teaching agendas contained in the appendices give you guidelines in the event you wish to design a strategic interviewing course for others in the organization.

Rambling, irrelevant questions usually fill interview time and result in a negative image for the company and poor hiring decisions. What is even more dangerous to a company is the manager who asks illegal or improper questions. Today's poor interviewers may hire the wrong candidates, and may also face the prospect of lawsuits. The time taken to study interviewing and to explore the issues presented in this book will not only improve the quality of the interview, it will also help improve the manager's overall communication skills.

Structure vs. Strategy

There has been an ongoing search for easy solutions to the interviewing dilemma, and the current gimmick is structure. Human resource managers must face the reality that interviewing isn't easy. There is no easy solution—no quick fix. Even when we counted on references, we had to conduct quality interviews. References alone couldn't tell us everything we needed to know. Similarly, interviews alone can't tell us everything we need to know. A structured interview particularly can't tell us everything we need to know. This book offers an alternative to structure.

Strategic interviewing is a new approach that fits between the highly structured (same questions posed to every candidate) and the highly un-structured (conversation with little direction or purpose). This book introduces the POINT process to help you create an interviewing strategy and an interviewing process that leads to more successful hiring decisions. Without oversimplifying the interview, the POINT process gives you a terminology that others in the organization may easily grasp.

Martin Yate's book, *Hiring the Best: A Manager's Guide to Effective Interviewing* (1987), plants an early seed for strategic interviewing. He refers to layering questions and writes, "Gathering information is the key to competent interviewing and nothing is more important than an ability to be flexible in your question techniques."[2] What Yate advises requires interviewers to plan for the interview through "gathering information," but he also asks us to change our plan once we are in the interview. In other words, we must be planned, intentional—but also flexible. Being planned, intentional, and flexible is the essence of strategic interviewing. A communication technique that facilitates strategic interviewing is the layered question. Layering questions means *reacting* to the candidate's response with a probe. For example:

Interviewer: "Describe how you managed to choose a major in history."

Candidate: "I always liked history courses. I'm fascinated by what happened in the past because it seems relevant to the present. My father was a high school history teacher. So I suspect he had some influence on me."

Interviewer: (*a layered response*) "What kind of influence did your father have?"

William Swan also discusses layered questioning in *How to Pick the Right People* (1989) when he talks about not turning the interview into an interrogation.[3] The last thing you want to do in a strategic interview is intimidate the candidate; interrogation—one probe after another—intimidates.

Some books espouse quick fixes in the form of structure. Arthur Bell in *Extraviewing: Innovative Ways to Hire the Best* (1992) writes, "The structural interview is a thoroughly planned, lock-step system of interviewing that guarantees virtually the same interview experience to each candidate. . . . All questions for a structured interview are asked in order and verbatim for each candidate."[4]

If interviewing were so ordered and "lock-step," we could program computers to do it for us. According to Robert Wilson in *Conducting Better Job Interviews* (1997), computers can do it for us. He mentions a program called ProSelect but cautions, "It's difficult to conceive of any computer-aided interviewing that doesn't also lead to less-than-rigorous training of interviewers."[5] What Wilson suggests is allowing computers to help us screen candidates. Once we establish the key skills or qualities we're looking for, computers can help us narrow the field, but that's the extent of their aid in the interview process. More and more human resource managers are disillusioned with the structural techniques posed by current books on the market and are looking for alternatives. Indeed the thought of computer programs making hiring decisions for us suggests we have allowed the pendulum to swing much too far in the wrong direction. A computer never replaces the strategic interview, even in the preparation phase of the process. A computer may aid us and become an important tool for the interviewer, but it will never replace the interview.

As a young interviewer for a major university, I received little or no training for my job. Because I was a good talker with relatively good interpersonal skills, my boss assumed I could interview. Working for an employment office that hired thousands of university staff, I soon learned there was more to interviewing than talking. Lots more. Many of the managers in your organization see interviewing as my boss did. They believe anyone can do it, and they think it can be done by the "seat of the pants." Part of your role in the organization is to erase this myth. **Your job is to help people respect the complexity of interviewing, to help them detach from the simplified solutions, and to show them ways to increase the odds of hiring the best people.**

THE DEFINITION OF AN INTERVIEW

In 1931 Walter Bingham and Bruce Moore described interviewing as a conversation with a purpose,[6] leading Richard Olson to devise what I've discovered to be the most inclusive and pragmatic definition of interviewing, namely:

A set of verbal and nonverbal interactions between two or more people focused on gathering information to decide a course of action[7]—to hire or not to hire.

Embedded in this definition lies the fundamental challenge interviewers face every day. What do we use to determine our course of action? Facts? Hard data? Look again at the definition. We determine our course of action from a "set of verbal and nonverbal interactions."

Verbal and Nonverbal Communication

According to communication theory, we pass along information in three primary ways:

- Visual
- Vocal
- Verbal

These three vehicles make up nearly 100 percent of our communication. I say *nearly* because a small percentage of communication comes through touch, which is not included in visual, vocal, or verbal messages. The handshake is one notable example that affects the interview. A strong handshake versus a weak handshake tells the interviewer something about the candidate. Interviewers sometimes miss this piece of information by quickly gripping the candidate's hand before he or she takes hold of theirs. Give the candidate one split second to initiate the handshake. By doing so, you will notice a strong, assertive handshake or a weak, looser grasp.

Visual communication includes every message we send to one another through the eyes. Eye contact, rates of blinking, facial expressions, gestures, posture, nearness of an individual to the speaker, physical appearance, clothing, and surroundings comprise examples of visual messages.

Skilled negotiators know when they've hit a nerve because the other party's blinking rate accelerates. A few quick blinks tell the negotiator that the person is considering something that was just said. High level negotiators understand the subtlety of visual messages and even resort to counting blinks! As interviewers, we, too, must learn how these obscure messages affect the interview. Like negotiators, we look for those subtle cues to suggest the feelings that lie behind the words. Unlike negotiators, we need not count blinks.

When someone walks into your office for the first time, thousands of visual messages bombard you and that person. These messages set up the interview. Strategic interviewing challenges you to manage these messages— to either make them work for you or to read them with more proficiency.

Practice Exercise

You are recruiting a top-level manager with experience in finance.

A man, dressed in a navy suit with a colorful tie, gray hair, and carrying a briefcase walks into your office for an interview. You are a woman, age thirty-five, who manages human resources for your organization. The man grips your hand firmly and greets you with a smile. His eyes take in the surroundings in one quick movement. He sits across from you, crosses one leg over the other and glances out the window behind your desk. He straightens the crease in his pants as you begin the interview. His fingers thump the top of his briefcase while you talk.

List everything you notice about this man.

How might you check the validity of the visual messages you've received?

What visual messages is the interviewer receiving?

- A nicely dressed, middle-aged man
- Darting eyes that quickly analyze the environment
- A firm handshake
- He sits easily and looks away

- He adjusts the crease in his pants
- He thumps his briefcase

What might the interviewer infer from these messages? The man's dress may indicate he takes the interview seriously. His fast review of the environment, without comment, could mean he puts little importance on this place. He may feel he'll be in this room for only a short time. The firm handshake gives the impression of confidence. He sits but doesn't maintain eye contact, which may suggest he's somewhat anxious. His smoothing of the crease in his pants may tell us he's someone who attends to details and can also suggest a certain uneasiness. The thumping on the briefcase may mean he's anxious to get on with the interview. He may see the human resources manager as the first step and the least important step in the process. He may see this interview as one he has to get through, but that it has less consequence than other interviews.

All these visual cues are inferences. They represent what may or may not be true until they've been verified. The trick is noticing the cues and then responding in certain ways to check each one out. How might you verify the visual cues?

- To determine if the man is indeed anxious, you might listen to his vocal responses. Is there a tremor to his voice? Does he stutter over his responses?
- To determine if he is in a hurry, you might ask, "What other pressing appointments does he have today?"
- To determine his attention to detail, you might ask strategic questions related to the detailed work you noted on his résumé.
- To determine if the man is confident, note how often his responses are defensive. Notice the sound of his voice when he talks. Does he speak without "um's" or other filler words such as "I think" or "I believe" before each statement? Does he end his sentences with an upward inflection, suggesting a question mark or with a downward inflection, suggesting a period?

How the Interviewer Might Interview Mr. Jones

If you find yourself face to face with this man, you can do several things to gain control of the interview:

- Begin the interview as an orientation. Let the candidate know what he'll be going through and who he will meet. Spend the first few minutes talking before you begin asking questions. Do not get defensive. Do not list your credentials or compete for the man's respect.
- If the man seems tense, you should relax. Later in this book you'll learn ways to relieve tension. Ask questions that get the candidate talking. Listen intently to what he says and respond without harsh probing. Your best responses are those

that develop rapport with the candidate—those that agree with him or give some information about yourself or the job.
- Watch the candidate's visual cues for changes. When he relaxes, ask more probing questions.
- Don't let the candidate's tension rub off on you. Your goal is to create a safe environment so your relaxed demeanor will rub off on him, not the reverse.

An interview with this candidate might proceed as follows:

Interviewer: "Good morning, Mr. Jones, we're so glad you agreed to see us about the Associate Financial Advisor's position."

Candidate: "Thank you."

Interviewer: "Let me explain what we plan to do today. After I have a chance to visit with you, you'll see Mark Peters, our marketing director. He'll help you understand the philosophy of the company. Later he'll give you a brief tour. After Mark, you'll meet with several more people who see the company in different ways. This is a large organization. Even though our administrative functions are head-quartered in the east, we span the entire country. Our staff has a broad view of the overall function of the company and often spends time in surrounding facilities. The people you'll meet today will share their perspective, which will help you understand us. How does that sound to you?"

Candidate: "Sounds great. I suppose I'll be here most of the day, then?"

Interviewer: "We'll try to be efficient with your time. A lot depends on scheduling. What time is your flight out?"

Candidate: "Six o'clock."

Interviewer: "That should be no problem. We'll get you to the airport in plenty of time."

As the candidate relaxes and understands more about what to expect, the interviewer might proceed into the actual interview. This interviewer decided not to employ a typical icebreaker (see Chapter 11) at the outset. The initial goal, based on the candidate's visual messages, was to move directly into an explanation of the process. The interviewer showed flexibility in order to get the most out of the interview. Once the candidate relaxes, the interviewer might move into the icebreaker in which the goal is to get the candidate talking about general things. Finally the interviewer eases into the more probing questions. By now the interviewer has developed a rapport with Mr. Jones, and the candidate seems more willing to share. Notice in our example the general nature of the comments the interviewer used to describe the process. If we're too specific and then realize this candidate won't suit our organization, we find ourselves boxed in with unnecessary interviews. All the candidate needs to know is he'll be seeing more than one person, and he'll meet his scheduled flight or next appointment.

Much of what this interviewer learned about Mr. Jones she picked up in those first crucial seconds of the interview. The interviewer immediately sized up the situation and changed her plan for the interview. This kind of flexibility marks a strategic interview—not a "lock-step," structural interview. **The interviewer changed her plan for a reason.** She facilitated Mr. Jones's ability to relax so he could participate freely in the interview.

Vocal messages comprise all the sounds we make that are nonwords, including long pauses or periods of silence. Voice modulation, pacing or speed of speech, word emphasis, nonword sounds such as uh-huh's, moans, laughs, and chuckles exemplify vocal messages. Accents whether southern, midwestern, or French give us vocal information about the speaker.

Practice Exercise

In the following example emphasize the underlined word. Listen for the altered meaning depending on your vocal emphasis.

I didn't say he <u>killed</u> the bird.
I didn't <u>say</u> he killed the bird.
I didn't say <u>he</u> killed the bird.
I didn't say he killed the <u>bird</u>.
<u>I</u> *didn't say he killed the bird.*

Looking at the example of Mr. Jones, we noted visual messages in the first few seconds of our meeting. Following close behind those visual messages come the vocal messages. They, too, bombard us with information.

When Mr. Jones said, "Thank you," how did he say it? Quickly or with a pause. A quick "Thank you" suggests impatience. I suspect, given Mr. Jones's visual demeanor, he responded with a quick, curt, "Thank you." That is another cue for the interviewer to spend the next several minutes orienting him to the process. Later the candidate says, "Sounds great. I suppose I'll be here most of the day." Does he say, "sounds great" as if it does sound great or does he say it with a sigh? "I suppose (*sigh—tired, no energy*) I'll be here most of the day" (*upward inflection*) tells you one thing and "I suppose (*upbeat, fast*) I'll be here most of the day" (*downward inflection*) tells you something else. These vocal messages tell the interviewer what to do next. In all probability, Mr. Jones made the statement with little energy. The interviewer realizes the best approach is to move into an icebreaker to try to ease the tension and develop a rapport with Mr. Jones.

Verbal messages include the words we actually speak. Correct or incorrect grammar reveals verbal information about the speaker.

According to social psychology research, these three categories of communication affect the communicated message in different ways.

- 57 percent of the power of the message comes through Visual
- 35 percent of the power of the message comes through Vocal
- 8 percent of the power of the message comes through Verbal

Visual and vocal communication comprise the nonverbal part of our communication; visual and vocal communication make up 92 percent of the power of a communicated message. In other words, you believe what you see more intensely than what you hear. A comedian put it nicely when he said, "You're acting so loud I can't hear you." Shakespeare's MacBeth said, "False face must hide what the false heart doth feel." MacBeth knew he had to control his visual expression to achieve his goal.

Most managers are surprised by these percentages. They're surprised because most of us spend a majority of our time worrying about the words. How many of you write down the questions you'll ask in the interview? You write down words and nothing more. Words are the least of our worries as far as communication is concerned. How we say those words carries the weight.

HOW DOES NONVERBAL COMMUNICATION AFFECT THE INTERVIEWING PROCESS?

In an ideal world we want the interviewing process to be as objective as possible. In such a world we seek real data on which to base our hiring decisions. We want facts. When a student in one of my classes saw the power of nonverbal messages, he exclaimed, "But that's not right!" It may not be right, but it's the way it is. According to the actual definition of interviewing, we decide to hire or not to hire based on a set of verbal and nonverbal interactions, not on facts. In the world of interviewing, nonverbal communication plays an active and dominant role in the decision-making process. It is a role we cannot ignore or shrug off or delegate to computers. In fact those troublesome nonverbal cues help us develop the strategy for the interview. They are integral to the POINT process.

My early experience with interviewing taught me that the interview is fraught with subjectivity. Not only are we subject to nonverbal messages, which may or may not reflect the true person, but we are also bombarded with our own biases and prejudices. And these affect how we interpret the messages. Auren Uris in *88 Mistakes Interviewers Make* (1988) lists subjectivity as the culprit when we make snap judgments and false assumptions.[8] How can we reduce the subjectivity of the interview?

Make Your Hiring Decisions More Objective

Current books on the market will have you believe that structured interviewing will help you reduce subjectivity. The premise is that all tendencies to be subjective can be erased by simply asking the same questions of each candidate. My response to this premise is try it. You'll find you cannot erase all subjectivity. We must accept the reality—as human beings we have frailties and those frailties enter the interviewing process. Once we face this truth, we can deal with interviewing realistically.

Furthermore if our goal is to erase subjectivity by asking the same questions of everyone, then let the computer interview for us. I fear computers will make far more hiring mistakes than we humans have made with all our subjectivity. From the very beginning as a novice interviewer, I saw how structure and its inherent inflexibility put interviewers in a box and suffocated the process.

Inference vs. Observation

The definition of communication is: *Behavior that transmits meaning from one person to another.*

This definition tells us that communication consists of *behavior*—some type of action and *meaning*—an interpretation of that behavior. When we interview, we employ one of the highest levels of communication available to us.

Effective interviewers must first be exceptional communicators.

In an interview we interact with someone we know little about, and we experience all the anxiety of first time communication. What is meaning for me may not be meaning for you. Until I know you better I have little knowledge of your meaning. For that reason we aim to keep the interview communication as basic as possible. We strive to deal with observation rather than inference. Unfortunately communication cannot happen without inference. It is something we all do. Like perceptions, however, awareness of inference helps us deflect it and gain meaning from it.

The following example, taken from a communication exercise used by communication consultants, will help you understand the power of inferences in communication.

Practice Exercise

Read the story. Answer the questions as follows: True = The story states this fact. False = The story states a contrary fact. Inference = This cannot be determined from the story.

Story

Mark and Mary Wilson turned out the lights in their living room when they heard a crash from the den. Mark went into the den and saw a man climbing out the window. The dog had the man's leg in his mouth. A scuffle ensued and the man escaped. Mary Wilson called a member of the police force.

Questions

1. *Mr. and Mrs. Wilson turned out the lights in their living room. T F I*
2. *Someone broke a lamp in the den. T F I*

3. *Mark and Mary Wilson didn't hear any noise from the den.* T F I
4. *The dog barked at the man.* T F I
5. *Mrs. Wilson screamed when she saw the intruder.* T F I
6. *A man was climbing out of a window in the den.* T F I
7. *The neighbors called the police.* T F I
8. *The man escaped before the police arrived.* T F I
9. *Mary Wilson went to the den when she heard the crash.* T F I
10. *The dog didn't bite anyone.* T F I

Let's look at the correct responses to these ten statements in terms of inference and observation.

1. I—You don't know if Mark and Mary are married. They could be son and mother or brother and sister.
2. I—Perhaps. We don't know.
3. F—They heard a crash.
4. I—We don't know if the dog barked or not. The only sound they heard was a crash.
5. I—Maybe there is a Mrs. Smith and she screamed. We don't know.
6. T—That's what the story says.
7. I—Maybe they called the police, too. We don't know.
8. I—We're not even sure the man got out of the window. We know he escaped, but maybe from the scuffle or from the dog.
9. I—We don't know where Mary Wilson went.
10. F—The dog bit the man's leg.

This example shows how easily we make inferences. Our goal is not to eliminate inferences; that's not possible. Instead we aim to keep an open mind while interviewing and recognize when we've inferred something and when we've observed something.

You may have noted that all nonverbal cues, whether visual or vocal, contain inferences. Yet, as you've seen, nonverbal messages make up 92 percent of our communication. Therefore meaning, in the definition of communication, happens 92 percent of the time from nonverbal cues. Meaning is fraught with inference and cannot be concluded as fact. Think about the thousands of nonverbal cues you get during a normal interaction with another person. It's impossible to check out all those messages. We must depend on inferences to help guide us. Otherwise we'd spend all our time asking people what they mean when they scratched their noses, frowned, or crossed their legs. We'd find ourselves unable to communicate by trying to attach meaning to everything a person does. We'd be lost in a forest of nonverbal messages and never find our way out. Fortunately we make these inferences naturally. Unfortunately for the interview process, we must bring that unconscious part of communication to a conscious level. When we do that the interviewer becomes sensitive to everything that goes on in the interaction between himself and the candidate and skillful enough to know when to pursue meaning and when not to.

THE POINT PROCESS

Understanding the effects of inferences and subjectivity on interviewing decisions will help you streamline your interview process. Understanding how to scale away superfluous information and stay focused on the individual and the job is the supreme challenge of the interview. The POINT process introduced in this book with its emphasis on *strategic* interviewing will move you closer to meeting that challenge. POINT stands for Plan, Open, INtentional, Test. Strategic POINTS surface from the time you realize you must make a hiring decision to the moment of the actual hire. This book takes you step-by-step through the POINT process of strategic interviewing. Throughout each chapter are examples of interviews. You may complete the practice exercises to further cement the skills. In section one we apply the POINT process to the job. In section two we apply the process to the candidate and in section three to the interview. Chapter 14 deals with interview nightmares. You will learn how to gracefully and professionally get through the worst kinds of interviews. Finally in Chapter 15 we'll look at the legal do's and don'ts. Strategically you pursue a certain line of questions based on what you've established is necessary for a particular job. But you must stay abreast of those questions that might lead you into dangerous legal territory.

The aim of this book is to show managers how to ask questions to get the results they want by practicing strategic interviewing within the framework of solid communication skills. The ultimate goal is to increase the odds of making the right choice.

NOTES

1. Bradford D. Smart, *The Smart Interviewer* (New York: John Wiley & Sons, 1987), p. 3.

2. Martin John Yate, *Hiring the Best: A Manager's Guide to Effective Interviewing* (Boston: Bob Adams, Inc., 1987), p. 68.

3. William S. Swan, *How to Pick the Right People* (New York: John Wiley & Sons, 1989), p. 120.

4. Arthur H. Bell, *Extraviewing: Innovative Ways to Hire the Best* (Homewood, IL: Business One, Irwin, 1992), pp. 72, 88.

5. Robert F. Wilson, *Conducting Better Job Interviews: The Skills You Need to Succeed in the Business World. Second Edition* (Hauppauge, NY: Barrons, 1997), pp. 36–37.

6. Walter Bingham and Bruce Moore, *How to Interview* (New York: Harper & Brothers Publishers, 1931), p. 3.

7. Richard F. Olson, *Managing the Interview* (New York: John Wiley & Sons, 1980), p. 8.

8. Auren Uris, *88 Mistakes Interviewers Make and How to Avoid Them* (New York: Amacom, 1988), pp. 8, 16.

2

Analyzing the Position

WHO ARE WE LOOKING FOR AND FOR WHAT?

The **P** in POINT stands for *Plan* in relation to the job. This chapter will explore the tools necessary to plan who is needed to do what job. Job descriptions alone do not give the manager a picture of the qualities and skills necessary to perform within an organizational culture.

Basic technical skills are easy to identify—a Bachelor's of Science in chemistry, a computer science degree, or passing the medical boards. When technical skills prove less obvious, employers might administer a simple test. Which interpersonal skills prove successful in your environment? Which pose more trouble? Are you looking for a person with a structured mind or someone who demonstrates more flexibility? When the whistle blows at five o'clock, are you looking for a person who packs up and leaves or one who rarely hears the whistle? Whether you're searching for an upper level managerial position or a first line supervisor, the organizational culture is a major consideration.

What is your organizational culture? New, growing organizations look for people with special drive and creativity that may be stifled in older, more established organizations. This chapter will explore differing organizations from a sociological standpoint.

Planning for job interviews takes time and energy. The planning steps cannot be ignored or shortchanged. One of the biggest problems I see in the classes I teach is not enough planning on the front end. We tend to get impatient, we're anxious to fill the position, and that impatience often leads us to hiring disasters. When you begin an interview without a clear picture of the job and the organizational culture, it's like walking in blindfolded. Either you hire someone terribly wrong or you don't hire anyone at all because no one seems to fit. Recently a class participant told me he'd never hire himself; no one, not even himself, suited him. He had set such high standards they had become unrealistic. This participant needs to improve his planning; he needs to realistically determine who can and cannot perform the job. Otherwise if he happens to hire a good candidate, it may be more a matter of chance than skill. Most human resource managers prefer not to hire on chance alone.

One organization I worked with required the interviewing team to develop a profile of its culture before interviewing candidates. This profile included a survey of what people wanted in the organization as well as past and future trends. The team spent the first six months developing this profile. This prework not only provided a thorough analysis of the organization but also provided a complete organizational overview for the candidate. Of course most organizations can't devote so much preliminary planning time to each hire. But organizations can and must do more. Rather than reacting when a top position opens, the organization could create such a profile every two to three years as a regular part of its self-study. Such a corporate analysis provides useful information for many aspects of the organization—including hiring, and it encompasses more than the annual report which merely reflects what happened during the year. The corporate profile examines the organization from the standpoint of its past, present, and future.

Those of us who have been in our jobs for long periods of time often take the organizational culture for granted. We're so close to it we don't see it. We could save a lot of time in the interview process if we'd step back and examine the world around us. Swan tells us "There's no better way to increase productivity, profit and morale than to hire the right people the first time."[1] As human resource managers, you know that's easier said than done. Your boss depends on you to produce the right people for the right jobs. It's like managing a huge jigsaw puzzle. The more facts we put into the equation, the greater our chances for success.

THE ORGANIZATION AS AN ORGANISM

For decades sociological literature talked about organizations as if they were large conglomerates of people, living and breathing as people do. The use of biological metaphors, however, has received heavy criticism because clearly the laws of social science and biological science differ. I concede to two main differences:

1. With people, death is inevitable; it is not so with organizations. Of course organizations die, but death isn't inevitable.
2. With people, development is linear; it is not so with organizations.[2]

Nonetheless, for the purposes of identifying the development of your organization prior to an interview, biological metaphors provide the clearest and simplest method, particularly when you look at growth. Studying the organization, identifying its culture, and profiling its needs are the planning steps human resource managers often skip.

- The Childhood Phase. This is the discovery phase of organizational growth. To a child everything appears new. As young children our primary function is to learn new things. We ask lots of questions, and we condone mistakes. In this phase the organization experiences fast successes and a few valleys before quickly succeeding again, like a child learning to walk. The organization values innovation, risk taking, enthusiasm, ambiguity, and good listening skills.
- The Adolescence Phase. Fast-paced growth marks this phase. The goal is to create more of everything, including buildings, people, and resources. It's a period of testing the organizational limits. In this phase people argue with one another (like warring hormones). But growth peaks. Profits increase to unexpected heights. The values that mark this phase are action, ability to manage conflict, ability to raise funds, independent thinking, and a willingness to act.
- The Middle-Age Phase. Organizations in this phase maintain the status quo and avoid rocking the boat. Mature organizations do what they have always done and rarely take risks beyond those limits. People resist change and avoid mistakes at all costs. The organization's growth pattern stabilizes to a comfortable level of achievement. Values come out of the past. Those people, who represent tradition and the way things were, reap the rewards. Change agents do not survive in this culture.
- The Senior Phase. Organizations, like people, reach a point in their lives when the old ways no longer work. People cannot run as fast or jump as high in their declining years. Similarly, organizations experience a lack of energy with time. In this phase things begin to go wrong. Growth decreases while revenues and demands diminish. As with people, for the organization to survive it must adapt to the world around it without implementing radical change. Organizations in the senior phase are often targets for takeovers. Survival dominates this phase.

Imagine hiring a high energy person full of new ideas for an organization in the senior phase. You might say, great! That organization needs an energetic person to shake things up. Unfortunately one person alone, even if that person is the CEO, cannot buck the culture. Culture represents a conglomerate of the values of the people in the organization. Those values develop and harden over time. One person, whose values clash with everyone else's and who purports change, is looked upon as a nuisance. "We can outlast him" is the prevailing attitude and more often than not that attitude prevails.

Terrence Deal and Allen Kennedy in *Corporate Cultures: The Rites and Rituals of Corporate Life* (1982)[3] describe another way to identify corporate culture. Each of the four generic cultures that Deal and Kennedy describe coexist in the phases of cultural life above. What Deal and Kennedy share shows the pervasiveness of organizational culture.

- The Tough Guy, Macho Culture. This culture consists of individuals who take high risks and get quick results. Tough guy, macho cultures tend to be young with a focus on speed and endurance. Survivors maintain a tough attitude. If you appear weak in a tough guy culture, you're dead. Some typical examples are law enforcement, advertising, and the film and publishing industries. This culture survives in the childhood or adolescent phase of organizational life.
- The Work Hard/Play Hard Culture. In this culture the employees are busy and active but at low risk activities and with quick feedback. The values in this culture are fun and action-oriented but within a specific low risk environment. The most typical examples are sales organizations. You either make a sale or you don't. Unlike the tough guy culture, no "stars" exist. Instead team performance pays off. The best performers are active people who thrive on quick, tangible results. This culture survives in the middle-age phase of the organization.
- The Bet Your Company Culture. In cultures with big stake decisions the goals are high risk, but feedback drags. Often years pass before employees learn about the success or failure of their decisions. Instead of putting careers on the line as tough guys would, the "bet your company" culture puts the whole company on the line and stakes itself to a future that's worth betting on. The best performers are people with stamina to endure long-term ambiguity. In these cultures you get major technological breakthroughs, but everything moves with amazing slowness. This culture survives in the adolescent phase of an organization.
- The Process Culture. This is your typical bureaucratic culture where people get little or no feedback on what or why they do what they do. Instead they focus on how things are done. The best examples are government organizations, banks, and utilities. People spend time calculating risks and finding the best possible solutions. Survivors in the process culture tend to be orderly, punctual, and attentive to detail. Doing things as they've always been done makes more sense than asking why. This culture survives in the middle-age or senior phases of organizational life.

Whether you are hiring an engineer or a first-line manager, you must determine the cultural environment in which the person will work. It helps to identify the personal qualities that will succeed in your organization, not the personal qualities you might happen to like in people. One mistake hiring managers make is to select people like themselves.

Several years ago I administered a personality inventory to city employees who worried about the city's inability to attract new business and who feared the community might dry up. The inventory showed personality profiles of the principal decision makers in that city exactly matching that of the city manager. The manager hired people just like himself and thereby shut out differences that might evoke creativity. This behavior marks a senior organization.

When human resource managers do all the hiring in an organization, they tend to select extroverted people who enjoy interaction. If the job requires working all day at a computer, the newly employed person won't last. Human resource managers must involve others in the hiring process. Today's organizations place hiring as one of the top decisions they make. They understand that human resource managers facilitate the process and use their professional skills to help the organization achieve the best results. But other key people in the organization must participate. A broad cross section of the company reveals information about its culture and gives candidates a clearer picture of what to expect if hired. The human resources manager is the coach; the others in the organization are the players.

A good coach learns about his/her team, trains and motivates them, understands the environment in which they'll have to perform, and makes sure everyone has the information they need to succeed. A good coach communicates with his/her team all along the way. I've learned from my classes that managers often do not see a résumé until moments before they interview. When human resource managers involve others in interviewing, they must give them the tools and information they need beforehand. Like a good coach, human resource managers must involve others in the process from the outset.

A chemical engineer hired into a middle-age organization characterized by the work hard/play hard culture should look different from a chemical engineer hired into an adolescent organization characterized by a tough guy, macho culture. Both engineers, however, might possess similar skills and experiences.

Let's look at an example of how culture affects hiring.

Case Study

Firm X—A legal firm in the midst of major staff unrest

History

The firm specializes in representing people in prisons who suffer from severe mental illness or mental retardation. Mac Smith began the firm six years ago. He started with a staff of himself and a paralegal. Smith's greatest strengths are his lobbying abilities, his dynamic personality, and his strong ability to persuade. He experienced success in raising awareness for his cause as well as raising money from the state legislature to fund the program. In a conservative southern state, Smith overcame great obstacles to achieve his goal.

In the early days Smith handled the cases himself as well as being the main point person for the legislature and for other potential funding sources. Most of the cases originated in the large metropolitan city where Firm X resided. Smith's paralegal handled all the business as well as the legal research. By the end of the first year, the caseload expanded beyond the metropolitan city to areas throughout the state. Smith hired several new attorneys and paralegals. Most of the staff came to Firm X because they believed in the cause, and they believed in Smith's drive. In a few short years Firm X grew to ten attorneys, two psychologists, a contracted psychiatrist, five paralegals, five secretaries, a computer programmer, and an accounting assistant. The caseload increased with equal rapidity.

Office Life

Smith tended to micromanage the office. After having begun the firm and nurtured its growth, he couldn't let go. Although he hired well-known and well-connected attorneys, he believed his way the best and only way to handle cases. He hoarded funding information and released occasional bits to the staff. Last year he hired an attorney-lobbyist, but he continued to be the front person representing Firm X. Legislators and business professionals connected him to the firm and no one else. The press quoted him, not the other staff. Smith's strengths lie in his intense drive and commitment to the cause, his willingness to work hard to accomplish goals, his persuasive power, his quick thinking, and his creativity. Smith's weaknesses include his inability to communicate, his lack of trust in his staff's ability, and his unwillingness to share information.

The office life reflected Smith's weaknesses. Staff worked to gain Smith's recognition and thereby to win his trust. They felt stifled and shut out. Conflicts among and between staff ran rampant. An intense gossip network formed. No one trusted anyone. Each felt he or she was working for an important cause, but survival depended on individual efforts. Some felt the clients suffered because of the staff's inability to work together. There was a high degree of frustration.

Fiery email messages flew from person to person. Staff meetings often turned into shouting matches.

Smith's Hiring Philosophy

Smith hired people like himself—strong-minded individuals with liberal leanings. He selected men and women who were outspoken to the point of rudeness. Once hired there was little time for orientation. Because of the intensity of the work, people ran from case to case or project to project in a frantic pace just to keep up. New people came into the workplace immediately running. They learned the nature of the culture the hard way—by being burned, usually by Smith. It wasn't unusual for him to ream someone out at least once not long after they arrived on the job. The ability to handle Smith's rancor became an unspoken part of the ritual. Loyalty to people didn't exist. Loyalty to the cause did.

Overall Difficulties

Smith was a highly charged taskmaster. His bold personality left little room for people skills. As the staff grew, the need for people management increased.

The fast changing nature of the organization put added pressure on the staff and on Smith. The stress of change caused people to revert to their "bad behaviors." No one cared about others enough to help reduce the stress. Each coped alone.

The people Smith hired mirrored his task consciousness. His lack of people skills filtered down to the people working for him. Once people realized he had no loyalty to them, they responded similarly. No one on the staff demonstrated the people skills to handle a group of strong-minded individuals. Each person looked out for himself or herself and let others perish.

The rapid change that marked past years continued into the present and was predicted to continue into the future. Smith's creative drive pushed him to search for new angles. He constantly toyed with the organizational structure—changing people's job responsibilities and turning the organization inside out.

Practice Exercise

What kind of organizational culture is Firm X?

What is the number one problem facing Firm X?

If you were Smith's consultant, what would you recommend?

How might Smith capitalize on his creativity while not ruining people along the way?

How might the office structure and environment calm down?

What kind of organizational culture is Firm X? To answer this question, let's look at the behaviors we know from the information above. Conflict dominates the interpersonal relationships within the organization. Growth in caseload and staff marches upward. A dog-eat-dog environment exists with low levels of trust and little tolerance for teamwork. From this information alone, we can characterize a Tough Guy culture in the Adolescent Phase of development.

What is the number one problem facing Firm X? As the consultant for Firm X, I was asked to conduct a team building retreat. Mac Smith thought if he could build a sense of team spirit (instead of a habit of stabbing each other in the back), he'd solve all his problems. This kind of thinking occurs in many organizations. Team building is the new quick fix. Having learned my lesson the hard way, I decided to investigate before launching a team building experience. Through one-on-one interviews, I discovered that team building was not the major problem facing Firm X. Instead, the major culprit was improper hiring in a fast-changing environment. When organizations experience rapid change, which is common in the Adolescent Phase, management of that change can spell survival or defeat. Management of change requires the right kind of people skills. In our example, we learned that Mac Smith lacked people skills, and he didn't hire persons able to fill that gap. Smith surrounded himself with task-conscious, independent people. Each clashed with the others in their ambitions and their personal visions.

If you were Smith's consultant, what would you recommend? Smith is the driving force in Firm X. From the beginning Smith demonstrated success in creating an organization that claims statewide respect and funding. His lack of people skills, his micromanagement, and his poor hiring decisions threaten to destroy what he created. Yet, he brings vision, excellent lobbying abilities, and creativity to the table. Smith is not a mediator. The way he handles conflict is to flame it. Smith needs someone between him and the staff to manage, recruit, train, and orient the people. Smith needs a highly qualified human resources (HR) professional. This HR professional must have the strength to withstand Smith's outbursts and to counsel Smith in his relationships with staff. He or she must possess strong listening and mediation skills as well as a high level of self-confidence.

How might Smith capitalize on his creativity without ruining people along the way? Bringing an HR professional into the mix at Firm X enables Smith to exercise his creativity without running the staff ragged. His ideas need not become fact until they are fully thought out. An organizational structure that enables a cross section of think-tank, brainstorming teams to consider new ideas gives Smith the opportunity to create safely.

Not until the HR professional is on board for at least one year can brainstorming teams form, however. In the early stages any kind of teamwork will likely prove difficult because of the lack of trust between and among the staff. Team activity is possible in an Adolescent Phase of development, but managers must introduce teams slowly and only for brainstorming purposes, not for basic decision making. In the case of Firm X the HR professional must first prove him or herself trustworthy, not a puppet or conduit to Smith.

Of utmost importance in the case of Firm X, the HR professional must demonstrate strong people skills, a high-level ability to handle conflict, and a strong working knowledge of team development.

Because Smith's hiring decisions in the past proved unsuccessful, the consultant should play an active role in designing a strategic interviewing process to find the right person to fill the shoes of the HR professional.

How might the organization and the office structure calm down? Smith must immediately remove himself as the staff's direct report. Until Firm X hires the HR professional, Smith should appoint an interim staff liaison—either one of the attorneys who demonstrated good people skills or an administrative person who is liked by the majority of the staff. This person might function as a buffer between Smith and the staff until the HR professional is found.

Organizationally the HR professional reports to Smith along with Smith's paralegal. The remaining professional staff report directly to the HR professional in a flat hierarchy. The organizational structure must remain fluid while Firm X continues to grow. New hires, including the HR professional, must demonstrate a high tolerance for ambiguity.

This case illustrates how the organizational culture, the organizational history, and the people who dominate the culture play an interactive role in people selection. Firm X shows us that when leaders do not pay attention to the culture and hire people based on gut feelings, they threaten to put the entire organization's future in jeopardy.

HOW TO DETERMINE YOUR CORPORATE CULTURE

The number of years an organization exists does not necessarily correspond to the phase of that organization's development. Apple Computer, Inc. exemplifies a company that began and stayed in the childhood phase.

As you look at your organization, use the following indicators to help you identify its phase of development.

Childhood. Growth is up and down like a seesaw. People spend a lot of time talking and listening to one another. Dress is casual. Hours on the job are sporadic, not rigid. Working conditions are uncomfortable and resources sparse. Job security is questionable. Everyday is different. People encourage risks and condone mistakes.

Adolescence. Growth soars upward without downward slopes. People are too busy to talk to one another and tempers flair. Hours are sporadic, not rigid. Dress is casual. Resources and working conditions are top of the line. Meetings are battles. People seem frantic as if growth may stop any day. People move up by stepping on others. Leadership is unstable.

Middle-Age. Growth plateaus and stabilizes. Hours are rigid and expectations about productivity are clear. Dress code is specific, whether formal or informal. Meetings are long and frequent. Top management expects and rewards communication across channels. The organization places high priority on teamwork. Mistakes are shunned. Creativity, innovation and risk get head nods but little action and no reward.

Senior. Growth takes a downturn. Meetings consume much time and energy. People fear risk and avoid mistakes at all costs. Every action is carefully considered and the ramifications are clear. Hours are rigid with high expectations for productivity. Dress is formal. Turnover is high. Leadership is stable. Conflict is minimal with decisions made at the top by people who agree with one another.

Practice Exercise

To determine your company's phase of development, answer the following questions:

1. *Over the past five years, what is the rate of growth (human and profit)?*
2. *List the behaviors that reap rewards. (Examine the people that have been promoted. What qualities do they possess?)*
3. *What do others say are the qualities that make your company successful?*
4. *How do people respond to errors?*
5. *How often do conflicts arise?*
6. *What happens during a conflict?*
7. *How do people dress?*
8. *What amount of time do people spend communicating?*
9. *How much meeting time is spent looking at past history versus creating new policies and procedures?*
10. *How do people feel about the future of the organization and their job security?*

Once you've determined your organizational culture, you need to look at the particular job you are trying to fill. The following example will guide you through the process.

Practice Exercise

What phase of development is this organization?

This organization experiences steady but minimal growth. It is part of a larger bureaucratic organization, but it maintains autonomy. Its role, which includes lobbying for funding and management training to government officials, gives it a unique place in the organization. The dress code is business attire. Meetings are frequent and usually accomplish little other than information sharing. People never question what's been done in the past and often base decisions on past behavior. New ideas are tabled. People say, "Hey, why fix something that's not broken." Orientation of new hires includes clear rules and basic understanding of policies and procedures, but most jobs are shaped by the people in them. Although the hierarchy is flat and delegation is frequent, staff has a clear picture of what the bosses expect. Staff know the parameters. People move up because they don't rock the boat, they go by the book, and they stick around. There's little reward for risk and mistakes are infrequent. Feedback is clear and specific.

The position this organization wants to fill is a first line supervisor who would manage a team of four field workers.

In addition to the basic educational and experience levels needed to complete the tasks in the job, this person must possess the following qualities: team player—goes by the rules, facilitator, ability to empower for delegation, action-oriented, good listening skills, not too ambitious, responds well to instruction.

Two people applied:

A. Janice Chappell. She worked five years at a major bank as a teller and moved up to branch supervisor. Her job includes working with the public as well as managing a staff of six. She enjoys detail work and has an undergraduate degree in business. As a branch supervisor she served on one of the larger bank teams where she represented her branch. That team brainstormed ideas for the bank as a whole. Ms. Chappell enjoyed the camaraderie of the team meetings. She liked learning what went on in other parts of the bank. Ms. Chappell is an independent thinker who works well on teams.

B. Ralph Gray. After he completed his undergraduate degree in marketing, he worked for six years at an innovative computer service business. He began working directly with customers and selling certain computer hardware and software. He quickly moved into a contract salesman position where he brought in over $100,000 in new client business to the company. He loves working with people and likes selling so long as he believes in the product. He has technical know-how as well as strong people skills. Gray supervised one assistant and enjoyed that experience.

Who would you hire in this position?

Before we determine whom to hire let's decide what kind of organization we're dealing with and what stage of development it is in. From the information we have this sounds like an organization in the Middle-Age Phase of development and in a Work Hard/Play Hard Culture. We know the organization values status quo and loyalty, not risk. But because the group operates autonomously from the larger bureaucratic organization, it gets fast feedback which indicates a Work Hard/Play Hard Culture; the work itself (lobbying) lends itself to a Work Hard/Play Hard Culture.

Looking at the candidates, Ralph appears competent and talented. He has been successful in sales which fits with a Work Hard/Play Hard Culture. But it sounds as though he might be an individual performer, not terribly responsive to a team environment. Teamwork is an important value in this organization. Ralph would fit better in a Work Hard/Play Hard Culture in either the Childhood Phase or the Adolescent Phase of development. There he'd be able to excel and use his innovative skills.

Janice, on the other hand, looks like a team player who has had experience in supervision with an organization in the Middle-Age Phase of development—banks. Janice also fits what the group is looking for, someone with good facilitation skills and someone who isn't too ambitious. Middle-Age Phase cultures promote slowly. Janice seems more likely to remain, contribute to the organization, and await her promotion before moving on. For this particular position in this particular organizational culture Janice is the better fit. Of course, we cannot confirm this decision until we interview both candidates. A strategic interview, focusing on the items we've isolated, will help us determine which candidate best suits this organization.

In this chapter we examined the environment—where the person will work and the qualities needed to fill that job. We looked at a case study that helped us understand the importance of organizational culture on hiring. We are now in a position to *Plan* the interview with the job in mind. The purpose of the strategic interview is to plan a strategy of action. Taking a closer look at the job is the first step toward developing that strategy.

The next chapter will examine the O in POINT, setting an Open tone for the interview and turning it into a conversation versus a one-sided interrogation.

NOTES

1. William Swan, *How to Pick the Right People*, pp. ix–x.

2. John Kimberly, Richard H. Miles and Associates, *The Organizational Life Cycle: Issues in the Creation, Transformation and Decline of Organizations* (San Francisco: Jossey-Bass Publishers, 1980), pp. 6–7.

3. Terrence Deal and Allen Kennedy, *Corporate Cultures: The Rites and Rituals of Corporate Life* (Reading, MA: Addison-Wesley Publishing Company, Inc., 1982), pp. 107–121.

3

Creating an Open Interview

This chapter will explore the O in POINT by examining *Openness* in relation to the job. By openness we mean more than telling the truth about what the job will entail. That is a given. Distorting a job to entice someone to work for you only leads to bad feelings, hiring fiascoes, and poor judgment on the part of the interviewer. Some managers gloss over the distortions, thinking the candidate will adjust once he or she is hired. It is those attitudes that frustrate human resource professionals. Although we want to put our best foot forward and show off our company, we must give an honest account of the job and its challenges. If you expect hard work in less than comfortable surroundings, tell the candidate. Of course, there's a flip side to everything. Last week I worked with a company that overstated the requirements of the job; they scared potential candidates off. We must find a realistic center point in which we discuss the job in an open and honest manner without overemphasizing or underemphasizing it.

In this chapter you will learn ways to create a sense of trust and openness in the interview. Looking at the job, you should consider the information you wish to share throughout the interview and sprinkle it in as you go. Interviewers who launch the interview with a long, detailed description of the job risk losing the candidate's interest. By balancing the interview with giving information and soliciting information, you place important facts about the job in strategic points all through the interview—rather than everything at the beginning or at the end. This kind of balance keeps the interview moving at a comfortable, conversational pace and enables the interviewer to share information when it can best be **heard**.

For many companies weekend work is an important hiring issue. One company I consult with requires new managers to work shifts in order to learn the company's business. Yet, when people resign, weekend work comes up most frequently as a reason for leaving. This is how interviewers often probe a candidate's willingness to work weekends:

Interviewer: "At XYZ Company we require weekend work for all new managers. Would you mind working two or three weekends a month?"

Candidate: "No, I'm fine with working weekends. That wouldn't be a problem for me at all."

Four things went astray in this approach:

- First, the interviewer told the candidate what to say. He explained the company requirement before finding out how the candidate felt about weekend work.

- Second, because weekend work is an essential part of the job, the interviewer must ask the question in an open rather than closed way. "Would you mind working two or three weekends a month?" is a closed question because the candidate may answer with a simple yes or no. Closed questions give the interviewer very little information.

- Third, the interviewer didn't tell the candidate anything about himself. Even though he shared information about the job, without sharing something about yourself, it's unlikely the candidate will open up. Instead the candidate will only tell you what you want to hear and what the candidate intends to reveal, nothing more.

- Fourth, the interviewer posed the question in a future-oriented manner, i.e., it is based on the candidate's assumption about future behavior.

The best predictor of a person's behavior is how they've behaved in the past.

When the candidate complains about working weekends once hired and perhaps exits the company because of the weekend work, this interviewer should not be surprised. He didn't delve into the matter strategically.

Let's look at a more strategic example.

Interviewer: "When I first started working here it was hard for me to adjust my schedule to working weekends. At first I resented not being able to join my friends for weekend activities. In what ways have you had to adjust your schedule in previous jobs?"

Candidate: "I had to adjust my schedule in my last job because I had to work weekends there, too."

Interviewer: "So you're saying in your last job you had to adjust your schedule to work weekends."

Candidate: "That's correct."

Interviewer: "What adjustments did you make?"

Candidate: "I had to change my routine a little, but since I'm single, that was easy."

Interviewer: "Adjusting your routine didn't bother you at all?"

Candidate: "The only real frustration was when my friends wanted to party on the weekends, and I had to either work or get up early the next morning. Then when I'd want to go out, they had to work. But since I didn't work every weekend it wasn't so bad."

Interviewer: "How often did you work weekends in your last job?"

Candidate: "Once a month."

Interviewer: "Our company requires you to work weekends every other month."

The first statement helped the candidate learn about the interviewer. From there the interviewer probed to see if weekend work might indeed present a problem. The interviewer did this by asking an open question about past weekend experience. "In what ways did you have to adjust your schedule in previous jobs?" Once the interviewer realized this candidate had no problem with a weekend schedule and had actually made the adjustments successfully in his/her last job, the interviewer divulged the actual weekend requirement in this job. Notice when the candidate said weekend work was fine since he or she wasn't married, the interviewer did not explore marital status. In Chapter 15 we'll look at legal issues. Although the foundation of strategic interviewing is to dig deeper and learn as much as you can beyond the superficial, there are some things we cannot "dig deeper" into. There's no law against listening, however. Candidates may tell you anything they wish, but interviewers must avoid pursuing sensitive areas.

HOW TO BE OPEN AS THE INTERVIEWER

Candidates, who interview for jobs, put themselves through one of the most stressful experiences any of us face in our lives. We sit across from a perfect stranger and smile as if we love being there. We "sell" ourselves to that person with all our fears of rejection on our sleeves. When offers do not flow in, it feels as if you're somehow not good enough—someone else must have been better. You gave it your all and failed. For many people this is an awkward and uncomfortable place to be.

Interviewers, too, face an uncomfortable situation. We must present our company in the best possible light, demonstrate the skills needed to accomplish the job, talk in a relaxed manner to someone we've never met before, and make a decision about bringing this person into our world after no more than a twenty- or thirty-minute visit. Both candidates and interviewers face each other with their anxieties hidden and their false smiles on display.

Who knows what other pressures may be at work—the candidate may have a hungry family and this may be his or her last chance for work or the interviewer's boss may have told him before the interview, "This person better work out. I'm getting tired of bringing in all these people." Skillful interviewers know how to deal with their anxieties and at the same time help put the candidate at ease.

The last thing we want to create in an interview is a defensive environment. Yet, some companies put candidates through intimidating cross-examinations as tests of their ability to handle pressure. Yate calls this style of interviewing the stress interview. "The constant barrage of tough, trick and negatively phased questions that constitute stress interviewing is designed to keep the candidates off balance while the interviewer evaluates poise and quick thinking under pressure."[1] These tactics fail because to get at the truth the interviewer must peel away the superficial. An intimidated person puts up barriers. One goal of strategic interviewing is to remove those barriers.

Furthermore many candidates take offense with games designed to intimidate. Candidates prefer an honest and open interchange. Today's job market has the best companies competing for the best candidates. These candidates interview you with much more intensity than in the past. During the baby boom era, companies faced a wealth of talent to fill their jobs. Good people came and went all the time. In today's tighter job market, fewer people are available to fill our jobs. Candidates often have two or three offers. As human resource managers we must impress the candidates with our professionalism, quality interviews, and honesty.

Larry Smalley lists the kind of questions that work in an interview and those that don't. Questions that don't work according to Smalley are leading questions and trick/psychological questions.[2] Once we recognize the inherent tension an interview environment presents, we are better able to cope with the anxieties. Human resource managers, who spend years interviewing, often lose this edge. They forget the uneasiness they felt when they first conducted an interview or when they themselves faced an interviewer. Showing respect for the psychological tension in an interview will strengthen the interviewer's skills and help release the candidate to share information he or she didn't intend to share. Therein lies the purpose of strategic interviewing.

PSYCHOLOGICALLY, WHAT HAPPENS DURING AN INTERVIEW?

Psychologists Joseph Luft and Harrington Ingham shed some light on what happens to people in an interview environment. In the 1950s the two psychologists coined the Johari Window theory. Luft and Ingham arrived at the name Johari from an amalgam of their first names and published several books, including *Of Human Interaction* by Joseph Luft in 1969. The Johari Window remains popular in psychological literature because it presents a simple way to look at human interaction.

Joe and Harry tell us people interact with one another on the basis of four quadrants:

	Known to Self	Not Known to Self
Known to Others	**Open**	**Blind**
Not Known to Others	**Hidden**	**Unknown**

Source: From *Group Processes: An Introduction to Group Dynamics, Third Edition* (pp. 57, 60) by Joseph Luft. Copyright © 1984 by Joseph Luft. Reprinted by permission of Mayfield Publishing Company.

- Open Area—Known to self and known to others. This quadrant contains the things you willingly share. As people get to know you, they learn more and more about you, and the Open Area widens. When you feel threatened, you close the Open Area and share little about yourself.

- Blind Area—Not known to self but known to others. This quadrant contains the things we don't know about ourselves, but others see. Think about your own blind spots. Who are the people who tell you about your hidden truths? Many people point out our blind spots, but we hear only those people we **respect**. To improve ourselves and learn more about how others see us, we must pay attention when people point out our blind spots. Blind spots include both positive and negative behavior. Interviewers often compliment the candidates' skills or experiences. Unless the candidates believe your compliments, they haven't actually heard you or they consider the praise meaningless. This doesn't mean you shouldn't compliment a candidate; instead interviewers must share genuine praise and in such a way the candidate believes the praise to be true.

- Hidden Area—Known to self but not known to others. Again, think about your own hidden area. Who are the people with whom you share your secrets? Family or friends? In reality we share with people we **trust**. The interviewer expects a candidate to share hidden information even though trust hasn't been established. After someone is hired, we wonder why that person didn't tell us certain things in the interview. From the initial handshake, the interviewer must establish trust. Candidates come into the interview wary. The interviewer and the candidate harbor hidden agendas in their hidden areas. Barriers exist on both sides of the table.

- Unknown Area—Not known to self and not known to others. In this quadrant we store our deep subconscious information. Maturity as well as a willingness to open up to others releases this information. When trust and respect are evident, information flows out of the unknown area. These are golden, "ah-ha" moments that rarely happen in an interview setting.

Psychological Challenges Interviewers Encounter

- Candidates walk into your office as strangers. You know little about them, and they know even less about you. During a very brief period of time you exert pressure on yourself to learn hidden information from the candidate and you expect the candidate to willingly share with you. At the same time, you must share the interviewer's blind spots with a person you hardly know. What is the likelihood of the candidate sharing hidden information with you? What is the likelihood that you will share your blind spots with this individual?

- Your goals and the candidate's goals differ. You're looking for someone to handle a certain job and its pressures and carry out responsibilities; they're looking for someone to provide income and benefits and certain psychological rewards for working. Understanding how those goals interconnect takes a willingness to verbalize the real goals. Most candidates prefer to answer your questions as they think you want them answered. They prefer not to tell you their honest goals. They prefer to keep that information hidden. You, too, prefer to keep certain aspects about the job hidden. Few human resource managers tell candidates everything about the job and company—there are certain things we all prefer to keep "inside."

- Because you and the candidate don't know each other, how do you know when the candidate is being open and honest? Skillful candidates know how to interview in order to appear sincere while they continue to hold their hidden information tucked away. We often experience difficulties discovering when our friends are honest with us; being able to discover when a stranger is honest presents a much more formidable challenge.

Based on the psychological challenges that will appear during the interview process, imagine a candidate walking into your office for an interview. What would that person's Johari Window look like? In all probability the candidate would have a tiny Open area with huge quadrants in the Hidden, Blind, and Unknown areas. How might your Johari Window look? Similarly, you probably aren't yet willing to open your open area too wide.

Knowing these psychological tensions will help you enter the interview environment realistically. Some interviewers ignore or discount the psychological barriers. They feel their effervescent presence can dispel any tension that might exist. Such beliefs prove naive and set the interview up for failure.

Let's look at an interview and see if we can determine how the Johari Window looks for both the interviewer and the candidate.

Interviewer: "Good morning, Mrs. Jones, I'm delighted to meet you. I was very impressed with your résumé." *Carole Jones's résumé was the most promising one we got. It looked as if she had the skills and experience we're seeking in this position. But my first impression leaves me a little cold. She took my hand in both of hers and shook it vigorously. She stood too close to me as she spoke, and her voice sounded desperate. I'm worried she might not hit it off with our clients.*

Candidate: "Oh, thank you very much. When I saw this position advertised, I thought it looked exactly like what I wanted. It seemed perfect for me." *I really want this job. I've wanted to work for this company all my life. To have a position come up like this in my field overwhelms me. I couldn't believe it when I saw it in the trade journal. I'm sure there are a lot of people interviewing, and I'm going to do all I can to stand out from the crowd.*

Interviewer: "Before we get into the actual interview, I was curious about your work with the Olympics as a volunteer. I worked for the Summer Olympics in Atlanta in 1996 and thoroughly enjoyed that experience." *My goal now is to see if I can get the candidate to relax. She still seems desperate and a little jittery. Maybe I can learn what is really going on with her.*

Candidate: "That had to have been one of the most wonderful experiences in my life. I worked on the public relations team during the Olympics in Los Angeles. I'd never been to California, but the opportunity presented itself and I couldn't say no and am glad I didn't. A friend of my husband's had been on an Olympic committee and somehow we managed to tag along. It was wonderful." *I don't want to spend too much time talking about this because all I did was sell parking tickets at a booth miles from the entrance. I was terribly disappointed not to get more involved. The man I talked to in the beginning really liked me and wanted to put me in the front office, but nothing ever opened up. I sure don't want to let on that I didn't get what I wanted from a silly little temporary job!*

Interviewer: "So you and your husband went to California?"

Candidate: "Yes. We spent six months there."

Interviewer: "And it was your first trip to California? It's a fascinating state, isn't it?" *I'm hoping this line of questions will not threaten her and maybe lead us into what brought her to our company.*

Candidate: "Oh fabulous. I've loved every place we've lived. But there, particularly. I toured parts of northern California while my husband worked with the committee."

Interviewer: "So you say you were part of the public relations team. Tell me what you did during the games."

Candidate: *I sure wish he'd move on to something else.* "That was such an experience. I met people from all over the world. (*Sigh*) I'd never seen anything like it before."

Interviewer: *She didn't actually answer my question. It sounds as though she wasn't too involved with the games.* "When I worked the Atlanta games, I really enjoyed meeting the people who came to Atlanta. I've never seen the city as ablaze with diversity and international fervor. I had a menial job, sorting the Olympic pins and getting them to the various distribution centers, but I didn't care. Just being part of something like that made it worth it."

Candidate: "You're absolutely right. I, too, didn't have much to do during the games. I sold parking tickets, but meeting all those people from parts of the world I'd only read about was thrilling."

This brief interchange shows how the interviewer attempted to get the candidate to open up. The interviewer wanted to find out what was behind the candidate's thick façade. The candidate aimed to keep that façade up. It took some delicate probing and sharing about the interviewer's own experiences to finally get the candidate to relax. Because of this candidate's strong desire to obtain this position, she will keep her hidden area well covered for as long as possible.

We can see from the above interchange that the interviewer and the candidate entered the interview with their open areas closed. Finally toward the end of the series of questions, the interviewer cracked his hidden area. Doing so encouraged the candidate to reveal a portion of her hidden area.

How do we get people to open up and trust us in an interview? One way is to open up ourselves. If we close our own Johari Window, other people won't open theirs. Opening your Johari Window does not mean that you spend the entire interview talking about yourself. You should spend no more than 20 to 25 percent of the interview time talking and that time limit includes talking about the job. In strategic interviewing, we do everything with a purpose. With a limited time for talking, we must strategically pick what we will say, when, and why. This leads to purposeful conversation.

PURPOSEFUL CONVERSATION

Purposeful conversation aims for openness and avoids statements like, "I will give you an opportunity to ask questions at the end of the interview." Ideally you encourage the candidate to ask questions as the interview progresses. Strategic interviews feel conversational—the interviewer asks a question, the candidate responds, the interviewer reacts to that response, the candidate asks a question, and so forth. Most of us relax more readily in a conversation than an interrogation. Allowing the candidate to toss in questions throughout the interview equalizes the flow of the interview. One caution—the interviewer must maintain control. If the candidate leads the interview, then you've lost track of your strategic plan.

To be strategic, every question and every response must have a purpose.

If the candidate asks you a question that deviates from your strategy, how should you react? Let's look at an example.

Interviewer: "You say you left your last job because it didn't offer enough challenge."

Candidate: "Exactly. I worked there for two years. I was constantly snowed under with paperwork and couldn't use the technical skills I learned in school. Granted it was an entry level position, but I expected more than just logging in data day in and day out. Is that something I'll have to do with your company?"

Interviewer: "Our entry level process improvement positions require paperwork as well. Data entry is a major part of the job for industrial engineers. Tell me how you handled the boredom in your last job."

The interviewer quickly answered the candidate's question without elaboration and then proceeded with probes to learn more about this candidate's response to less challenging jobs.

The following example incorporates openness and purposeful conversation and demonstrates the interviewer's skill at staying on target.

Interviewer: "I noticed you worked as a receptionist at the Baker Law Firm. Give me an example of how you handled a difficult client problem." (*A probe that addresses past behavior*)

Candidate: "Once when a client came in to see one of the attorneys, I had to explain that the lawyer was still in court, and we had no idea when he'd be back. The client got real mad because he drove from another town specifically for this appointment. He demanded to be reimbursed for the hours he wasted."

Interviewer: "How did you handle the person's anger?"

Candidate: "Of course we couldn't reimburse him, and I told him that. We have real strict policies about billing, and I try to make sure I tell people what our policies are. He stormed out of there and said he'd find a lawyer who would show more respect for his time."

Interviewer: "How did that interaction make you feel?"

Candidate: "It didn't bother me because I knew the man was mad and didn't really mean what he was saying. Those things happen. I am usually unruffled by things like that. I don't let them bother me." (*Pause*) I thought this job was for a paralegal. How much contact with the public would I have?"

Interviewer: "We deal with clients every day either on the telephone or face-to-face. Sometimes we have to tell the client they can't have what they want. We strive to maintain a good relationship even if we refer the client elsewhere. It sounds as though in your dealings with people, you do not let their anger affect you, right?" (*Quickly answers the question, tells something about the job and paraphrases to get back on track*)

Candidate: "That's right."

Interviewer: "When someone is that angry, I have a hard time holding my feelings in check. I get uptight. How do you manage to keep from getting upset when someone yells at you?" (*Opens his/her Johari Window*)

Candidate: "One thing I try to do is look at it from the person's point of view. Like with the guy I just mentioned. I told him I'd be upset too if I'd driven that far. I let him vent. When he realized there wasn't much I could do, he left. I really think he wasn't as angry as when he arrived. At least I didn't feel he was angry with me."

Several important things happened in this interchange:

• The interviewer began with a general question to focus on dealing with uncomfortable situations involving the public. The response gave a clear example of an event, but didn't reveal specifics. In fact, had we stopped with the candidate's first response, we might have thought she didn't handle the public too well because the man stormed out of the office, still angry.

- When the candidate asked about the amount of time that would be spent dealing with the public in this job, it threw off the interview. The interviewer wished to find out more about what happened to the angry man and specifically how that interchange affected the candidate. Instead the interviewer quickly answered the question and sprinkled in a few details about the job. This diversion took some of the heat off the candidate. Had the interviewer responded, "Please save that question. I will describe the job in detail later," the interviewer would have lost the opportunity to open up the interview and would have placed the candidate in the witness box. Even if a candidate asks you something you know another interviewer plans to discuss, answer quickly and add something like, "When you talk to Mr. Jones, he'll provide detailed information on the computer system."

- Notice how the interviewer got back on track at the end of the response to the candidate's question when the interviewer said, *"It sounds as though in your dealings with people you don't let their anger affect you, right?"* The interviewer added a paraphrase from the previous response to lead back into the planned line of questioning. This is what we call "piggybacking" the candidate's response.

- The Johari Window was opened when the interviewer said, *"When someone is that angry, I have a hard time holding my feelings in check. I get so uptight."* This kind of sharing enabled the candidate to provide a more detailed account of how she handled the angry man. The candidate acted as if she were instructing the interviewer on good communication skills in a crisis.

Practice Exercise

1. *Draw your Johari Window when you're about to interview someone you've never met.*

2. *Draw an imaginary Johari Window for the candidate who will walk into your office for a job interview. How open do you expect that person to be?*

3. *List the things you can do to help candidates relax and become more open in the interview with you.*

Some interviewers are too relaxed. They slump in their chairs, loosen their ties, and prop their chins on their palms. After all, why should the interviewer experience jitters; it's the candidate who has the most to gain or lose. Right?

Wrong. The time, money, and energy given to the interview process demands that we give it our full attention. When we lose the edge and become too relaxed, we no longer use the skills needed to conduct a strategic interview. Once in my career, an interviewer ate a sandwich while we talked. That gave me a poor impression of the organization and the interviewer. As we strive to increase the level of comfort in the interview environment, we must not let the pendulum swing too far in the opposite direction. Openness in the interview doesn't mean a reduction in professionalism.

Strategic interviewers stay on their toes, listen, respond, and probe at all times.

Informal Traps

One question human resource managers often ask relates to interviewing during a meal. If we take a candidate out to lunch or dinner, how do we handle the interaction? Think about your own Johari Window when you must eat with a stranger. Eating is an awkward experience. Some of us recall our mothers telling us, "Keep your elbows off the table" or "Don't blow on your coffee." Interviewing and eating do not mesh comfortably. Yet, to be hospitable we must take candidates out for meals; it is expected. One participant in my class shared a funny incident that happened when he took a candidate to dinner. He and the candidate sat down to eat. The waiter placed the gravy on the table. Just then the candidate began to eat the gravy. That left the interviewer in a quandary. Should he tell the candidate he's eating the gravy or simply ignore him? Should he ask the waiter for more gravy or go without? An awkward social moment occurred. Of course, after the first taste, the candidate probably realized he was eating the gravy but didn't know how to gracefully stop.

Another problem we face as interviewers is we may not remove our interviewer hats. We can't think, *Well, since I'm taking this candidate to lunch, I can talk about anything. I don't have to be on my toes—like the other people.* This is an incorrect and dangerous assumption. In fact these informal settings are full of traps. Interviewers are most vulnerable during these informal times because we are tempted to cross the legal line, so to speak. It's so easy during a meal to ask a candidate about his family life, for example.

So, what do we do? Remain interviewers, but not interview? Absolutely. Talk to the candidate about the community—perhaps about restaurants in the area. Answer the candidate's questions, but do not try to conduct a strategic interview in this environment.

What makes strategic interviewing a challenge is that each interview depends on the person sitting across from the interviewer. What worked with the last candidate won't work with this one. Unlike structured interviewing where you ask the same questions of each candidate, strategic interviewing requires you to stay alert. You cannot perform a strategic interview eating a sandwich, watching a computer screen, answering a telephone, or enjoying a glass of wine at dinner. Most strategic interviewers sit on the edge of their seats, their eyes and ears alert. As soon as you let your strategic defenses down, you miss a golden strategic moment. In an ideal strategic interview there is a reason for everything you do or say. That kind of attention requires all your energy as an interviewer.

In this chapter we examined the importance of Openness in a strategic interview, and we saw the strategic reasons interviewers open their Johari Windows. Through purposeful conversation, you aim to encourage the candidate to tell you something he or she hadn't intended to tell you. In the next chapter we will look at INtentional listening. We'll examine how to respond to key job-related points while avoiding the pitfalls of perceptions and groupthink.

NOTES

1. Yate, *Hiring the Best: A Manager's Guide to Effective Interviewing*, p. 77.

2. Larry Smalley, *Interviewing and Selecting High Performers* (Irvine, CA: Richard Chang Associates, Inc., 1997), p. 27.

4

Identifying Probe Points

HOW AND WHAT DO I ASK?

The **IN** in POINT refers to *INtentional listening* in relation to the job. In this chapter we will identify key words that trigger deeper questioning. These are your probe points.

Good interviewers spend 75 to 80 percent of their time responding (listening) and 20 to 25 percent talking or soliciting.

If you spend the majority of your time talking, you have not conducted a quality interview.

The goal of the strategic interview is to peel away the superficial and dig deeper. This chapter will provide concrete examples of how to listen with intentionality for the purpose of getting beyond the superficial. You will also discover ways to overcome perceptions and groupthink.

First and foremost we must know when and what to probe. Carol Hacker in *The Costs of Bad Hiring Decisions and How to Avoid Them* (1996) instructs us to get off to a good start by deciding what you need to know and what you want to ask each candidate.[1] This is where your planning and homework come into play. The work you do prior to the interview determines your success during the actual interview. As human resource managers you spend much of your time preparing people to interview others. Included in this preparation is teaching them how to plan for the interview. As noted in Chapter 2, the human resources manager alone cannot plan for the interview. A cross section of people within the organization must look at the job together and make strategic decisions about what is needed to be successful in that job. By strategic decisions we mean selecting some things and ruling out others—isolating those key factors that produce success in this job. Strategic interviewing requires forethought. Some interviewers want to probe everything. Too much probing not only exhausts the candidate, but it also tires the interviewer. In this chapter the strategy in strategic interviewing takes shape.

For example, if you identify **teamwork** as an important value in your organization and a skill that is needed for success in the job, the following may occur:

Interviewer: "Tell me about your work on the capitals project with XYZ Company."

Candidate: "That was a challenging team project. We had to pull together disparate groups and make them work as a team. At first people resisted, but we managed to win the trust of key players and finally succeeded."

Interviewer: "How did you manage to win the trust of key players?"

Candidate: "We identified the key decision makers, met with them, and sold them on the project."

Interviewer: "So you're saying you met with certain people and sold them on the project?"

Candidate: "Yes, I met with one team leader, myself. At first he was reluctant. But when he heard the vision of the organization, he came on board."

Interviewer: "What do you mean by vision of the organization?"

Candidate: "I explained to him that the new vice president saw teamwork as the most vital quality in the organization. This guy had been around for a long time. He was clearly going to be a difficult nut to crack. We knew without him we'd never get the others on board. I explained to him that performance and promotions would henceforth be based on working with other groups rather than individual performance."

Interviewer: "So if the team leader didn't respond positively, his evaluations would be adversely affected?"

Candidate: "That's correct."

Interviewer: "How did your team design the process to bring people on board?"

Candidate: "We didn't do that as a team. Each of us met separately with the resistant team leaders and went from there."

Interviewer: "If I understand you correctly, this project contained no team preparation for these meetings."

This interview could go on for several more questions. But it's now clear to the interviewer that this candidate did not have a team experience. Instead a group of people in the organization coerced another group to behave in certain ways. The interviewer probed until the candidate revealed what he actually did in that project.

Let's look at another example.

This interviewer wants to determine how the candidate responds to demanding bosses and ambiguous leadership. The interviewer is looking for an independent worker who will take initiative even when not given direction. These are the key strategic points the interviewer sets out to discover.

Interviewer: "I see you've worked for three different companies over your career. Tell me about your relationships with your different bosses."

Candidate: "At the Marks Company my boss was fairly new on the job. He'd been there just a couple of years and seemed unsure of himself. Since that was my first job out of college, I, too, was unsure of myself. I needed some guidance. Clearly I wasn't going to get it from him."

Interviewer: "So, how did you handle that situation?"

Candidate: "At first I took things to my boss, but when I realized he wouldn't make a decision and things would just sit, I had to do something. There was a guy there who had been with the company for years. He wasn't my boss or even in my department, but I started having lunch with him in the cafeteria. I picked his brain about the company. He saved my life."

Interviewer: "When you say you 'picked his brain,' what exactly do you mean?"

Candidate: "Well, being so new I really wasn't sure about the organization at all. He told me some of the history and the low-down on the way things really worked. He told me what not to do as far as the things that would definitely get me fired. He described some of the other people in the company, the higher-ups, and helped me understand what their goals were. I didn't exactly take specific questions to him, like I did my boss. But I was getting a picture of the way the operation functioned and that helped me make the decisions I needed to do my job."

Interviewer: "In other words, you still took your individual questions, like when to submit such and such form or what price to put on a certain order, to your boss, but you learned more about the overall organization from this other person."

Candidate: "That's sort of correct. It was a gradual thing. Not something I planned, exactly. What happened was I didn't need to take as much to my boss. Also, since my boss and I were about the same age, we became friends. Before long he shared some of his insecurities about working in this company. He'd never had a decent orientation either. I told him some of the things I'd learned. We taught each other as we went."

Interviewer: "What you've described in your relationship with your boss sounds like an ideal situation. You were fortunate you had someone who didn't feel threatened by you."

Candidate: (Laughs) "It wasn't so ideal at first. I was very frustrated with my boss. Every night I went home with a headache. But, I loved the job and the opportunity it afforded me. I decided I had to do something to make it work. Oh, yes, at first my boss was threatened by me. I was a little too demanding, and I'm sure I wore my frustrations on my sleeve. I'm not one to cover my feelings too well. Especially then. I was so green. But, once I made the decision to do something, I felt less frustration and after a while things fell into place. Charlie and I are still friends. We've stayed in touch all these years."

This interviewer found out what he or she needed to know. The candidate took initiative when it became necessary and found a way to be successful in a difficult situation with ambiguous leadership. The candidate recognized his own culpability in the situation, not blaming it entirely on the boss, and he changed his behavior to make a difference. As the interview progresses, the interviewer may uncover other situations where leadership was ambiguous and perhaps where leadership was not as congenial as with this candidate's first boss.

How to Determine What to Probe

To peel away the superficial requires interviewers to probe deeply in certain areas. Interviewers must ask themselves as the interview progresses, *Is there anything else I can ask related to this line of questioning? Have I found out everything I need or might more information help me get a clearer picture of what I'm looking for?* In the last example the interviewer found out a lot, but we still do not have a clear picture on some aspects of leadership. Furthermore, the candidate opened a door we might wish to explore. That door dealt with the candidate's ability to manage his emotions. If dealing with difficult bosses is an issue, then the interviewer might explore that area further as follows:

Interviewer: "You said a few moments ago that you sometimes wear your feelings on your sleeve. What did you mean by that?"

Candidate: "I'm a pretty open person. When people make me angry, I usually let them know. Sometimes I don't say anything right away, but they know by my reaction. I've had people tell me I'm easy to read."

Interviewer: "Share an example in your career when one of your bosses made you particularly angry."

Again, as we probe this avenue, we enter territory the candidate probably did not intend to divulge. But by now, we've developed rapport with the candidate, allowed him to share lots of information, and reached a point where sharing becomes easier. If the candidate seems resistant to share or continues to avoid giving specific examples, the interviewer may need to relax this line of questioning and come back to it later.

Time constraints pressure us to identify the areas of utmost importance and to select which interviewer will focus on what. It is not possible for each interviewer to probe everything. As most interviews typically go, one interviewer asks a few questions about an area and then moves on to another area. The candidate faces a second interviewer in that organization who asks many of the same questions. When this happens, the organization loses an opportunity to probe deeply because each interviewer gets no further than the surface.

When human resource managers travel to campuses to recruit new hires, they basically *screen* candidates (i.e., reduce the candidate pool). In other words, they cannot develop a full strategic interview and thereby cannot determine in that interview if candidates are ideally suited for the job—only that they might be. Usually they meet with candidates for fifteen or twenty minutes. They've done their homework, reviewed the résumé, and identified key strategic points related to the position and the person. But with so little time, they can only address one or two points. The other points go unanswered. When the candidate comes to the site, the interview becomes strategic. If, on the other hand, everyone asks the candidate the same questions, then we've gotten no further than the initial screening.

The opportunity to get beyond the superficial and come closer to a successful hiring decision happens on site with a team of interviewers who have strategically planned and interviewed the candidates.

How to Get Beyond the Superficial with Strategic Probes

Let's say your organization experienced problems with turnover because people did not expect to relocate to a small community. Often interviewers approach this problem in the following manner.

Interviewer: "How do you feel about moving?"

Candidate: "I've lived in many communities, so moving is not an issue for me."

Interviewer: "Pleasantville is a small town and doesn't offer as many opportunities as Detroit. Would you be comfortable living in a small town after having lived in a big city for five years?"

Candidate: "Detroit was great while going to school. I enjoyed the nightlife and the social opportunities. But, I really prefer living in a quieter place, like Pleasantville."

Notice how the candidate simply answered the questions as the interviewer wanted them answered. We don't really know how this person feels about living in Pleasantville or how the candidate might adjust to the small town.

Let's look at a more strategic approach to this same interview.

Interviewer: "Tell me what it's like living in Detroit."

Candidate: "It's very exciting living in a big city. While going to school in Detroit, I enjoyed the nightlife and everything that went on all the time. But it's not a place I want to live for the rest of my life."

Interviewer: "What kind of place do you want to live in for the rest of your life?"

Candidate: "I like smaller communities, like Batesville, where I grew up. I enjoy knowing the guy in the drugstore who fills my prescriptions and the fellow who gives me coffee each morning at McDonald's. In Detroit you really don't get to know anyone, even the people in your neighborhood."

Interviewer: "So you're saying you like the personal contact with people that a smaller community affords you?"

Candidate: "Yes, I miss that."

Interviewer: "You also mentioned enjoying the nightlife in the larger city. How would you adjust to a lack of nightlife that smaller communities can't offer?"

Candidate: "That won't be an adjustment for me. I grew up in a small town where nightlife didn't really exist. We went fishing and hung out downtown as kids. I like going to the movies and now that I'm married I don't enjoy partying like I did in college."

This candidate sounds like a good risk for a move to Pleasantville. The interviewer learned that he's married, grew up in a small town, and enjoyed hobbies small towns offer. In the second series the interviewer asked open-ended rather than closed questions. Open questions enable the candidate to share more information about himself. The questions in the second series built on the candidate's responses (piggy-backed) and probed beyond what the candidate said.

When time constraints face the interviewing process, as they usually do, it is essential that the interviewer explore particular areas of concern and allow other interviewers to explore others.

THE INTERVIEW PROCESS

Once you've established the culture where the candidate will work and have a good understanding of the job at hand, you and your fellow interviewers must determine the key areas to probe.

Remember most job seekers are better prepared for the employment interview than the people who hire them.[2] Colleges and universities place great importance on finding jobs for their graduates. They spend untold hours teaching students how to interview. The colleges pay less attention to how long a candidate remains in the job and more attention to getting the graduate hired in the first place. You, on the other hand, must find the right candidate for the right job. As colleges better prepare candidates and as candidates go out into the workplace and learn ways to improve their interviewing skills, the challenge facing human resource managers mounts.

Several important points:

• Interviewing preparation related to the job and pre-interview planning should be done as a team. All interviewers must have a clear understanding of the goals.

Each should agree on the skills and qualities each is looking for. This interview team makes the decisions about the interview process, that is, who will take the candidate on a tour, which interviewer will focus on what area, whether to conduct team interviews, and when and how to entertain the candidate. Some companies review résumés as a team rather than individually. Team analysis of the job, of the résumés, and of the process gives a broader perspective. Your team members may notice something on a résumé you missed. Your team members know certain aspects of the job you may not know. Human resource managers must include on the interview team people who work in similar jobs in the company, people who will work with the candidate, and people from other departments who will interact with the candidate. The team should mirror a cross section of the organization. Each team member brings unique and different knowledge and perspective to the table.

• All the planning in the world won't replace the interview. And just like any other situation in life, Murphy's Law applies to interviews. Even after you've planned, consulted with others, considered all contingencies, something unforeseen will happen. If you focus and listen carefully to the candidate's responses, you will probably uncover a piece of information that the résumé and the previous discussions with your colleagues didn't reveal.

Skillful interviewers brace themselves to make strategic adjustments. Let's look at an example of a strategic adjustment. In this scenario the interviewer began with the goal of determining how the candidate responds to direction. As the conversation progresses, watch how the interviewer alters the goal.

Interviewer: "Tell me about the people you admired as bosses in your previous jobs."

Candidate: "I can think of one boss that I really admired. She ran the restaurant where I worked as a freshman. She worked all the time, even gave up her home life for the job. Whenever decisions needed to be made, she was there to help out. She never allowed the employees to wander aimlessly. I remember once when I was there alone, she asked me to look over the schedule and draw up a rotation for the waiters. I realized we were short because one waiter called to say he wouldn't be there. I contacted the boss immediately, and she filled in. Now, that's my idea of commitment."

Interviewer: "Clearly you admired this boss. So, your idea of commitment is working all the time and filling in during emergencies."

Candidate: "That's right. She really was a team player."

Interviewer: "In your view, then, a team player is someone who takes over when things don't go as planned."

Candidate: "I sometimes think that's necessary."

Interviewer: "What else could this manager do other than take over in emergencies?"

Candidate: (*Pause*) "I really don't know. She seemed to jump right in there. We never worried about things because we counted on her to respond."

In this instance, the candidate expressed little understanding of delegation or of crisis management. The candidate admired someone who reacted to problems; he did not take a proactive approach. Rather than probe about the candidate's response to direction, the interviewer pursued another course and discovered the candidate's ideas on leadership and teamwork.

At the end of this interview, the interviewer will need to tell the next person on the interview team about the concepts that were covered and those that remain unexplored. The next interviewer might need to adjust his or her questions accordingly.

You might ask, "Won't that kind of strategic adjustment mess up the entire plan for the day?" We cannot become so wedded to a plan that we allow important information to go unexplored. Our plans must have some degree of flexibility. Making strategic adjustments is a natural part of the interview process. If the team has a clear view of the bigger picture and knows the direction each interviewer will take, members are in a better position to make strategic adjustments.

• Some responses signal red flags. Legally you cannot ask questions about age, marital status, plans for a family, religion, or national origin (see Chapter 15 for a full list and a discussion of legal issues). But nothing prevents you from listening. Some candidates will tell you they're married or have children. A skillful interviewer moves the conversation away from these sensitive areas and back to the strategic plan.

• If, at the end of the interviewing process, you all agree wholeheartedly on one candidate, you cannot breathe a sigh of relief. Instead this wholehearted agreement may signal another kind of problem. This is where "groupthink" threatens to enter the interviewing process.

WHAT IS GROUPTHINK AND HOW DO PERCEPTIONS AFFECT THE INTERVIEW?

To understand groupthink, we must first examine perceptions.

A perception is an unidentified feeling that is not based on fact.

R. Cleve Folger in *The Right Choice: Hires That Meet Your Agency Needs* (1993) discusses the halo effect—that positive feeling we sometimes get when we instantly like someone. "You should challenge yourself to ignore these external characteristics in order to determine the internal strengths of your candidate," Folger advises.[3]

Ignoring perceptions is about as easy as ignoring breathing. Perceptions and assumptions make communication possible. Whenever we communicate, we face a bombardment of sensory data. Our mind sifts through all this information and quickly puts it into categories. The way those categories exist for each of us depends on our previous experiences. This process is not something we turn off or on. Therefore we must understand how to recognize perceptions and deal with them.

How Do You Handle an Interview when You've Been Zapped by a Perception?

When a candidate walks into your office and something turns you off, a perception has zapped you. Perhaps the person slumps her shoulders or doesn't quite look at you or barely grasps your hand during the handshake. Your mind responds, "This person won't do."

You've got twenty minutes to probe key strategic areas that you and your team identified prior to the interview. After being zapped by a negative perception, managers simply put their strategic interview aside, march forward with a few cursory questions designed to confirm their perceptions, and end the interview as quickly as possible. By doing so, these interviewers risk not hiring a potentially good candidate. Perceptions are never 100 percent right or wrong. Our job is to recognize when a perception has zapped us and keep from falling prey to them.

Many people reach the top of the management ladder based on their intuition and ability to read people. They trust their gut feelings. They're proud of their ability to "size" people up in short order. They expect you to do the same. Unfortunately no one has that kind of ability. The people who profess these skills are unsuccessful as many times as they are successful (but you don't hear about their failures!). Our job as human resource managers gives us a unique respect for human differences and frailties. We've learned that if it's too easy, something else might be at work. We must recognize and teach others who interview about the power of perception.

Believe it or not the most difficult perception pitfall is the positive perception. When people impress us favorably, many times we ignore their negative responses. We sit back and relax. Our carefully planned strategic interview flies out the window. After all, this person is a definite "yes," right? Unlike negative perceptions we often end up hiring the positive perception, and these are the people who come back to haunt us. As with negative perceptions, we need to put our guard up against ourselves and finely tune our listening antennae. Awareness is ninety percent of the battle.

One example from one of my classes illustrates the power of perception. An interview team prescreened college students on campus for their entry-level management positions. One candidate stood out positively. The interviewer asked the candidate to join the interview team for lunch. During lunch the candidate clearly showed a lack of attention, a lack of knowledge about the company, and some inappropriate people skills. The interviewers glanced at one another, grateful for the lunch, and decided not to invite the candidate for a site interview. What happened here? During the twenty-minute interview the candidate displayed a positive perception. The interviewer did not conduct a strategic interview; instead he made a hasty decision. Later, given more time at lunch, he saw his mistake. Even during a brief interview as you might experience on college campuses or in employment offices, you must focus on strategic probes and not let perceptions take control.

Perceptions and groupthink go hand in hand.

Groupthink is when everyone decides to do something *stupid* together.

Groupthink happens as a result of peer pressure. The most famous example surfaced during the Bay of Pigs in the early 60s. "The Kennedy Administration Bay of Pigs decision ranks among the worst fiascoes ever perpetrated by a responsible government," wrote Irving Janis, who coined the term "groupthink."[4] President Kennedy asked each of his top advisors what they thought about invading Cuba. The CIA and the military, intent on carrying out the Bay of Pigs (which had been concocted during the Eisenhower administration), informed the President that the operation would succeed. Rather than buck the military and disappoint a new President, each advisor agreed to the operation. No one shared his concerns. The invasion proved a dismal failure.

Groupthink happens in an interview when the candidate impresses each individual with a positive perception, and the interviewer allows his or her perceptions to prevail. Often organizations allow their individual feelings about a candidate (positive or negative) to seep out before all the interviews are completed. When we pass the résumé on to the next interviewer, we say something like, "This is a real winner" or "You're really going to like this candidate" or we give a thumbs-up or thumbs-down. A reason for multiple interviews (besides letting several key people meet the candidate and join in the decision making) is to get different perspectives and deaden the threat of perception. This works when we stay alert to groupthink and when we avoid sharing our assessment of a candidate until all interviewers finish.

Managers must remember they are dealing with highly skilled candidates who answer questions with poise and skill. If you adhere to your strategic plan and don't get swept away with the positive image, you can break through the façade and combat groupthink.

You might say, aren't some candidates so outstanding their selection is obvious? Perhaps. But, the interview process is fallible. You never really know how candidates will perform in a function until they actually perform the function. Only when you interview for human resource candidates, whose jobs are to interview, will performance during the interview serve as a test. No candidate is so perfect we see nothing negative.

If your group cannot come up with a single reservation, then you should question whether you interviewed strategically and are wary of groupthink.

Groupthink happened to me several years ago. I worked for a large department in a major university. The vice president decided to give everyone a chance to interview the final four candidates for director of that department. Over fifty people interviewed the finalists. The people interviewing ranged from secretarial staff to upper managers and everything in between. Each of us selected the same individual. Together we shared no reservations in our choice. The vice president hired that person, and he turned out to be the worst director in the history of our department. In retrospect we recognize we fell prey to a subtle and dangerous culprit–groupthink, and strategic interviewing got lost in the process!

Let's look at how groupthink works.

Practice Exercise

Mark walks into the conference room and announces, "Well, clearly we all know which candidate is the best. I don't even see why we're meeting. Lucy can do the job so let's get on with hiring her."

Sam responds, "Yeah, Mark, you're right. Lucy really overshadowed the others. There's no question about that."

Margaret adds, "She had all the credentials and I liked her, too; she's got my vote."

You're perplexed. You liked Lucy. You found her attractive and intelligent. But when you asked her to explain how she handled conflict, she said, "Oh, I rely on good interpersonal skills. That always works." You probed further and couldn't get a hold on her ability to deal with conflict. Her responses lacked depth. You couldn't seem to get her past the surface. You began wondering about the extent of Lucy's experience. Since your organization is in the Adolescent Phase of development and conflict arises all the time, you worry about Lucy's ability to succeed. Everyone turns to you.

Mark says, "So, Pete, what do you think about Lucy? Can we make it unanimous?"

If you were Pete, what would you do?

Groupthink strikes hard. Are you willing to buck everyone else? Are you willing to be the gadfly? Some of us rationalize our concerns, think we're exaggerating what we see, talk ourselves out of the negative, convince ourselves that yes, indeed, Lucy is great. Others have little difficulty bucking the system. Much depends on your personality. But either way, we must tune into groupthink.

One way to diagnose groupthink is to notice when you've heard nothing negative. If that is the case, groupthink is alive and well. Usually once you share your concerns, others follow. Both Margaret and Sam probably noticed problems with Lucy, but they kept quiet when they heard Mark's enthusiasm. If the team thoroughly discusses everyone's concerns and decides to select Lucy, they have hired her with their eyes open and have given Lucy a better chance to succeed.

This team should bring Lucy in for a second interview. Considering the nature of this organization, Lucy's ability to handle conflict is critical. But would you make that suggestion if you were Pete? If you do, prepare yourself for Mark's response, "Why waste our time and spend the money to bring her back? Everyone likes her. I think we should just hire her and get on with the work around here. Come on, Pete, admit you liked her, too."

This argument prevails among managers and results in poor hiring decisions and high turnover. Strategic interviewing requires forward-thinking managers. Yes, bring Lucy back even if it costs the company a little extra time and money. Doing so reduces the risk of a much more costly hiring mistake. As the human resources manager you'll need to help people see the value in bringing Lucy back.

In this chapter we learned how to INtentionally listen for key job-related points, and we saw the effects of perception and groupthink on the interview process. Next we'll look at how the interviewer Tests the job fit with the candidate's skills.

NOTES

1. Carol A. Hacker, *The Costs of Bad Hiring Decisions and How to Avoid Them* (Delray Beach, FL: St. Lucie Press, 1996), p. 60.

2. Hacker, *The Costs of Bad Hiring Decisions and How to Avoid Them*, p. 63.

3. R. Cleve Folger, *The Right Choice: Hires That Meet Your Agency Needs* (Indianapolis, IN: The Rough Notes Co. Inc., 1993), pp. 95–96.

4. Irving L. Janis, *Groupthink: Psychological Studies of Policy Decisions and Fiascoes* (Boston: Houghton Mifflin Company, 1982), p. 14.

5

Testing the Fit

This chapter will explore the **T** in POINT by *Testing* the job fit against the candidate. We've looked at how to Plan for the job, how to be Open when interviewing candidates, and how to INtentionally listen. After we've done all those things and have strategically interviewed candidates, we must make a decision. Is this candidate suitable for this job? This question becomes the bottom line in any interview, and it is the most difficult to answer.

FINDING THE RIGHT FIT

One of the hardest decisions an interviewer makes is rejecting a talented candidate because the person doesn't fit the job you have open. This part of the interview process mimics finding the missing piece in a jigsaw puzzle. You must stay focused on the job and be realistic about the demands of the job to determine whether a candidate fits. Often managers rationalize as follows: *I know this person is overqualified for this job, but they're so talented, they'll soon get promoted. I hate to lose such a good person. Our company needs people like this.*

Watch out! Ask yourself these questions:

- How quickly can someone expect promotion within our organization?
- Will this person find a job in another company before we can reasonably expect to effect a promotion?

- If the job doesn't meet the candidate's skills, how soon will boredom and burnout set in?
- What are the morale implications regarding our other employees if we promote too quickly?

This chapter will help managers learn how to test what they've learned about candidates to determine if they are right for the job. It will also look at the manager's tolerance for empowerment and present examples of candidates with different skill levels competing for different kinds of jobs.

We want people who will grow in our organization, but not until these people develop in their current jobs. If there is no growth potential in the current job, and we hire the person anyway, we do a disservice to the candidate and to the organization. Recently a manager told me he wouldn't hire anyone who didn't demonstrate some measure of improvement in his/her previous jobs. Just having a job isn't enough. That philosophy sounds great, but how can people fresh out of school show this kind of self-improvement? Often these candidates lack experience related to their professional endeavors. Many young people, however, work during school. In the service industry at a minimum-wage job, what did the person do? I've seen many young people who got promoted to store manager, head cook, or chief bookkeeper during a summer job. If they spent each summer flipping hamburgers or filing folders and never amounted to much more, what are the chances they'll take the initiative to excel in your job? Remember the best predictor of future behavior is past behavior.

But, you say, those young people weren't interested in the "menial" jobs. As you examine candidates and the skills they present, be careful not to fall prey to "I'll do better in the future because that's where my interest lies." Base your decision on some past behavior. If this same person excelled in school, but not in his/her summer job, that may serve as an indicator that indeed when the task is interesting, he/she may perform.

To determine fit we must examine those factors that spell success in the job and see if this person meets the test.

Candidates Who Are Oversized

When I worked for a university employment office, I interviewed candidates for many kinds of jobs. In this university town, people finished school and remained in the community. They applied for whatever jobs we posted regardless of their qualifications. After all, why couldn't a Ph.D. in English perform as a secretary?

Once I interviewed a young man with a graduate degree in physics. He applied for a lab technician position. He worked in the Physics department as a graduate assistant and wanted to remain. Let's look at how that interview went.

Interviewer: "I see on your application you worked for five years in the Physical Science lab as a graduate assistant. What are you looking for after having had that experience?"

Candidate: "I knew when I finished my degree, the department couldn't hire me onto the faculty because the university prohibits hiring its own graduates. But I love the people in the department. It's a great place to work. I'm more interested in being around good researchers than in doing the research myself."

Interviewer: "So you're saying you are not interested in doing research?"

Candidate: "Perhaps someday I will want to jump into a research project again. But right now, after just finishing my dissertation, I want some time to do something else."

Interviewer: "And what might that something else be?"

Candidate: (Shrugs) "I suppose logging in data and performing experiments at the direction of someone else."

Interviewer: "After having led a research project yourself and taught classes as a graduate assistant, how will you feel in a position where you simply respond to someone else's instruction?"

Candidate: "I know what you're getting at. But, I like working in this lab and I know that a time will come when I can pursue my own projects. I'm just not ready to do that now."

Interviewer: "And when do you expect that time to come?"

Candidate: "Probably in a few years. Right now I'm happy washing out test tubes and chilling out for a while."

Interviewer: "After spending five years completing a graduate level degree, it must be frustrating to step back to a lab tech position where not even a college degree is necessary. I know I'd be very frustrated."

Candidate: "I tried to get a research job at other universities but none came forth. You're right. It is sometimes frustrating, but I'm willing to pay the price until something comes along in my field. I'm in no rush."

Sure, and when another university calls in six months, this candidate will exit and rightly so. The candidate might be extremely talented and personable, and we wish we could give everyone a job. Unfortunately unless we want to spend all our time interviewing, we must find people who match the job at hand. In this case we have an oversized candidate for an undersized job.

One organization I work with requires all candidates to have a minimum 3.0 Grade Point Average (GPA). Candidates with a 3.7 or 3.9 GPA look excellent. They achieved near perfection in school, often in highly technical fields. That near perfection suggests they excelled in research or design or some other complicated application of their study. Often these candidates have had few practical jobs. They've had experience in research or design as co-ops or interns. Usually their main focus during their tenure in school is study. They've rarely worked at McDonald's. In other words they may not have been successful in the more practical aspects of living. This particular company hires first-line supervisors into highly practical positions that require flexibility and little opportunity to use technical know-how. Over the years, the human resource managers recognized that persons with high GPA's become frustrated early into their tenure and often leave in the first year. Those with more balanced experience and more average GPA's achieve more success. Again, we must match the candidate with the job. A very bright candidate may be unsuitable for the practical, hands-on job. This doesn't mean we don't want smart people. It means we want a different kind of "smart."

Candidates Who Are Undersized

What about a situation where you have an undersized candidate?

Interviewer: "I see from your résumé that you have a degree in music theory and experience in public relations. Describe in more detail your duties in your last job."

Candidate: "I prepared press releases for the theater and I took photographs at events. I worked primarily with the media to make sure the theater got top publicity. I won two awards for advertising in national magazines. I also worked with groups and shared information and brochures about the theater. I became a mouthpiece for all the performances."

Interviewer: "When you say mouthpiece, what do you mean?"

Candidate: "I just talked the performances up with all my friends and made sure the press understood what we were doing."

Interviewer: "You didn't make formal presentations about the theater's activities?"

Candidate: "We had a development office with staff whose job was to make formal presentations. They went around and talked to civic and cultural groups and people like that. I really didn't get involved in those presentations unless they needed some type of publicity."

Interviewer: "So by publicity you're talking about preparing materials to be mailed or for press releases and talking informally to people you know."

Candidate: "Right. Once I got a company to give money to the theater. I talked to a friend of mine who was a CEO, and he donated $1000."

Interviewer: "Tell me how that went, talking to your friend about giving money."

Candidate: "It wasn't so hard. My friend wanted to support the arts. When I told him about the theater and all the things we do, he gladly opened his pocketbook. I enjoyed bringing in that kind of financial support."

Interviewer: "When you said there is a development office with staff. Are you saying, their job is fund-raising and yours is public relations?"

Candidate: "That's right. But, of course, if I'm able to raise a little money, they're happy."

Interviewer: "We're looking for someone whose primary job is to raise money and increase membership in our organization. Another person on the staff handles the public relations."

Candidate: "I'm excited and challenged by new things. I've been doing public relations now for six years and am ready to take the step toward development. I'd love the opportunity to try. My experience in public relations gives me an idea of how to approach people for money—that is, how to target them. I see the jobs as interrelated."

Interviewer: "Tell me how you've been challenged by new things in your work."

Candidate: "I came into the job with the theater with no experience in public relations. My music theory degree taught me about the arts. I knew and understood the language, but I knew nothing about how to write press releases or deal with the media. I struggled to write copy the average public could understand and to win the respect of the press. Musicians often use ninety dollar words to describe performances."

Interviewer: "How did you learn the business of public relations?"

Candidate: "I had a wonderful mentor who guided me along with patience. I also attended as many continuing education courses as I could."

Clearly this candidate is talented. The person won awards for well-designed and well-placed work and shows initiative and enthusiasm. The job, however, specifies skills in fund-raising and membership development. This candidate raised a small amount of money purely by coincidence. The person never developed a fund-raising or marketing strategy and has a limited understanding of the rigors of development. The match isn't there.

Even so, some managers make the strategic decision to teach a talented candidate the basic skills as long as the candidate demonstrates enthusiasm for the job. Determining the fit for your organization requires you to consider how much time you are willing to spend as a mentor.

EMPOWERMENT AND MENTORING

James Brewer, Michael Ainsworth and George Wynne developed a power management model that applies to a manager's thinking when evaluating his or her own ability to empower. In *Power Management: A Three-Step Program for Successful Leadership* (1984), the authors discuss empowerment in terms of task and human relations dimensions. (See Figure 1.) Applying the principles from this model, human resource managers can evaluate their inclination to train the untrained candidates.

Stage 1: Directive Stage. Employees arrive fresh with limited skills but a high willingness to learn. They need and want direction. Managers focus on task. The manager teaches the employee the task and sticks by the new person to assure adequate performance. The term "micromanagement" comes into play here, but employees appreciate the direction. Managers spend a great deal of time with the employee in the Directive Stage.

Figure 1
Power Management Model

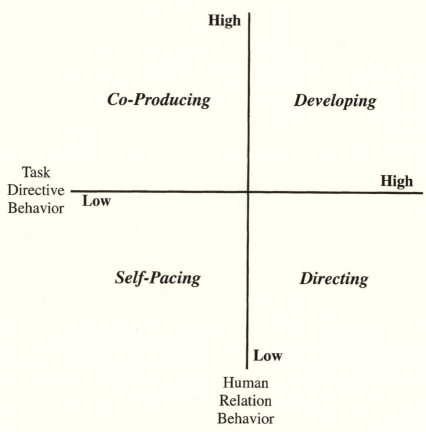

Source: From *Power Management: A Three-Step Program for Successful Leadership* (pp. 83, 88–90) by James H. Brewer, J. Michael Ainsworth, and George E. Wynne. Englewood Cliffs, NJ: Prentice-Hall, Inc., 1984. Reprinted by permission.

Stage 2: Developing Stage. In this stage the employee generally understands how to perform the task, but lacks confidence in doing a successful job. The employee depends on the manager for input and support. The manager focuses on developing the employee's confidence in doing the task by stepping back (no longer micromanaging) and allowing the employee to fumble. The manager praises correct performance and supports and guides the employee through errors. Mistakes are okay. The manager allows the employee to stretch in order to demonstrate that mistakes happen, and we learn from them. The manager becomes the employee's safety net, remaining accessible to help the employee through good and bad times.

Stage 3: Co-Producing Stage. At this stage in the employee's development, the ability to complete the task and confidence in doing so match.

The employee functions but without total independence. The manager stretches and teaches the employee to the point that he or she accomplishes the task with nearly as much ability as the manager. In the Co-Producing Stage the employee relies on the manager merely as a final checkpoint or for modest tweaking.

Stage 4: Self-Pacing Stage. When the manager notices the employee's work no longer needs review, the manager lets go. The employee makes decisions that match or excel the manager's and both the employee and manager have a high degree of confidence in the employee's performance. In this stage the manager knows the employee will accomplish the task with skill and confidence at a high level of achievement. Complete empowerment happens at the Self-Pacing Stage.

Let's look at applying this model to the interview process. Human resource managers, who do strategic hiring, must consider the job from every angle. They must ask themselves: Are we willing to take an employee under our wing—mentor him or her through the entire process of empowerment from directive to self-pacing? Or do we hope to hire an employee at the Developing or Co-Producing Stage? Who will actually do the mentoring? We need to carefully consider these questions early in the hiring process.

Often managers overlook these considerations. If they hire someone at the directive stage, frustration sets in when the employee falters without solid guidance. The employee's morale drops and a bad hiring decision results. The manager's expectations of the employee's abilities and the employee's actual abilities didn't match.

Human resource managers can guide other managers into making the tough decisions. If you have a talented candidate who needs direction and the manager wants to hire the person, you need to counsel the manager. The choices are:

- Hire the talented person. Managers often advocate doing this. They're tired of interviewing, and they like the person they see. They don't consider the time involved in training. Once they understand they'll need to "direct" this person for several weeks, take them under their wing, "develop" them for several more weeks before the candidate reaches the same point where another, more adequately trained candidate might have been on the first day, they often reconsider. If the manager still wishes to hire the undersized candidate, you've enabled them to do so with open eyes.

- Don't hire the person. This decision also carries risk. Weeks of interviewing still might not produce someone with the skills you're seeking. Sometimes you find candidates with technical knowledge but with inadequate interpersonal skills. Again, human resource managers can guide others through these tough decisions. Sometimes managers place too much weight on technical know-how. The job itself might require less technical ability and more interpersonal ability—such as teamwork, flexibility, or strong communication skills. Human resource managers scrutinize the job with a "third" eye and help managers see the skills that are needed and those that are peripheral. Again a team of people within the organization can make these decisions with more objectivity than the direct manager alone. Together the team weighs the consequences of continuing the interview process or of hiring someone who must go through extensive training before becoming productive.

When does the organization make the decision to hire undersized candidates or not? Ideally the team should consider this issue when identifying the skills and abilities they are seeking—before they've looked at the first résumé. If they set their standards too high, they may need to revisit them and make modifications. Teams must be careful, however, not to modify their standards too quickly. If your team decided certain skills are needed to perform successfully in a job, those are the skills you seek through your strategic plan. You should not alter those specifications to fit the candidates you end up interviewing.

The following candidate is interviewing for a management training position. The requirements for the job include strong interpersonal skills, a working knowledge of the principles of management, a demonstrated ability to speak before groups, and experience as an adult educator. Jonathan Price applied.

Interviewer: "Mr. Price, thank you for coming in this afternoon. I've reviewed your résumé and see you've been a Baptist minister for the bulk of your career. What prompted you to apply for the management training position?"

Jonathan: "I've grown tired of the ministry. I'm really not sure what my next career might be, but it's going to be something different. When I saw your ad, I decided to take a chance. The job sounded fascinating."

Interviewer: "What fascinated you about the job?"

Jonathan: "I love to teach. Part of what I did in the ministry was Christian education. I taught all age groups and thoroughly enjoyed it. I'm also a professional storyteller. I enjoy capturing people's attention and spinning a good yarn. I love making people laugh. This job, as I see it, might give me an opportunity to use both those skills. I can teach things people yearn to know but do it in an interesting, entertaining way."

Interviewer: "So you see this job as teaching and entertaining?"

Jonathan: "Indeed I do. I love public speaking. I've had many courses on speaking before groups. As a minister I had to prepare a sermon every Sunday. I perfected it and struggled with trying to make what I said interesting enough to hold attention. That wasn't easy."

Interviewer: "What made you decide to abandon the ministry?"

Jonathan: "I've done what I can there. I've gone as far as I can. I'm looking for new challenges. The ministry doesn't offer the challenges it used to in the early days. I'm a person who loves new things and thrives on every day being different. I will remain in the ministry and continue to help and minister to people. I'm sure I will do that the rest of my life. But, I'm ready for a new adventure."

Interviewer: "What challenges do you anticipate in the job we have open?"

Jonathan: "Everything will be a challenge. I will have to learn what I'm teaching.

I've had no training as an adult educator or in the field of management. All of it will be new and a wonderful learning opportunity for me."

Interviewer: "Help me understand when you've faced a similar daunting challenge in your previous career."

Practice Exercise

Look at the preceding interview.

1. *Examine the candidate's responses. From what the interviewer learned, at what stage of empowerment will this employee begin?*
2. *Examine the interviewer's questions. How did the interviewer learn the candidate's level of skills?*
3. *List additional questions the interviewer might ask to determine the stage of empowerment without focusing on future behavior. (A question focused on future behavior might sound something like this: "Tell me how you might go about teaching a management class.")*
4. *Would you recommend Jonathan for hire?*

At what stage of empowerment will Jonathan Price begin? Let's look at the skills Jonathan Price has that match the requirements of the job.

- The interview tells us he has strong interpersonal skills.
- His experience as a minister as well as his efforts to continue his education tell us he has demonstrated an ability to speak before groups.
- He experienced teaching through the Christian education program at the church.

What skills are missing?

- He lacks any knowledge of the principles of management.
- He admitted he lacks experience or knowledge in adult education.

Based on this analysis, Jonathan Price would clearly enter the job at the Directing Phase. He'd need to spend time sitting in on classes to learn the way to facilitate an adult group in a workshop setting. He'd need to spend time learning the content of the material he'd be teaching.

How did the interviewer learn about Jonathan's level of skills? The interviewer asked open questions leading Jonathan to discuss his abilities:

- What prompted you to apply for this job?
- What fascinates you about this job?
- What challenges do you anticipate in this job?

Notice, the interviewer never asked, "Why would you apply for a job so unrelated to your field?" Such a question would put Jonathan on the defensive. The interviewer made sure the questions probed but did not offend.

What additional questions might the interviewer ask to determine stage of empowerment? We need to know more about what Jonathan did during the Christian education experience. We don't want to get into sensitive areas, but we want to learn if Jonathan taught adults and how he handled those classes. This will help us understand if he's on the verge of moving out of the Directing Stage as far as adult learning is concerned or embedded in the early stage.

Furthermore, as a minister Jonathan probably had to manage people in some fashion (even if it was just one church secretary). What experiences did he have in that role? What did he learn from those experiences that might translate into management training?

Would you recommend Jonathan for hire? Without answering the questions we've identified in the practice exercise, it's hard to tell, but from what we know, we'd have to say no. Jonathan brings a lot of talent to the position, but moving from a minister to a management trainer without anything in between seems quite a stretch.

Furthermore, Jonathan's view of education seems naïve. His desire to entertain as well as teach suggests a lack of understanding of quality adult learning. We'd need to learn more about what he means by asking him for specific examples in which he taught and entertained.

CO-OPS AS A WAY TO TEST FIT

Many companies offer co-op positions to help young people apply technical skills to a work environment. Co-ops come into the organization at the Directive Stage and managers know that. Managers spend time with the young person, help them learn the organization, and guide them through each decision. Many co-ops work on teams and experience the value of teamwork firsthand. These experiences help in two ways: first, the young person learns your organization and how to function in your culture and second, if you hire the person, he or she immediately enters the organization at the Co-Producing Stage.

Simply because someone worked as a co-op in your organization, however, doesn't necessarily mean that person will fit into the job you may have open. To determine fit, you still must conduct a strategic interview.

Some co-ops find it hard to blend in with the organizational culture. Perhaps your organization is in the Middle-Age Phase of development and the co-op is a creative, energetic person who likes to experiment with new ideas. Frustration sets in if the ideas sit on the boss's desk. Nonetheless, co-op programs give the organization a way for employers and employees to try each other out.

Let's look at an interview with a former co-op named Mary Steward.

Interviewer: "I see you worked for two semesters with XYZ Company as a co-op. Tell me about that experience."

Mary: "My professor got that job for me. I wanted to work in a technology environment, just to see how things went. There were several choices for co-opting. I interviewed for all of them, but I liked the sound of this company best."

Interviewer: "What attracted you to this company?"

Mary: "I tend to be a creative person. I want to try new things all the time. I like to take what's always been done and turn it upside down, just to see if there's a better approach. The guy I talked to before I took the co-op job had lots of energy. He was young, out of college just a few years. He said one day was never the same as the next at XYZ Company. He made the job sound exactly like what I wanted."

Interviewer: "So, when you went to work for XYZ Company, what did you experience?"

Mary: "It was much as I expected. There was lots of activity. Mark, my supervisor, showed me the ropes and explained how things worked. Basically it was a very informal environment. I could approach anyone with questions. I liked that a lot."

Interviewer: "It sounds as though XYZ Company met your expectations for being a creative company."

Mary: "Well, it did and it didn't. I learned a lot while I was there. I saw how my technical knowledge played a role in a real company. That felt good. People counted on me for the new, more advanced information. But I also learned that being energetic isn't necessarily being creative."

Interviewer: "What do you mean by that?"

Mary: "People seemed to run around doing lots of stuff, but there wasn't any reason for what they did. There didn't seem to be any logical pattern for the work. If I had an idea, they'd say, 'Try it.' No one asked if the idea was any good; no one seemed to care if the idea worked or not. I felt at loose ends."

Interviewer: "Are you saying people basically did their own thing and let you 'play' at your job, so to speak?"

Mary: "Yeah, that's it. But I sorta felt everyone was playing at their jobs. I couldn't get a handle on the organization's overall vision. It was a new company and maybe they were still searching for that vision, but I really felt lost."

Interviewer: "So how did you handle being in an organization like XYZ?"

Mary: "First, I talked with my professor. He suggested I look for my own direction. He said new companies often flounder for a while, but working there can be exciting. We talked at the end of each month, and he helped guide me through it. Before long I realized how I could make a contribution."

Interviewer: "I noticed you worked for XYZ Company again the following semester. What made you decide to work for them again?"

Mary: "I liked the challenge. As I grew more accustomed to the culture at XYZ, I started finding my own place there. By the end of the first co-op, I hated to leave. That's why I returned."

Interviewer: "How did your second experience go?"

Mary: "Much better. Since I knew what to expect, I came right in and began working. Also, after having more classes, I felt better equipped to handle the job."

Interviewer: "It sounds as though your co-op experience started out a little bumpy, but you gained a lot from it."

Mary: "I really did. It was probably the most worthwhile thing I did while in school."

Interviewer: "So what made you decide not to apply for a full-time position with XYZ Company after you graduated?"

Mary: "Actually, I did apply. But they didn't have an opening. Like I said they're a small company, and they have limited opportunities for either new hires or for growth within the company."

Practice Exercise

Examine the preceding interview.

1. *What did you like about the candidate?*
2. *What concerns do you have about the candidate?*
3. *How do you think Mary will fit into your job and your culture?*
4. *Would you recommend Mary Steward for hire?*

What did you like about Mary Steward?

- She knew the kind of company she wanted to work for. As a co-op candidate, she recognized a creative company and made her selection based on what she knew she wanted for her co-op experience. She seemed to go into the interview process with a plan.

- When things didn't work out the way she expected, she sought help from her advisor. Through his guidance, she found a way to become a contributing member of the company's team.

- She knows herself and her creative energy.

What concerns do you have about Mary?

- Mary Steward seems to need a lot of latitude. She wants a job where she can initiate ideas and see those ideas happen. Many organizations don't have immediate feedback. Most organizations don't allow newly hired persons to jump in and change things. Mary admitted she likes to turn things upside down. Depending on your company, this may be a liability.

- Mary Steward adjusted to XYZ Company and fit well into their culture. How she might adjust to another culture, one not quite so new, might present a problem.

How do you think Mary will fit into your job and your culture?

- The first question you'll need to ask is what kind of culture do you have? If your company is in the Childhood or Adolescent Phase of development, Mary might fit in nicely. If you're in Middle-Age or Senior Phases of development, Mary might become frustrated and leave after a short period of time.
- You'll also need to ask yourself if you're in a Tough Guy culture or a Work Hard/Play Hard culture. Either of these cultures might suit Mary Steward's style. If you're in a Bet Your Company or Process culture, she might become frustrated because of the delay in feedback. She indicated she likes to know what's going on quickly.

Would you recommend Mary for hire? Even if Mary Steward seemed suited to your culture, I wouldn't recommend her for hire. The main concern I'd have would be her willingness to stay with the company. If XYZ contacts her, it seems she would be inclined to go there. You may say, XYZ doesn't have an opening. That's true, but as a young organization, they'll create an opening for her if they liked her. She seemed suited to their organization, liked working there, and ended up contributing. There is no reason for the interviewer to believe she wouldn't go there if offered a job. The risk is too great.

Mary probably would need less direction than many candidates because of her co-op experience, but she's still new. The time and energy to bring her in and train her would cost the company too much if she turned around and left in six months.

Most organizations prefer to hire candidates with basic skills. The energy we spend on training new candidates shrinks all the time. New demands on us as managers require that we find people ready to jump into the job, preferably at the Co-Producing Stage. All new hires spend a short time in the Directive and Developing Stages, but those with solid skills quickly move out. Hiring a candidate who takes more time to develop might enable you to mold the person to fit your job, but the trade-offs may be too high. In the fast-paced world of today's business, hours of training and mentoring are a luxury most managers cannot afford.

In summary, as you test the fit, several factors come into play:

- Do I have an oversized candidate for an undersized job?
- Do I have an undersized candidate for an oversized job?
- If I judge the candidate to be undersized, how much time am I willing to devote to training?
- How will this candidate fit into the company culture?
- A reasonable fit matches the basic skills needed to do the job at an entry level. Anything less than that requires managers to analyze the job in terms of more intensive training.

This section focused on applying the POINT process to the job. We Planned with all aspects of the job and organization in mind. We set an Open tone for the interview by sharing information about the job and ourselves and by being purposeful in our interview conversations. We INtentionally listened for key job-related points and braced ourselves for the effects of perceptions and groupthink. Finally we Tested the job and the organizational culture against the candidate's skills to determine fit.

In the next section we will apply the POINT process to the candidate.

6

Résumé Screening

This chapter will explore the **P** in POINT by *Planning* for the interview with the candidate in mind. The yardstick for each probe is whether the question fits this particular candidate. If a question fits any candidate, not this one in particular, you haven't asked a strategic question.

Strategic interviewing designs questions with a specific candidate in mind. Questions like, "Where do you want to be in five years?" or "What made you decide to apply for a job with XYC Company?" are not strategic because you might ask that question of anyone who walks into your office. "What factors led you to choose a degree in English literature?" is more candidate-specific. As we recognize the power of the interview, we see the importance of each question we ask. Loose, unnecessary questions waste interview time and give the appearance of being unprofessional.

Recent hires in my classes tell me they noticed quality interviewing; it became a key criterion for making a decision to join a company. Companies that asked canned questions or asked what the candidate expected didn't win the candidate's respect.

RÉSUMÉ SCREENING

Planning questions for the candidate requires a careful analysis of the résumé or application. Since you've already established the job qualities you're looking for, you're now in a position to examine the résumé with particular goals in mind. Does this person meet the basic requirements of the job? Does this person demonstrate the qualities we've listed for performance in our organization? Michael O'Driscoll and Paul Taylor call this a job analysis.[1] They talk about structuring the interview within the framework of the particular position you wish to fill. Although they use the term "structured" interview, they often relax the structure and encourage interviewers to show flexibility in the interview. In fact, they set the stage for what we're calling strategic interviewing.

Let's look at an example.

XYZ Company is seeking an entry-level management position. The candidate must show flexibility, demonstrate strong communication skills, act as a team player, take the lead, and relocate to South Carolina. Peter Long submitted his résumé.

Peter Long
32 Nadder Ridge
Philadelphia, PA
(214) 997–2039

OBJECTIVE: To obtain an entry-level management position

EDUCATION: University of South Carolina
Bachelor of Arts degree, May 1999
GPA 3.1. Major in psychology, minor in business administration

HONORS: Dean's List, 1997–1998
President's List, 1996
Golden Key National Honor Society, 1996
Woodrow Scholarship, 1997–1998

ACTIVITIES: President, Psi Chi (Psychology Honor Society),
1996–present
Volunteer coach at the Columbia YMCA

WORK EXPERIENCE:
6/98–9/98   Philadelphia General Hospital
Lab orderly
* Labeled the vials
* Put data into the computer
* Made material requests

6/97–9/97   The Opera Company of Philadelphia
* Prepared publicity material
* Sold ads for the program
* Coordinated the board meetings
* Answered the telephone

6/96–9/96   Marshall Law Firm, Philadelphia
                 * Served as a runner, delivered mail, answered telephone during
                 lunch hours, and made appointments

PERSONAL DATA: Born in Philadelphia
                 Interests: music, recreational sports
                 Willing to relocate

Practice Exercise

1. *Review Peter Long's credentials. Examine Peter Long in terms of his flexibility, communication skills, teamwork, leadership, and willingness to relocate.*

2. *What gaps or red flags do you see from Peter Long's résumé?*

3. *If you were the manager of XYZ Company, would you ask Peter Long for an interview?*

4. *What probe points would you address (after the icebreaker)?*

Let's examine Peter Long's résumé together.

Task 1: List the points in the résumé that fit the qualities needed to fill this job.

Educational achievements

• BA in psychology with a minor in business administration
• Honors as a student

Flexibility

• Worked one summer as a hospital lab orderly

Communication skills

• Runner for the law firm
• Sold ads for The Opera Company
• Volunteer coach at the YMCA

Team player

• Participated in recreational sports
• Volunteer coach at YMCA

Leadership

- President of the Psychology Honorary Society
- Sold ads for The Opera Company
- Coordinated board meetings for The Opera Company

Willingness to relocate to South Carolina

- Went to school in Columbia

Task 2: List the items missing or in need of more in-depth attention.

- He attended school in Columbia, South Carolina but returned to Philadelphia every summer.
- He has no clear supervisory experience.
- He has no clear teamwork experience.
- His interpersonal skills appear good but could use more probing.

Task 3: Interview or Not Interview? Looking at this analysis of Peter Long's résumé, would you recommend interviewing him? Yes. On paper he possesses all the qualities XYZ Company is looking for.

Task 4: Probe POINTS. Where would you aim your initial series of questions when you interview Peter Long?

Because XYZ Company is a Middle-Age organization that places a high value on loyalty, being willing to stay in the job for a period of time is important. Furthermore XYZ Company invests time and money training all new entry-level management hires. Therefore, as a manager interviewing Peter Long, you must determine his willingness to live in South Carolina and attempt to discover what brought him to the south in the first place. Your primary goal is to determine his staying power.

With these key points in mind, focus the interview on Peter and peel away the superficial to learn more about his potential fit in your entry-level management position.

Let's look at how to address the most uncertain issue—his staying power.

Interviewer: "I see from your résumé that you worked each summer in Philadelphia. What made you decide to return home?"

Peter: "My parents live in Philadelphia, and they wanted me closer to them during the summers."

Interviewer: "So, it was your parents' decision for you to return home?"

Peter: "Not exactly. I just knew they wanted me at home, and I knew I could get a job there."

Interviewer: "What were your chances of getting a job in Columbia?"

Peter: "Pretty good. Most of my friends worked down here. But I also had friends in Philadelphia, and my girlfriend came home, too. I enjoyed being home during the summers."

Interviewer: "It must've been difficult for you to come to school so far from home. I went to school fifty miles from my house and still had difficulty adjusting."

Peter: "It was hard at first, but I was excited to go someplace so different."

Interviewer: "How did you deal with the initial difficulty?"

Peter: "I was young. Sure I was homesick, but so was everybody. My roommate came from Charleston and even though his home was closer, he still missed everybody—his friends and all. We became buddies. That helped."

Interviewer: "So you really knew no one in Columbia when you came here?"

Peter: "Not a soul. I got a small scholarship. When my parents and I came down to look at the school and the town, we all liked what we saw. So that was it."

Interviewer: "How do you feel about living in Columbia now?"

Peter: "It's a nice town. I still like it."

Interviewer: "And what do you like about it?"

Peter: "The campus is beautiful. The old oak trees and the shaded lawns are great. I love the winter, but I have trouble with the summer heat. Wintertime is great because it's cool, not freezing like at home. I also like the people. Southerners are so friendly."

Interviewer: "So, you like the cold but not freezing winters. How did you cope with the heat while you lived in Columbia?"

Peter: "I suppose I never experienced the worst of it. I left in June and by the time I came back, it had cooled down some."

Interviewer: "It can get pretty hot down here, especially in August. I often wish I had a place to escape to for a few weeks. After a while, though, you get used to it. Earlier you mentioned that you knew you could find summer work in Philadelphia. Now that you've finished school, what made you decide to apply for a full-time job here instead of going home?"

Peter: "I have friends down here, and I just wanted to stay."

Interviewer: "I thought you had friends up there, too."

Peter: (Looks away) "I do, but a lot of them have moved away. My girlfriend got a job at a big company nearby. And a couple of my other friends are looking for jobs around here. The job market is better in this area than in Philadelphia, which is somewhat depressed."

Interviewer: "Are you saying because your friends stayed here and more job opportunities exist here, you didn't apply for jobs in Philadelphia?"

Peter: "That's right. I want to work in this area."

Let's examine this interview. The interviewer learned Peter has a girlfriend. It seems wherever the girlfriend is, he goes there. When she went home to Philadelphia in the summers, he did, too. Now, she's working in the south, and Peter wants to work there, too. We can't ask more about the girlfriend or his future plans. If he marries her, he might remain in the south and continue working for us. If he breaks up with the girlfriend, guess where Peter will probably go? You're dealing with probabilities here and in all likelihood, *based on Peter's past behavior*, he'll return to Philadelphia. Even though he looks like a good candidate in terms of his experience, hiring him would be a high risk for long-term employment. At some point either Peter will marry his girlfriend or she will separate from him, and he will settle in his own place. Peter's concern about the summer heat suggests he might select a place north of us if it weren't for the current pull of his girlfriend. If we want to hire someone with staying power, Peter might not be the best choice.

The rest of Peter's résumé looks appealing. He was a good student. In the interview you liked his honest and open responses. The decision not to hire Peter will be difficult. The question XYZ Company must ask is whether Peter is worth the risk. A person like Peter could become a long-time employee, but he may also leave in six months if his personal circumstances change. His attachment to the area seems tenuous. With all the training XYZ Company devotes to entry-level management positions, you will likely decide to reject Peter.

Had Peter shown more enthusiasm for living in the south, XYZ Company could justify hiring him. Had he stayed one summer in Columbia, particularly his last summer, and worked independently from his Philadelphia connections, XYZ Company could justify hiring him. Human resource managers must look at his past behavior, not what they hope someone will do in the future.

Until he becomes more stable, Peter would be better served in a faster-moving company that places less emphasis on longevity. Peter and XYZ Company aren't a suitable match.

Screening the résumé helped the interviewer identify the gaps and recognize where to focus the interview. Résumés provide a wealth of information even though they're often produced with guidance from career planners or friends and mentors. The résumé is the first hint you have of the person behind the façade. As you study the piece of paper, ask yourself, what does this person count as important? What kinds of things matter to this person? Where are his or her priorities? The résumé cannot answer all your questions; it merely points you in the right direction to focus your strategic interview. From Peter's résumé alone we saw that location was an issue. The résumé told us he was from Philadelphia and worked there every summer—a definite red flag.

Let's examine another résumé.

MARY COLE
2912 Bayonet Court
Port Hueneme, CA 93041–2160
Home: (805) 984–1121   Office: (800) 669–4562 ext. 776

OBJECTIVE: A career with a world-class organization in a growth industry where my abilities and drive will lead me through an outside sales position and into management.

EDUCATION: B.S. Business Administration, Marketing
California State University, Northridge

EXPERIENCE: Outside Sales Representative   July 1989–present
Tri-West, Ltd. Santa Fe Springs, California
An Armstrong Resilient Flooring Distributor

- Sold over $2,400,000 in sales in the last four years while product lines were being reduced
- Increased market share every year
- Established strong relationships with accounts through the sale of resilient sheet and tile, laminate, rubber and vinyl flooring products
- Sold, managed, and developed 130 accounts which incorporate residential, commercial, builder, and tenant improvement flooring markets
- Conducted sales and installation meetings to introduce new products and promotions and to insure customer confidence and preference of existing products and programs

Outside Sales Representative   May 1987–June 1989
Budget Rent-A-Car   Van Nuye, California

- Increased sales and market share every year
- Increased car rentals from automotive dealerships, automotive repair businesses, body shops, and hotels by building strong relationships
- Supervised an assistant and operational personnel to develop the highest quality service and customer satisfaction

Retail Sales Manager   June 1985–June 1987
Gary's Custom Optik Northridge and Westwood, California

- Sold eyewear in the fast-paced, trendy Westwood Village to the conservative, established clientele of Northridge
- Managed sales people and laboratory personnel

PERSONAL: Married with 2 children

In this instance XYZ Company is a newly formed Internet business that launched two years ago. The owners are looking for a dynamic person to lead the sales team. They want someone willing to take risks, with a high level of tolerance for ambiguity in leadership, a creative drive, and an ambitious nature. The company's future is tenuous. Since launching, they have tripled their staff, but a buyout might change the nature of the company, and the owners are not adverse to the buyout potential. The new sales manager must jump into the job immediately with little orientation or training. Therefore a person with well-developed sales skills is necessary. This company can't spend time "directing or developing" someone.

A company analysis indicates XYZ Company is in the Childhood phase of development and in a Tough Guy culture. The owners wish to hire someone at the Co-Producing or Self-Pacing level.

Practice Exercise

1. *List the qualities you see on the résumé that fit this job.*
2. *List the gaps or items that are missing.*
3. *Would you recommend Mary for an interview?*
4. *If yes, what probe points would you pursue?*

Task 1: List the qualities from the résumé that fit this job.

• Strong sales experience. Mary can walk into the job and begin working. She's clearly at the Self-Pacing level.

• Mary's proved herself a risk taker by working on a commission since 1989. She sold $2.4 million of the product even though the product line was being reduced. Her approach included direct sales as well as developing relationships with similar industries.

• Mary not only sells products but she teaches others how to sell. The Childhood phase of XYZ Company will require Mary to help others become part of a sales team.

Task 2: List the gaps or items that are missing from the résumé.

• Mary seems to have worked for stable companies. There are no indications she's experienced the short-term pace indicative of Internet businesses.

• The résumé doesn't give us any indication of Mary's tolerance for ambiguous leadership. Two owners run XYZ Company. They don't always agree. Conflicts arise. Mary will need to deal with this kind of tension.

Task 3: Interview or Not Interview? Mary's strong experience in sales as well as the ambition her résumé shows suggests XYZ Company should interview her.

Task 4: Probe Points. There's no need to probe whether or not Mary knows about sales. We may want to discover *how* she managed to sell $2.4 million in four years with a shrinking product line. Answering the how might shed some light on her creativity and drive.

Of greater importance to XYZ Company is Mary's tolerance for ambiguity and her ability to handle conflict. Let's examine how the interviewer might address those issues after the initial icebreaker.

Interviewer: "Tell me about your relationship with your boss at Armstrong."

Mary: "Actually I had several bosses. I worked as the outside sales rep and as such I reported to Lanny Wilkins. Lanny was the VP for Sales. Several years ago I expanded my job beyond sales into teaching and orienting new reps. That put me under the auspices of Sandra Lewis, the VP for Human Resources. I had two offices. I floated from one to the other depending on my days on the job."

Interviewer: "Are you saying you had two distinct jobs?"

Mary: "I didn't see them as distinct. I saw them as complementary. My work in sales training helped create interns who in turn sold the product. That's how I "sold" the sales end of my work to Lanny. He used to be one of these people who believed the only way to sell is to be out in the field, knocking on doors. When his reps were in the office, he got nervous."

Interviewer: "You had to sell your boss on a new aspect of your job. How did you do that?"

Mary: "I learned that convincing someone isn't too hard when you use good sales techniques. For example, I figured out what Lanny wanted. His bottom line was an increase in market share. He cared little about anything else. It's what he constantly talked about. After I'd been there awhile, I presented a clear proposal to him showing how we'd increase the market share and potential share with better sales training. In the past what little sales training people got wasn't done by anyone who worked in sales. The HR people told them where their territory was and said, 'go.' I showed Lanny what we could accomplish with better training, and I wanted to do the training as a way to enrich myself. We launched a pilot program and that was it."

Interviewer: "How did the HR people respond to this new idea?"

Mary: "That, too, was a little tricky. I found the HR people had become a little territorial. They didn't like the idea of anyone interfering with their program. At the same time, they needed help. We had unusually high turnover in the sales force; one reason was the lack of training and frustration among the sales team. Lanny and I talked to Sandra. Again, it took some convincing, but she finally agreed to the pilot."

Interviewer: "Once you got the program approved, what kind of difficulties did you encounter?"

Mary: "The usual things—turf issues. That's when I suggested that I become 'jointly housed.' That had never been done before in the company and the idea took some time to absorb. Eventually, though, it all worked out."

Interviewer: "What do you mean by time to absorb?"

Mary: "First I had to win the trust of the HR staff. They had information I needed, and I couldn't succeed without them. I pulled out my very best communication skills to try to show them we were playing the same game, and everyone would look good if we succeeded. It took some time, but they finally came along. For the first program I asked an HR staff professional to join me. We worked wonderfully together. That created a sense of teamwork and a willingness on everyone's part to help out."

Interviewer: "How did you manage to relate to two bosses with two agendas for you?"

Mary: "First I had to help each one see that what I was doing would benefit their individual departments. That was key. Then I made sure both knew everything that was going on. I sent memos and communicated directly with each one much more frequently than I had when I worked just for Lanny. This went on for several months. Now, I rarely see either of them. At first it took time away from the work to keep everyone on top of things, but I knew I had no choice. There were a couple of rough spots, especially the first quarter when the sales dropped drastically because I was not in the field."

Interviewer: "How did you handle the rough spots?"

This interview gives XYZ Company a clear picture of Mary's initiative and creativity. She knows what she wants and is willing to take risks to get there. Once she sets a goal, she looks for the possibilities to meet the goal. She broadened her job even though it meant working with a potentially hostile staff and having to appease two bosses. Mary handles conflict by anticipating it and nipping it before it happens.

Based on what we've seen on Mary's résumé in addition to this interview, Mary looks like a good candidate for the sales manager position in XYZ Company. There's another important probe point, however, we haven't addressed. That point is Mary's tolerance for working in a company that might dissolve in a year or six months. We know Mary takes initiative and has an excellent ability to sell her ideas, but we don't know what makes her want to change jobs, particularly to a less stable company.

Let's look at how the interviewer might explore these points.

Interviewer: "I noticed from your résumé you've worked for Armstrong for ten years. What precipitated your interest in a change?"

Mary: "I've done everything I can at Armstrong. When I changed the nature of my job from direct sales to training and management, I stretched myself. I've been doing that now for over three years. There's really no place else for me to go at Armstrong. The top VP's have been there forever, and I don't see any of them moving on anytime soon. Even if they do, I may not be the one selected."

Interviewer: "So are you saying you're looking for a promotion in your company, but one isn't available?"

Mary: "I suppose a promotion would be nice, but I really think I'm tired of Armstrong. I don't have the energy I once had for the products or for the company. It's a great place to work. I've enjoyed the experience, but I've gotten kind of stale."

Interviewer: "What do you mean by stale?"

Mary: "When I first started working for Armstrong I had new ideas floating in my head all the time. I was excited to go to work everyday and try out something different. Now, I don't seem to have those sparks. I do the same thing nearly every day. I've gotten bored with the job. A promotion would put me in a different position with a different focus, but I don't think it would provide the spark I'm looking for. I want a total change. Something that will turn me on again."

Interviewer: "And what might that something be?"

Mary: "I'm interviewing with only high tech companies. I'm excited by the newness and the challenge of working in an industry that remains an unknown. Nobody knows what will happen next. It's reactive and proactive at the same time. The fast-paced, creative energy is pulling me. That's why I'm interested in XYZ Company."

Interviewer: "So you believe the high tech industry will give you the spark you're looking for?"

Mary: "I know it."

Interviewer: "How have you prepared for the risks?"

Mary: "If you mean the company's risks, I suppose I recognize I could be working one day and on the street the next. That's a little scary, but I've put away enough money—at least one year's worth—in preparation for this. My husband and I talked about starting our own business several years ago, but with two kids, we didn't want to take that much risk. Instead, we agreed for me to tuck some money aside as insurance and when the time was right, make the move. That's why I'm ready now to leave the security of Armstrong and see what's out there."

Mary indeed looks like a good candidate for the sales manager at XYZ Company. She has weighed the risks, understands the tenuous nature not only of this company but of the industry in general. Apparently she's done her homework. Since XYZ Company is not looking for someone to remain for many years, Mary fits the bill. She may indeed leave after several years to fulfill her dream by starting her own company. She has the kind of drive and spirit to do that. But in a company in the Childhood phase like XYZ the fact that she might leave at some foreseeable point in the future doesn't matter. What matters is finding talented people willing to jump in there, create, and give for one to two years, and then move on.

Practice Exercise

Examine the following résumé and answer the questions below:

1. *What do you like about Mike?*
2. *What red flags do you see?*
3. *Write two probe questions to address the gaps and red flags noted.*

MIKE BLAZER

543 Jackson Dr   PO Box 342
Milwaukee, WI   Madison, WI
(414) 795–3212   (608) 858–9823

JOB OBJECTIVE

To obtain an entry level accounting position

EDUCATION

Accounting Major: Bachelor's Degree received May, 2000
University of Wisconsin, Madison, WI GPA 3.19 GPA in Major 3.46

Major Course Work Includes:

- Intermediate accounting, auditing, accounting information systems
- financial management, cost accounting, budget and executive control
- corporate taxation, strategic management, interpersonal communication

Computer Experience: Lotus 123, COBOL, SQL, ADA, Networks, Windows, MS-DOS

EXPERIENCE

Forsythe and Johnson, Inc   Madison, WI
Accounting Data Entry Clerk   May 1999–August 1999

Ran gamut from accounts receivable to check issuance. Reconciled South Carolina Broker Tax forms and differences in agents' monthly reports. Cleared payroll checks on computer records and reconciled bank accounts. Mediated disputes between employees. Interviewed prospective employees for the Accounting Department. Developed ideas that redesigned part of the computer system. Researched Accounting Department's function and made a system work flow chart to help with the reassignment of job descriptions.

University Athletic Department
Mail Room Assistant   Spring/Fall 1997

Metered athletic office mail and ticket office mail. Made photocopies for athletic administration and ran various errands.

HONORS   Dean's List
              Fellowship of Christian Athletes, Activities Committee
              Intramural Sports
              Reformed University Fellowship

What do you like about Mike?

- He achieved a high level of academic success
- He has broad computer experience
- He worked one summer as an accounting clerk with extensive duties

What red flags do you see from Mike's résumé?

- What did Mike do during the summers of 1996, 1997, and 1998? People often omit jobs they consider menial or less meaningful. All jobs are meaningful, especially those that helped us develop into the person we've become. When you see periods of time when the person didn't attend school, wasn't in the military, or didn't work, find out what the person did. For some, staying at home with the children was a meaningful experience.
- The duties listed as an accounting clerk seem lofty, i.e., would a temporary student worker really mediate disputes between employees, interview prospective employees for the department, and redesign a part of the computer system?
- Mike seems to be an excellent student, but what else does he do? What leadership positions has he held? He was on the activities committee of the Fellowship of Christian Athletes, but what does that mean?

Two probe questions. Because probes must be open questions, be sure to write open questions that address the issues raised above. For example: "What other summer jobs did you have while in school?" or "Tell me what you did on the activities committee of the Fellowship of Christian Athletes" or "How did you mediate disputes between employees at Forsythe and Johnson?"

Sample Form: Résumé Screening

From the résumé do the following:

1. List the candidate's knowledge and experiences in relation to the skills you're looking for.
2. What knowledge or experiences are missing in relation to the skills you're looking for?
3. How does it appear the candidate interacts with others?
4. Would you recommend this person for an interview? If yes:
    a. What would you use as an icebreaker in this interview?
    b. What probe points do you want to explore with this candidate?
    c. Develop two questions that would help you extract the type of information you need to help you reach a decision.

In this chapter we POINTed to the candidate by planning our strategic interview with the candidate in mind. In Chapter 7 we will POINT to the candidate by looking at interview examples that include Openness. In the initial set of questions with Peter, the interviewer learned about a girlfriend without asking. How did the interviewer do that? Peter opened up and was honest in his responses because the interviewer was honest as well as focused. In the second interview example, Mary shared her long-term goal to start a business with her husband. That was something she probably didn't intend to share. The way the interviewer asked the questions enabled her to open up. In Chapter 7 we will look at examples of how to Open the interview.

NOTE

1. Paul Taylor and Michael O'Driscoll, *Structured Employment Interviewing*, (Brookfield, VT: Gower, 1995) p. 13.

7

Demonstrating Openness

In this chapter we will explore the O in POINT as we look at *Openness* in relation to the candidate. If you never share information about your likes, dislikes, and who you are, why should a candidate do so?

The ultimate goal of a strategic interview is to strip away the superficial. To achieve that goal requires trust.

As we saw in Chapter 3, trust comes through openness. I'm never going to open my Johari Window if you don't open yours. The interviewer must take that first step; we cannot expect candidates to automatically open up. Some do, of course, and when they do, we're grateful, but most withhold as much information as possible.

Getting the candidate to open up during the interview becomes the interviewer's greatest challenge.

GETTING CANDIDATES TO OPEN UP

If the interviewer opens up and the candidate remains closed, then you may have problems. Some people take longer to trust than others. The struggle in the interview is to facilitate openness. It's frustrating when you do everything you can and the candidate still remains closed. In Chapter 14 we will look at ways to overcome difficult interview situations, including times when the candidate doesn't talk. Human resources managers who have interviewed for many years understand this frustration.

If you give a person every opportunity to share but the person refuses to

do so, you've learned something about that person. That in and of itself is valuable information.

A strategic interview appears conversational. This chapter will provide you with examples of how to probe in a conversational manner and thereby create trust. We will also examine interview situations where either the candidate or the interviewer refuse to open up, and we will study alternatives for dealing with those situations.

Let's begin with an example. XYZ Company, a credit institution, wants to fill the position of financial manager. The institution is in the Middle-Age phase of development and fairly bureaucratic. Movers and shakers are not successful in this organization. It is a conservative, secure company.

Let's look at an interview with Libby McMillian and analyze what we like or dislike about the interviewer's strategy.

LIBBY MCMILLIAN
543 West 99th Street
Bronx, NY 10245
(212) 778–4325

OBJECTIVE: To obtain a position with a company where I can use my verbal and mathematical skills.

EDUCATION: FORDHAM COLLEGE
BA English, May 1988
Cumulative Index: 3.7

University College of London
1985–86 Academic Year

Bronx High School of Science—Honors Diploma

HONORS: Graduate Magna Cum Laude
Dean's List Manhattan College (1st Honors each semester)
Honor's List, University College of London (both semesters)
Epsilon Sigma Pi Honor Society, Manhattan College

EXPERIENCE:

10/86–present   **Saks Fifth Avenue, New York, NY**

Divisional Credit Manager, Credit Authorization/Customer Service
Assumed partial to full managerial responsibility for the department in all aspects of operation: approving sales, interfacing with customers, coordinating the paperwork, and monitoring the department production and performance on a daily basis.

Divisional Credit Manager, Customer Service
Performed various managerial tasks; assumed full responsibility for evening and weekend staffs, interviewing, scheduling and preparing reviews (25–30 hrs per week)

Divisional Collection Manager, Collections
Assumed part-time responsibility for a collection division and appropriated work to the full-time staff (Summer 1987)

10/82–9/86   **Ambassador Supermarket, New York, NY**

Front End Manager
Coordinated cashier activities, taking monetary pick-ups and handling customer complaints. On occasion assisted with bookkeeping (30 hours per week)

1985–86   **University College of London**
Tutored secondary level mathematics (20 hours per week)

1985–86   **Advertising Age Agency, New York, NY**
Summer Intern: Assisted with typing, reception, and general office work in various departments Winter, intercessions

PERSONAL: Typing 50 wpm, Wordstar. Hobbies: Classical piano, singing, aerobics, and jogging

Interviewer: "You've held your position at Saks for a long time. What brings you into the job market?"

Libby: "If you've ever been in a job for a long time, you know how much you can get in a rut. I just decided to explore what might be out there. Saks is a great place to work, and I've gained excellent experience, but I'm ready for something different."

Interviewer: "Tell me what you do at Saks."

Libby: "I'm a full-service manager. I have ten credit managers who work under me. We try to keep the company from falling prey to bad customer debt. But we also have to keep the customers happy. Of course, some customers are such a drain on the company, we're better off without them. Others have a short-term financial problem. In these cases we can often help through counseling and budget management. Those are the fun ones."

Interviewer: "Your job sounds full of challenges. Tell me what you want to do now."

Practice Exercise

1. *What did you like about this interview?*
2. *What did the interviewer learn about Libby?*
3. *What was the interviewer's strategy?*
4. *How might you improve the interview? Give two different responses to Libby.*

What did you like about this interview? The interviewer asked solid open questions and got the candidate talking.

What did the interviewer learn about Libby? The interviewer learned what Libby wanted to tell. Libby's reason for suddenly wanting to leave a job she's had for over ten years is rather vague. All we know is she's interested in change. But, why now? What kind of change? The interviewer let her get away with canned responses.

As for what she does, her job sounds interesting and full of challenges.

Why would she want to leave it? The interviewer let her gloss over her work experiences and present only the good stuff. We really know very little about what she did or why she wants to leave.

What was the interviewer's strategy? This was not a strategic interview. Why not? First, there was no strategy. The interviewer asked general questions that he/she could have posed to any candidate. The interviewer did not piggyback Libby's responses. Instead the interviewer went on to other questions. As far as we can see, there was no strategy here. Even the response, "Your job sounded full of challenges" was too general a statement to be a paraphrase. A paraphrase might be, "So you enjoy doing financial counseling?"

How might you improve this interview?

- Make the interview strategic. Develop key probe points and pursue those. In this instance two probe points might include the candidate's decision to leave her job and the candidate's willingness to accept change in a new company.
- Respond to what the candidate says by piggybacking her responses and by being more open and empathetic as an interviewer.
- Balance the interview with questions concerning Libby's outside interests.

Let's look at a second interview with Libby.

Interviewer: "You've held your position at Saks for a long time. What brings you into the job market?"

Libby: "I just felt it was time for a change."

Interviewer: "What sort of change are you looking for?"

Libby: "Something different."

Interviewer: "I've worked for twenty years at XYZ Company. My job changed a number of times during those years, just like yours did at Saks. I went from a first-line supervisor to a vice president. Change can be exciting and scary. When I recently moved into my present position, I wasn't so sure I wanted to make the move. Tell me what makes you want to change at this point in your career?"

Libby: "There's really nothing specific. I'm just ready."

Interviewer: "So, there's nothing specific." (Pause) "I see from your résumé that you enjoy a variety of activities in your spare time, from classical music to aerobics. Tell me how you usually spend time away from the office."

Libby: "I like to stay in shape. That's why I jog and go to aerobics. Otherwise I listen to classical music."

Interviewer: "What about your singing? How do you make use of your singing talent?"

Libby: "I sing in a community choir, have for years."

Interviewer: "I love music too, and I've attended a number of concerts in the city. What musicians are your favorite?"

Libby: "No one in particular. I like all classical music."

This candidate is one we've all experienced. It's maddening. You give her every opportunity to share information, and yet she remains closed. Her brief answers shed little light on her interests. The interviewer tried several things. First the interviewer shared personal work experiences where change occurred, hoping the candidate would open up. This didn't work. Next the interviewer went to safer subjects, the leisure activities. This didn't work. It's clear this candidate prefers to remain closed.

Some other things the interviewer could do to help the candidate open up:

- Reality test. When you reality test, you *test the reality* of what the candidate just said. You want to avoid paraphrasing with a tone of voice that suggests disbelief. In this example when the candidate insists there's nothing specific to make her want to change jobs after more than ten years, the interviewer might say, "Clearly there must be some reason you're looking for a job now, and you didn't look for one five years ago." If the candidate still says nothing pushed her to explore jobs at this stage in her career, the interviewer could test reality further, "So, you're saying that after more than ten years with Saks, there's nothing that prompted you to interview for a new job, nothing in your career options with Saks or in your private circumstances?"

- Silence. When candidates give very brief answers as she did when asked what sort of change she was looking for and she said, "Something different," the interviewer might have responded, "Like?" and waited. The wait seems endless to you, but usually it provokes a response. If you count to ten slowly, and the candidate still hasn't said anything, you must go on.

- Share your frustration. "Surely, there must be some specific change you're seeking," or "I'm frustrated. You've worked for a company for ten years, held different jobs with that company and now you seem reluctant to share your reasons for seeking a new job." Sharing your frustrations tells the candidate if they don't open up, the interview could end badly for them.

Show Empathy During the Interview

Carl Rogers, the notable psychologist, defined empathy as getting in the other person's skin.

Empathy strives to understand what it feels like to be the other person.

In this case, you might ask yourself, why is this person so closed? Is she nervous about the interview? If so, do everything you can to help her relax. If you don't detect she's nervous, then you might consider other things. What do you know about Saks? How have they treated their employees?

Are they cutting back? Has there been a takeover? My guess is this candidate was downsized in some way and is reluctant to share that information. As companies streamline, they often lay off excellent employees because jobs disappear. Divulging the fact that you were laid off isn't easy. If you suspect this happened to this candidate, share examples of people your company hired who had been laid off or of people you know. This kind of sharing might trigger a willingness to open up.

Rogers says that empathy must include three components:

- Consistency—Your verbal and nonverbal responses must match. If you say one thing and your face or your voice or your posture say something else, the candidate won't open up. When candidates remain closed and you've tried everything you can think of, ask yourself what your nonverbal cues communicated. Sometimes our frustrations show, and we don't even realize it.

- Nonjudgmental—For empathy to work, you must never appear judgmental. If your voice or your face suggest sarcasm or disbelief, you've communicated a judgment. To get into the candidate's skin—to really understand where they are and encourage them to open up—we must be totally neutral and supportive.

- Congruent—Rogers tells us that we must be ourselves. Congruence and being genuine go hand in hand. In other words, if you're frustrated, you must say so. Your nonverbal behaviors will give you away, so why not just say it? When you share your genuine feelings, the candidate is more likely to do so as well.

LEISURE PURSUITS VS. WORK ACTIVITIES

Learning about a candidate's technical and educational background without exploring leisure interests restricts your picture of a person. It's like always seeing someone in a business suit and never in casual attire. Intersperse the technical questions with questions about hobbies. What does this person like to do besides study or work? These questions are easier to answer, and they strategically give us a peek at the real person behind the candidate.

For example if teamwork is important to you, take note of the person's involvement in team sports. If the person prefers lone activities in his/her leisure time, what makes you think the candidate will be an effective team player? If, on the other hand, the job you have open requires hours of work behind a computer screen, then candidates who played basketball or soccer in their spare time might not be good choices.

Your job as an interviewer is to find out as much as you can about the total person.

Taylor and O'Driscoll explain in *Structured Employment Interviewing* (1995) that the difference between a structured interview and an unstructured interview is the former relies on job-related questions that stem from a job analysis while the latter places more weight on creating rapport.[1] Strategic interviewing blends the best of Taylor and Driscoll's structured and unstructured interviews. While a thorough job analysis plays a dominant role in the strategic interview (as we noted in Chapter 2) and most questions deal with experiences on the job, the strategic interview also focuses on the candidate's life outside of work. Strategic interviewers balance the various aspects of a person's life to determine significant behaviors.

I've had people tell me they are very different at home than they are at work. Sometimes we believe we are two different people; we believe we're more "ourselves" at home. In reality we spend a large percentage of our waking life in work settings. It would take a tremendous amount of self-containment to be a totally different person eight or more hours a day. Talk to your spouse; you may learn you behave in similar ways at home as you do at work. Indeed the leisure activities you select complement the activities you pursue at work. Most of us conduct lives at home and at work that intermingle with what we either consciously or unconsciously desire.

Claire Raines tells us in *Beyond Generation X* (1997) that the new crop of employees, born after 1960, place greater emphasis on leisure pursuits than older employees. They bristle at the thought of work becoming their total and complete lives. After having witnessed their own parents working sixty-hour weeks, bringing work home, not having time to devote to their families, they vow not to become workaholics. Raines says, "They will tell you with *conviction* they want a lifestyle with more balance, that they want to work to live—not live to work."[2] Competing for the best candidates means showing them we have an interest in more than their work life.

If managers devote the entire interview to work-related questions without exploring community involvement and leisure pursuits, the interview becomes stiff and reveals only one side of a candidate. Interviewers create an open environment for the interview and build trust when they balance questions dealing with work and leisure.

Let's look at an interview with James Suddreth.

JAMES SUDDRETH
231 Peachtree Rd.
Atlanta GA 30303
(404) 231–2991

CAREER OBJECTIVE: To find a career in my field

EDUCATION: Georgia Institute of Technology
Bachelor of Sciences degree in Chemical Engineering,
May, 2000 Minor in Business Administration
GPA: 3.42

HONORS: Recipient of Kimberly Clark Engineering Scholarship
                 Recipient of Martin Marietta Freshman Engineering Scholarship
                 Tau Beta Pi, National Engineering Honor Society
                 1998 American Chemical Society

WORK EXPERIENCE:

6/98–present   Intern, BNA Engineering, Atlanta GA

- Successfully completed group projects involving cost performance and other
  criteria for evaluation of innovative technologies in the area of waste treatment
- Developed several computer generated tools using Microsoft Excel for material
  balance unit operation modeling

6/97–9/97   Ridgeway Packaging Systems, Inc, Atlanta GA

Package handler—Unloaded packages from vans and trailers onto conveyer
belt

ACTIVITIES:

President of the American Institute of Chemical Engineers, student chapter
Participated in intramural activities including tennis, basketball, and football
Volunteer tutor in math and chemistry
Member of the College Republicans

HOBBIES: Play racquetball, baseball, and basketball
                  Teach Sunday School
                  Tennis with my wife

Interviewer: "I noticed you worked on a group project with BNA Engineering. Tell me what it was like working with a group."

James: "Because I was the new kid on the block, being the intern and all, I enjoyed watching the seasoned engineers at work. I'd usually sit back and wait before I offered suggestions because the other people had been there so long."

Interviewer: "What happened when you made a suggestion?"

James: "Well, the only time I really spoke up was when the group came up with a new cost performance measure. I felt the measure left out a major part of the waste treatment program. When I finally pointed out the oversight, most people listened."

Interviewer: "What do you mean by most people?"

James: "There was one guy who dominated the group. He brushed off my concern, saying that it had been considered. But the others stood up for me. They said we needed to test the cost performance measures against the system before we moved ahead."

Interviewer: "So how did you feel about your contribution to that team?"

James: "Because I finally spoke up and the majority of the team seemed to appreciate it, I felt pretty good. Even though I was an intern, the rest of the team seemed to respect my opinion."

Interviewer: "It is intimidating to come into an established work group as an intern. Even though you didn't share your concerns right away, it sounds as if you had the courage to do so when the opportunity arose. That must've taken a lot out of you."

James: "Actually not so much. I'm used to teams. Now that I think about it, I suppose I was too naive to realize I was taking any sort of risk."

Interviewer: "What other teams have you participated on?"

James: "Mainly sports teams, no other work teams."

Interviewer: "Tell me about your experiences on sports teams."

James: "When I played basketball at Georgia Tech, I realized I was really entering foreign territory. The team was dominated by the seniors. As a freshman, I didn't have much say about plays or my position."

Interviewer: "How did you handle being the lowliest low on the team?"

James: (Laughs) "I suppose I was too dumb to realize I was so low. I just forged ahead, made suggestions, and before I knew it, I was one of the team leaders. It was funny. I was the only freshman the seniors shared play analyses with."

Interviewer: "I played soccer in college and had a similar experience. The seniors dominated the team. I remember asking if I could play goalie when the regular goalie was injured. You'd think I asked if I could jump on the moon."

James: "Did you get to play goalie?"

Interviewer: "Yeah, thanks to the coach. As it turned out, I managed to help win the game."

James: "That just goes to show. Age doesn't necessarily mean people know everything. I respect age and when I worked on that team at BNA, I kept quiet and listened to the 'experts.' But I suppose I was taught at home that I had something to offer. When the time is right, I just jump in."

This interview illustrates the way an interviewer creates openness and trust by encouraging the candidate to talk about experiences outside the workplace. By so doing the interviewer learned more about this candidate's view of teams as well as his view of himself as a contributor to teams. When the interviewer picked up on the sports teams rather than discounting them, the candidate responded openly. Furthermore, the interviewer created trust by sharing what happened during his or her experience playing soccer.

OPEN VS. CLOSED QUESTIONS

Most experts will tell you that interviewers should only use open-ended questions. They say this because we, as interviewers, want to get the candidate talking. Open questions encourage the other person to talk freely. Closed questions narrow the field of response. In a strategic interview we select an open or closed question with a purpose. If indeed you want the candidate to talk, ask open questions. If, however, you do not need as much information on a particular issue, ask a closed question.

What Is an Open Question?

Open questions encourage the respondent to answer with more than a single word response, more than a yes or no.

Not all open questions are posed as actual "questions." Some are statements that infer a question by the way they're stated.

Most open **questions** begin with the words *who, what, where, when, why,* and *how.* **Statements** requiring an open response often begin with *tell, describe, give,* and *share.*

Communication literature cautions us not to begin questions with the word *why.* Our goal in asking open-ended questions is to get people to open up. *Why* questions tend to cause defensiveness, i.e., "Why did you leave your last job?" or "Why are you applying for a job with us?" In our example with Libby who refused to open up, imagine asking "Why are you applying for a job with us," or "Why are you leaving Saks?" Surely her responses, although closed, would become even more guarded. You may say, don't *why* questions get to the meat of the matter quickly? Perhaps. But what you risk is taking a closed person and closing them further or causing an otherwise open person to shut down. *Why* questions require the candidate to "defend" something—in these instances either what happened in their last job or their choices of places to apply. When we feel as if we must defend something, we become defensive. Another way to ask those two questions might be: "How did you reach the decision to leave your last job?" or "What attracts you to our company?"

Practice Exercise

Turn the following why *questions into questions that don't begin with the word* why.

1. *Why did you major in economics?*
2. *Why did the company you worked for fold?*
3. *Why did you decide to sell your own business?*
4. *Why do you like to play field hockey?*
5. *Why did you take a job for less money?*

Some ways to ask the questions above without using *why*:
Why did you major in economics?

• Tell me what attracted you to economics.
• What is it about economics that you enjoy?
• How did you select economics as a major?

Why did the company you worked for fold?

- Tell me what happened to the company that folded.
- So, your company folded, what happened?
- What kinds of things caused the company to fold?
- How might the company have prevented folding?

Why did you decide to sell your own business?

- What factors led you to decide to sell your business?
- Selling your business must have been a difficult decision. Explain to me what happened.
- How did you reach the decision to sell your business?

Why do you like to play field hockey?

- What do you like about field hockey?
- When did you begin playing field hockey?
- Describe what you like about playing field hockey.

Why did you take a job with less money?

- What led you to take a job with less money?
- Taking a job for less money must have been difficult for you. Help me understand what made you do that.
- How did taking a job for less money make you feel?

Notice from these examples of responses that do not start with the word *why*, we may ask harder or softer questions. Depending on the sensitivity you anticipate, you would choose to ask either, "What led you to take a job with less money?" (harder) or "Taking a job for less money must have been difficult for you. Help me understand what made you do that." (softer).

A successful conversational interview balances open and closed questions. If you've just asked three or four open questions, you may decide to give the candidate a rest. In a conversation, it is rare for one person to talk the entire time and the other to listen. Conversational interviews strive for a ratio of 75 to 25 percent talking to listening, not 99 to 1 percent and not 50–50. If you find yourself talking too much, you know you've failed as an interviewer. At the same time, if you've only asked one question in twenty minutes, you might also wonder about the quality of your interview.

When Is It Appropriate to Ask Closed Questions?

Every question in a strategic interview has a *purpose*.

Furthermore, you select the form of questioning—open or closed, for a strategic reason. You would opt to ask closed questions in the following circumstances:

- The candidate is talking too much, rambling.
- Time is running out and you want to signal the candidate to shorten the responses.
- You need a piece of specific information, such as a home address or a telephone number.
- You wish to paraphrase or clarify something the candidate said.
- You've asked too many open questions and want to give the candidate a break.

The following example shows how an interviewer balances open and closed questions. The candidate isn't talking too much, but the interviewer decides to throw in a closed question because it changes the pace of the interview.

Interviewer: "What led you to apply for our position?" (*Open*)

Candidate: "I spotted your ad in the trade magazine. The job sounded perfect for me. I've had experience in journalism and as a social worker. Being able to blend both of those skills is my dream."

Interviewer: "So you saw our ad and believe it will give you a chance to balance your journalism and social work skills?" (*Closed*)

Candidate: "Absolutely. I love writing and couldn't work in a job without some writing component and some creating aspect. But I've really missed the sense that what I'm writing will make a difference."

Interviewer: "Describe what you've enjoyed about your journalism career." (*Open*)

Candidate: "I love discovery. When I interview people for a piece and learn something new, it's so exciting. My work with the Investment Magazine led me to interview CEO's from all over the country. I discovered what made them successful."

Interviewer: "How do you see your yearning for discovery fitting our position?" (*Open*)

Candidate: "The newsletter editor must visit the courtrooms and listen to the cases. My interest in the social sciences will flower doing this. I've always been interested in the legal system, but more importantly in those people abused by the system. Learning all this and writing stories about it will satisfy my need to discover."

Interviewer: "As well as your need to make a difference?" (*Closed*)

Candidate: (Laughs) "I hope so, but I've had enough experience in social work to recognize the limitations."

Interviewer: "How have you used your social work experience in the past?" (*Open*)

Candidate: "Not as much as I'd like, but it seems to always come out."

Interviewer: "Give me an example of when your interest in social work came out while you worked for Investment Magazine." (*Open*)

Candidate: "There were many examples. One that comes to mind is when I had to do a piece on investing in the developing countries. While working on that story, I learned how powerful the American dollar is to these countries. Do you realize that $100 would support a child in Haiti for a year? That amazed me. My piece ended up centering on this aspect of investment rather than the usual financial focus on the need for diversity in our portfolios or how much money you can make in these countries."

Interviewer: "So you're saying you often focus on the social implications rather than the strict financial implications—like whether to invest in a mutual fund or not?" (*Closed*)

Candidate: "That's been my pattern."

Practice Exercise
Turn the following closed questions into open questions.

1. *Do you enjoy working with others?*
2. *Did you move away from the city because of the smog?*
3. *Could you explain for me your decision to major in history?*
4. *Would you mind talking about your work with the Tanner Company?*
5. *Which area interests you more—management, team facilitation, or human resources?*
6. *Are you interested in planning or design?*

Questions one and two in the practice exercise illustrate **genuine closed questions**. The candidate could simply respond with a "yes" or "no." One way to open these two questions is as follows:

1. *How do you feel about working with others?*
2. *Tell me what you like about living outside the city.*

Questions three and four illustrate **disguised closed questions**—those most people would not answer with a yes or no, but would respond to openly. Because the interviewer closed questions three and four, psychologically the interviewer said to the candidate, "Don't tell me too much," which may or may not be the interviewer's intent. If you don't want the candidate to tell you too much, ask a genuine closed question. If, on the other hand, you do want the candidate to talk, ask an open question.

There is no strategic reason for asking a disguised closed question. Examples of opening questions three and four follow:

3. *Explain your decision to major in history.*
4. *What were your principal duties at the Tanner Company?*

Questions five and six illustrate what I refer to as **closed-multiple choice**—they require a narrow response. You might strategically select this type of question after you've asked open questions that elicited several responses you want to sharpen. Examples of open questions for five and six follow:

5. *Looking at your job experiences, what kinds of work do you enjoy?*
6. *What aspects of project work interest you the most?*

In this chapter we looked at ways to create trust and openness by demonstrating balance throughout the interview. The interviewer shares likes, dislikes, and experiences and encourages the candidate to talk about recreational activities as well as work activities. We also saw how empathy can help interviewers understand where the candidate is and thereby encourage the candidate to share. Interviewers strategically choose open or closed questions to get candidates talking or to take the pressure off candidates. In Chapter 8 we'll explore the communication skills that point the candidate toward deeper disclosure.

NOTES

1. Paul Taylor and Michael O'Driscoll, *Structured Employment Interviewing*, pp. 13–14.

2. Claire Raines, *Beyond Generation X: A Practical Guide for Managers* (Menlo Park, CA: Crisp Publications, 1997), pp. 37–38.

8

Practicing INtentional
Listening Skills

When you INtentionally listen to the candidate, the candidate will lead you
through the interview. You never have to worry about your next question
because the candidate provides the prompt from one question to the next.
This chapter explores the **IN** in POINT and gives examples of how to use
candidates' responses to either probe further or to transition to another
area that you wish to explore. Using this method, every interview is different and every question is strategic.

**The most essential component of strategic interviewing is intentional lis-
tening.**

REACTING TO WHAT CANDIDATES SAY

Richard Olson in *Managing the Interview* developed a process to react
to a candidate. Olson's process calls for the interviewer to listen, restate,
and give feedback.[1] I've expanded that process as follows:

- Hear what the candidate said
- React in some way—probe further, paraphrase, reflect, summarize, reality test,
  present a flip side
- Give feedback

Hear What the Candidate Said

Hearing what the candidate said may seem obvious to you. But human resource managers who have spent years interviewing know how hard this is. As listeners, we face numerous barriers. Some of these barriers include:

1. We assume in advance that what the speaker is about to say is uninteresting or unimportant.
2. We start to formulate what our next question will be.
3. We mentally criticize the speaker's delivery.
4. We disagree with something the speaker said and begin to formulate our rebuttal.
5. We hear only the factual data and tune out the rest.
6. We tune out certain words, expressions, or phrases.
7. We jump to conclusions, right or wrong.
8. Our minds simply wander.

The mind thinks four times faster than the average person can speak.

The goal in the strategic interview is to harness this thinking toward the interview.

Reacting to What the Candidate Said

By reacting, you tell the candidate you're listening, and you set up opportunities for strategic questions. You cannot react if you fall prey to any of the above barriers. How can you paraphrase what the candidate just said if you didn't actually hear it? Most interviewers leave out this middle step because they haven't heard the candidate. For example, when a candidate says, "I brought in $10,000 in sales in my first year," interviewers often respond, "That's great." In other words the interviewer didn't hear what the candidate said and therefore gave feedback. That missing middle step ascertains and affirms what the candidate actually said. When we leave out the middle step, it appears we didn't really hear what was said and often we didn't.

In one of my classes a participant role-played the interviewer and began with an open question. The candidate responded in great detail. The interviewer nodded as the candidate spoke. When the candidate finally finished, the interviewer asked another open question dealing with a totally different topic. At that point I intervened and said to the participant-interviewer, "What did the candidate just say to you?" He looked at me in amazement and said, "I have no idea." How did I know the interviewer didn't hear the candidate? I really can't read people's minds. Even though this interviewer's nonverbal signals suggested he was listening by nodding, the fact that he didn't respond to anything the candidate said told me he had checked out. He left himself with no choice but to ask the next question or as many of us do, give meaningless feedback like, "That's great."

Some people protest and say, yes, I've heard what the candidate said, but I just didn't react. The reality is if we don't react, we **appear as if** we didn't hear. We particularly want to avoid not reacting when we've heard what's been said. In real life, it's hard to hear everything that someone says, and we will find ourselves checking out no matter how hard we try. When that happens (hopefully occasionally) we must move on and strive not to let it happen again. In other words, we definitely want to react when we've heard and save our "non-reactions" for those few times when we couldn't control our wandering minds.

Think how often your spouse comes home and you ask, "How was your day?" You may be in the middle of doing something else when your spouse answers. After he/she describes a miserable day, you say, "How nice" or "Good." Your spouse probably shrugs and walks off. And we wonder why so many marriages struggle with communication issues.

Strategic interviewing requires us to finely tune our antennae and really hear the candidate.

The following interview shows what can happen when we don't intentionally listen.

Interviewer: "I noticed you worked for a short time at XYZ Company. What made you leave when you did?"

Candidate: "As soon as I came to work I realized the job wasn't what I expected. I had little authority to act and was placed in a position to make critical decisions."

Interviewer: "I see. Tell me what you did when you worked for that company."

Candidate: "I was an accounting associate. I was responsible for keeping track of all the bills and paying them on time. I was also responsible for invoicing and for making sure our books balanced."

Interviewer: "Did you have other people working for you?"

Candidate: "I supervised the department. There were fifteen people including myself. We were responsible for all the bookkeeping and for maintaining the computer system."

Interviewer: "What are you looking for in a new job?"

Notice how this interviewer went from question to question with little regard to the candidate's response. When we do that, we're unable to strip away the superficial and find out what is really going on with the candidate. Furthermore, the candidate eventually talks less. When people feel as if they aren't being heard, they shut down.

Let's look at a more strategic interview with the same candidate designed to strip away the superficial.

Interviewer: "I noticed you worked for a short time at XYZ Company. What made you leave when you did?"

Candidate: "As soon as I came to work I realized the job wasn't what I expected. I had little authority to act but was placed in a position to make critical decisions."

Interviewer: "What kind of job did you think you were getting when you accepted the offer?" *This question picks up on the first thing the candidate said. The interviewer chooses to probe.*

Candidate: "I was told I would be responsible for the bookkeeping department. I thought I'd be doing the hiring, firing, and oversight. But as it turned out my boss micromanaged everything."

Interviewer: "What do you mean by micromanaged?" *Again the interviewer chooses to probe and responded to the last thing the candidate said.*

Candidate: "Every decision I made had to have his approval."

Interviewer: "To help me understand, give me an example of where you felt your boss's approval of something wasn't necessary." *The interviewer is probing again, trying to get specific information. By using the technique "give me an example," the interviewer hopes to understand what the candidate just stated.*

Candidate: "Bills came in every day. I put them in the ledger. It was pretty straightforward. But my boss insisted I show him the ledger at the end of the day so he could okay the entries."

Interviewer: "Are you saying, then, this boss's constant oversight of your work was suffocating you?" *This time the interviewer chooses to paraphrase what the candidate says. Notice this paraphrase is a closed question looking for clarification.*

Candidate: "It nearly drove me crazy. I started doubting myself."

Interviewer: "What did you do to keep from going crazy?" *Now the interviewer probes again and this time with an open question that leads directly from what the candidate just said.*

Candidate: "I talked to the boss. I shared my frustrations and asked for some modest freedom. We had a good talk, and I thought we'd reached an agreement."

Interviewer: "I applaud you for taking the time to talk to your boss. What happened after you talked?" *Finally, the interviewer gives feedback to the candidate for a specific behavior—not general feedback. Then the interviewer follows with a new probe.*

Candidate: "Oh, it lasted about one day. He began looking over my shoulder again almost immediately. I realized then the problem was his and not mine. There wasn't much I could do to change who he was."

Interviewer: "So after you realized the problem was your boss's and after you tried talking with him, you decided to seek a job elsewhere?" *A summary draws this series of questions to a close.*

Candidate: "Yes, I decided I'd done all I could do."

Interviewer: "It sounds as though you made the best decision for yourself and your boss." *The final statement gives feedback.*

In this scenario the interviewer learned how much supervision this candidate can tolerate and what the candidate did to improve the situation with the boss. Notice, the interviewer refrained from giving feedback until the end of the interview when the interviewer said, "I applaud you for taking the time to talk to your boss" and "It sounds as though you made the best decision for yourself and your boss." Sometimes interviewers sprinkle in feedback sooner, but that depends on what the candidates say and whether the interviewers feel as if they've exhausted the topic. Notice also how the interviewer balanced the interview with open and closed questions. This helped soften the pace of the interview and encouraged the candidate to share (see Chapter 7). Finally, notice how every response the interviewer gave was based on something the candidate said. A skilled strategic interviewer never has to worry about where the next question will come from.

INTENTIONAL LISTENING SKILLS—THE MIDDLE STEP

The following listening skills enable the interviewer to stay focused, strategic, and on target. These skills help the interviewer INtentionally listen and achieve the middle step in Olson's reacting process.

Probe. Ask a question related to what the candidate just said. For example:

Candidate: "I love to work with people."

Interviewer: "What do you like about working with people?"

Probes are open, never closed. Examine all the probes in the example about the employee's decision to leave his job. You'll see the interviewer formulated each as an open question. In the last chapter we learned there are strategic times when an interviewer selects to close a question—but never during probes. **The ultimate goal of a probe is to find out more information about something. Closed questions, by their very nature, cannot probe.**

Practice Exercise

*Write a **probe** for each of the following candidate responses*:

Interviewer: *"What is the most important aspect of the job you're seeking?*
Candidate: *"It has to be challenging."*
Your response:
Interviewer: *"What makes you want to work for XYZ Company?"*
Candidate: *"I want to work for a progressive company."*
Your response:
Interviewer: *"Describe some of your professional successes."*
Candidate: *"I was elected spokesperson for the team."*

Your response:

Interviewer: *"I noticed on your résumé that you held two jobs last year, one for a short time. Tell me what happened in that job."*

Candidate: *"My boss was real hard to work for. I worked hard but we just couldn't get along. So I got another job."*

Your response:

Interviewer: *"What are your future educational plans?"*

Candidate: *"I want to further my education, but I'm not ready to go back to school right away."*

Your response:

Paraphrase. Restate what the candidate just said. Paraphrases need not be in question form, but they must have an understood question mark at the end. Paraphrases show candidates you heard what they said, and you want to clarify the meaning. For example:

Candidate: "I like working with figures."

Interviewer: (*paraphrase*) "So you prefer working with figures versus something else?"

Candidate: "I'm better at figures than most people, but I like other things as well."

Interviewer: (*paraphrase*) "If I'm understanding what you're saying, you feel you're skilled at working with figures, but you enjoy doing other things as well."

Candidate: "That's correct."

Paraphrases are closed statements. The first response ends with a question mark to indicate a question. The last response doesn't end with a question mark, but the interviewer is prepared for the candidate to respond in a contrary manner. We don't want to make the mistake of being so sure of what we've heard that we paraphrase without listening for clarification. **The purpose of all paraphrases is to clarify.**

Practice Exercise

Write a paraphrase for each response below:

Candidate: *"In my last job I had lots of freedom."*
Your response:

Candidate: *"I really enjoy working with people rather than sitting in front of a computer all day."*
Your response:

Candidate: *"My hobbies include reading and skiing. I usually go to Denver once a year for a week-long skiing trip. It's become a family tradition."*

Your response:

Candidate: *"I traveled a lot in my last job, rarely had time to do anything at home except pack my suitcase. I loved the work and the experiences once I got to wherever I was going."*

Your response:

Summarize. INtentionally listen with a series of paraphrases to summarize what you've heard so far. Usually you choose to summarize when:

1. The candidate gives you a great deal of information.
2. You want to check to make sure you understood everything the candidate said.
3. You wish to check to see if you've completed your questions in a certain area before you transition to another area.
4. Your mind checks out. We must remember the mind thinks four times faster than any person can speak. It's natural, therefore, to occasionally check out. We simply can't help it. No matter how hard we try, we will occasionally find ourselves at a loss to recall what the candidate just said. Summarize whatever you've heard to get back on track. I always say, when in doubt, summarize.

Interviewer: "What did you enjoy most about working for the Chicago Press?"

Candidate: "I loved the people. They were helpful and never seemed to mind answering my questions. I felt like a novice because I hadn't worked for six years when I landed that job. No one acted like I was either out of it or behind the times. They gave me materials, listened to my ideas, and helped me learn the ropes. I also liked the way the office worked. The supervisors let us work our own hours. No one checked on you so long as you met your deadlines. I felt respected there."

Interviewer: "So you're saying you like to work with people who show you respect by listening to your ideas, helping you when needed, and leaving you alone to do your job?"

Notice how the interviewer took everything the candidate said and put it into a succinct sentence. But the interviewer also added the sense of a question. A paraphrase and a summarization both connote questions. The candidate must confirm what you just summarized.

Practice Exercise

Interviewer: *"Looking over your career, tell me what prompted you to move from sales to training."*

Candidate: *"I suppose it was a number of things rather than just one event. I had worked in direct sales from the time I sold magazines in high school. It seemed no matter what career options I pursued, I fell into sales. I suppose that meant I was good at it. Anyway, after working for six years with XYZ Company, selling the product, traveling from pillar to post, I became restless. I wanted to challenge myself to do something else. I began teaching people how to better use the product. I was interested in selling it, but I became more interested in product retention by teaching others how to better use it. This was a new idea at the time and created lots of interest among the management team. One thing led to another and before long, I was teaching the sales force about product retention and creating new ideas for usage."*

Your summary response:

Reality Test. Often candidates say something that seems unrealistic to you. Alert interviewers pounce on these lofty statements and "test the reality" by a series of probes and paraphrases. For example:

Candidate: "I don't mind working overtime every night if that's what it takes to get the job done."

Interviewer: (paraphrase) "So, you're saying working overtime never bothers you?"

Candidate: "My philosophy is to get the job done no matter what it takes."

Interviewer: (reality test) "I noted in your last job you said you didn't have to work overtime. Now you're saying you will work overtime if that's what it takes to get the job done. In what jobs have you worked overtime regularly to complete the tasks?"

Candidate: "My last job wasn't as challenging as it could be. I didn't need to work overtime to complete my tasks. I suspect the demands of this job would require overtime work. I've never had to work overtime regularly, but am willing to do so."

Interviewer: (reality test and probe) "Most jobs should not require overtime work if they're properly staffed. In what ways do you perceive the responsibilities of this job that make it more demanding than your previous job?"

In this example the candidate asserts a willingness to do something the person has never done before. Going back to the basics of interviewing, we know that future performance is based on past performance—not on what a candidate *thinks* they can do. The interviewer tests the reality of the candidate's assertion and determines what makes the candidate believe those behaviors are necessary in this job. An interviewer's antennae rise whenever a candidate speaks of future behaviors that have not been tested. Reality testing keeps you from falling prey to candidates who say things they believe you want them to say. Often interviewers who are not alert allow these lofty statements to go untested. We respond with something like, "That's great," or "I'm glad you feel that way because we do occasionally require overtime in this position."

Practice Exercise

Write "reality tests" for the following series of responses.

Candidate: *"Even though I've never worked on teams, I love people and a job that enables me to interact with others is exactly what I am looking for."*

Your reality test:

Candidate: *"When it comes to hard work, I'm the one. I'm the kind of person who never gets tired. I could work eighty hours a week and you'd never know it."*

Your reality test:

Candidate: *"I absolutely value my family. I have a wife and two young kids who mean the world to me. But when the job enters the picture, the family comes second. That's something I really believe in."*

Your reality test:

Flip Sides. Strategic interviewing requires you to look at things from every angle. When you determine a positive side of things, for instance, when you ask what someone liked about their previous job, it's important for you to also examine the negative (or flip side), what the candidate found challenging in their previous job. Remember one of our strategic interviewing goals is to get the candidate to say something they hadn't intended to say. Showing just one side is the candidate's goal; ours is to see as many sides as possible.

Interviewer: "I see from your résumé that you supervise fourteen engineers in your current position. Describe what you've learned about supervision."

Candidate: "I learned a lot about supervision in my last two jobs. I enjoy the challenge of helping people meet their goals. I love being the pivotal person making the key decisions. When questions arise, people depend on me for answers. That's part of leadership, in my opinion. Supervision and leadership go hand in hand. I suppose I like being in the center of things."

Interviewer: "So you enjoy running the show?"

Candidate: "You might say that. I've had leadership positions for the past fifteen years. Being part of the leadership team keeps me thriving."

Interviewer: (*flip side*) "What do you see as some of the challenges of leadership?"

Candidate: "Well, people don't always respond in the way you want them to. I suppose there have been times when I've gotten frustrated with performance. I hate firing people; not to say I haven't done it over the years, but it's not something I enjoy. I believe there's always something that can be done to help a person do the job. One of the biggest challenges in leadership is helping people bring their strengths into the company."

The interviewer could go on with this line of questions for quite some time. The candidate provided rich responses, full of topics to pursue. Sometimes it's hard to know whether to continue in the positive or to look at a flip side. In this instance the interviewer may have asked right before the flip side response, "Tell me what you thrive on in leadership." Had the interviewer posed this question, he/she might have spun off in a totally different direction, making it difficult to return to the flip side. To determine whether to pursue one area or another by either asking a flip side question or staying where the candidate is, you must do your homework. You must know where you want to go. What areas were you planning to pursue? If you don't look at the flip side, you might miss something important before moving in another direction. In this instance, by asking the flip side question, the interviewer got a deeper understanding of this candidate's view of leadership and supervision.

Practice Exercise

Interviewer: *"Tell me about your experiences on the Excel project with the management team."*

Candidate: *"I led a group of sixteen people. We met twice a week for the first six months of the project. Then we cut down to once a week. The experience taught me a lot about how to manage a group, especially one that large and that diverse. I enjoyed the sharing and the amount of experience in the room. Often I'd leave a meeting overwhelmed with how much the people knew in our company. The project was a great success. Afterwards we celebrated as a team. It was hard to break up when the project ended."*

Interviewer: *"Team work can be a rewarding experience, especially when groups work so well together."*

Candidate: *"I had no idea when I began the project I would enjoy the experience so much. At first I was daunted by the challenge. But now I have to say that it was one of the most valuable experiences in my career."*

Your flip side response:

Reflecting. INtentional listening means hearing more than the words. It requires you to **reflect**. Reflecting will enable you to produce the openness you need to make the interview successful. Reflecting requires you to reflect (as a mirror reflects) the feelings you hear behind the words. For example:

Candidate: "My job with the ABC Company was too much work."

Interviewer: (*reflect*) "It sounds as if you were overwhelmed with the responsibilities in your job with ABC."

As with paraphrasing and summarizing, when you reflect, a question is always understood. You mirror back the feeling you **believe** you heard. In this case the feeling you heard was *overwhelmed*. The person must affirm that feeling for it to be real.

To reflect, interviewers must ask themselves, what *feeling* do I hear?

As we said earlier people express their feelings through nonverbal cues—the visual and vocal part of their communication. To reflect, interviewers sensitize themselves to these subtle messages.

Practice Exercise

Write a reflecting response for each statement below.
Rephrase the feeling, not the content, in the following candidate responses.

Candidate: *"I really don't like doing the same thing over and over."*

Your response:

Candidate: *"Working the night shift was too much work."*

Your response:

Candidate: *"Between my scholarship and my part-time jobs, I managed to pay for my entire college education."*

Your response:

Candidate: *"When I decided to leave my last job, my supervisor told me I could come back at any time. I really couldn't believe she felt that way."*

Your response:

Let's look at possible responses to the practice exercise on reflecting. What feeling is suggested in the first candidate statement about doing the same thing over and over? Boredom, frustration, exhaustion? Any of these might work. You might respond, "It sounds as though doing the same thing over and over bores you." If, on the other hand, you had said, "In other words, you don't like doing the same thing over and over," you've paraphrased but not reflected. Reflecting requires you to state a **feeling** response.

The second candidate statement suggests exhaustion or frustration. You might respond, "Night shift work tires you?" If you had said, "So you don't enjoy the night shift," you would have paraphrased. There's nothing wrong with a paraphrase, but not when you're trying to reflect a feeling.

In the third statement we hear pride. "It sounds as though you're very proud of financing your college education."

For the fourth statement, we might reflect honor. The person was honored their boss thought so highly of them. You could reflect by saying, "You felt honored your boss held you in such high esteem."

A reflection is more than a paraphrase. As we have seen, each of the responses in the exercise could have been a paraphrase. Interviewers opt to reflect when they want to go deeper and when the feelings are too obvious to ignore.

Let's examine an interview where the interviewer uses all the INtentional listening skills. In this example, the position to be filled is for a medical director of a major hospital. The candidate is someone who has worked at the hospital for five years as the director of radiology.

Interviewer: (*probe*) "As director of radiology, Dr. Smith, what have you enjoyed about working for St. Michael's?"

Candidate: "I enjoy the support of the administration. I've worked in two other hospitals in my career, but I find St. Michael's the most responsive to the needs of the physician. Last year when I desperately needed a new technologist in my department, but hadn't included the position in my budget, the administrator went to bat for me."

Interviewer: (*paraphrase*) "So, you're saying, unlike the other hospitals where you've worked, this one supports the medical staff?"

Candidate: "I believe this administration sees the medical staff as part of the team. It's not 'us against them' like in so many other places. Here, I feel we're all interested in giving the patient the best possible services."

Interviewer: (*paraphrase and probe*) "In other hospitals where you've worked in the past, you've apparently experienced this 'us against them' approach. How did you cope with that kind of thinking?"

Candidate: "Unfortunately, I played right into it. I became territorial, watching out for myself and my colleagues, never willing to share or pool resources. The atmosphere was tense rather than collegial. It was not an atmosphere I could have survived for the long haul."

Interviewer: (*reflect*) "It sounds as if you felt protective in that kind of atmosphere."

Candidate: "Yes, protective and paranoid. We feared others were going to take something away from us. I did my job but with a sense of independence instead of interdependence like I've felt at St. Michael's.

Interviewer: (*probe*) "I noticed you worked in the previous hospital for six years. If it was so difficult there, what kept you on staff?"

Candidate: "Sometimes we don't realize how bad it is until we go someplace else. I wasn't that unhappy at the Veterans' Hospital. I worked for a great chief."

Interviewer: (*reality test*) "Help me understand. You worked in a place where you felt protective and paranoid, felt you could get stabbed in the back, but you weren't unhappy?"

Candidate: "Well, I suppose I wasn't exactly happy. I was just in a zone—doing my job and minding my own business."

Interviewer: (*probe*) "What made you decide to leave the Veterans' Hospital?"

Candidate: "The offer for chief of radiology came up at St. Michael's. I wanted to move up and the timing was perfect."

Interviewer: (*paraphrase and reality test*) "So, you didn't leave the Veterans' Hospital because you were unhappy but because a new offer arose?"

Candidate: "That was the primary reason, but I suppose my unhappiness played a role, too."

Interviewer: (*summary*) "To summarize what you've said, you were unhappy at the Veterans' Hospital because of the lack of support from the administration, but you liked the people in your department so you stayed there until an opportunity arose for a promotion elsewhere."

Candidate: "Yes, that's a good summary."

Interviewer: (*flip side*) "You've told me what you like about St. Michael's. What kinds of things are not so good, that could cause the same kind of unhappiness you experienced in the past?"

Candidate: "Well, no place is perfect. The administration, although supportive, does fall prey to putting a premium on the bottom line."

Interviewer: (*probe*) "Bottom line?"

Candidate: "We're constantly trying to look at the most efficient way to do things—sometimes that efficiency is translated into cheapest. That kind of thinking leads to poor quality care for the patients."

In this interview, the interviewer used all the INtentional listening skills to strip away the superficial. The candidate began with a rosy picture of the hospital and his feelings toward the administration. As the interview progressed, the interviewer wondered if this candidate would be likely to move on when unhappy rather than take risks in a negative environment. The candidate seemed to adjust and blend into a negative environment rather than make waves. As the interview proceeds, the interviewer should explore this issue in more depth to determine if this candidate will be a 'yes' man for the hospital or someone with some creative drive.

One note regarding the INtentional listening skills—too much of a good thing won't work. In other words, interviewers must skillfully use probes, paraphrases, summaries, reality tests, flip sides, and reflecting. Imagine how frustrating it might be to a candidate if the interviewer only paraphrased or only reflected. As the example above illustrates, when the interviewer balances the responses, he/she uncovers more information and keeps the interview strategically challenging for the candidate.

There's purpose behind each choice: You choose to probe when the candidate gives you general, not specific, information; you choose to paraphrase to show the candidate you understand; you choose to summarize when the candidate bombards you with information; you choose to test reality when something the candidate said doesn't jive; you choose to flip sides when you hear only one angle; and you choose to reflect when you sense something deeper going on or when you clearly sense a feeling being expressed through nonverbal messages.

This chapter taught us the importance of reacting to what the candidate says by using INtentional listening skills. By reacting we enrich the interview and move beyond the superficial. In Chapter 9 we will explore the T in POINT by testing the candidate in relation to the job and the candidate's performance during the interview.

NOTE

1. Richard Olson, *Managing the Interview*, p. 57.

9

Testing the Candidate

Socrates said that wisdom is knowing what you know and knowing what you don't know.

This chapter will explore the **T** in POINT in relation to the candidate. The interview tells us some things but not everything. The trick is knowing **what** things we can ascertain in an interview and **what** things we cannot.

Determining a candidate's skills and abilities in relation to a particular job puts interviewers in an uncertain place. Sometimes we make rash judgments about things we couldn't possibly know from an interview. Other times we try to determine much more than is necessary. In this chapter we will explore ways to test the candidate's skills and abilities according to the job we're trying to fill. When you evaluate the candidate, you return to those skills you listed for the job that cannot be taught, and you measure them according to the interview responses. You also evaluate the candidate in relation to reference information, test scores, assessments, and presentations.

Rosse and Levin in *High Impact Hiring* (1997) caution us to be realistic in our selection process. They say, "The lesson to be learned to improve your hiring decisions is to stop looking for the 'best' performer. Instead start your hiring process by identifying performers whose qualifications predict they can do the job effectively."[1] This recommendation helps us look at the interview in a more realistic light.

I have known human resource managers who travel to major colleges to recruit candidates, return after several days of interviews, and say, "I just couldn't find anyone to do the job." If this happens, we must ask ourselves several questions:

- Do we know what we're looking for? If a suitable candidate walked in, would we know it?
- Are we asking for too much? Are our requirements for experience stretching what college students are able to accomplish at this stage of their careers?
- If we feel we're being realistic, and we indeed know exactly what we're looking for, is the school providing an educational foundation suitable for our jobs?

EVALUATING THE CANDIDATE

Some human resource managers turn to testing to determine whether or not a candidate can do a particular job. Employment testing, so common today, didn't exist twenty years ago. Before you pull the tests off the shelf and hope they will save you from the fallibility of interviews, beware. Tests cause almost as many problems as interviews, the most common of which is legal. Are the tests racially and culturally biased? When we talk about Test in this chapter, we're looking strategically at the entire process of determining if a candidate suits our job. We're not looking at administering particular tests. In reality, tests illustrate another example of structural interviewing because some managers use tests as a way to avoid making difficult decisions. They rely on the test to decide for them.

One organization with which I consult uses tests to determine the candidate's technical know-how. Persons in the organization tell me they would probably fail the test, even given their experience with the organization! Why spend time and money on a test that screens out many good people? Again, many human resource managers look for easy solutions; testing sometimes fits that bill. In this organization a few candidates didn't measure up technically. Rather than go back and examine the schools from which they recruit, they instituted an across-the-board testing program.

Just like anything else, testing has its place. No test, and no computer, can replace the interview; no test, and no computer, can make that difficult decision for us to hire or not to hire. But what tests can do is help us screen candidates in the early part of the recruiting process. Some jobs require a basic skill level that schools do not necessarily provide or that the résumé or application cannot tell us. In these instances a simple test helps managers screen out candidates who lack those skills.

The best kind of testing is a simple test designed to prescreen for basic skills.

Tests designed to measure the soft skills are less valid. Numerous costly consultants profess to test your candidate's psychological ability to do the job. It's easy for managers, human resource and others, to fall into these traps. The complexity of the human mind and human behavior outsmarts any test we may try to employ.

We must avoid letting any kind of test box us in or eliminate the value of the interview. Rosse and Levin tell us there are two ways to approach an interview: seat-of-the-pants gut feeling and a highly quantitative process. They say neither works.[2] In this chapter we'll look at a third way—a strategic determination of a candidate's skills by his or her interview performance.

Based on everything you've seen on the résumé and the responses you've heard in the interview, the basic question is whether this candidate can do the job. This is the fundamental decision we're struggling to make. Ultimately we must determine what skills are missing and if our organization is willing to teach someone who lacks those skills.

Human resource managers sometimes spend a good portion of the interview time probing technical areas. Technical skills are learned in reputable schools. If you recruit in schools you respect, you trust the candidate will be able to perform technically. If candidates cannot perform, you should take your recruiting program elsewhere. Strategic planning for the interview begins with identifying the schools (vocational or higher educational) that produce technically competent candidates for the job.

Similarly, if you're searching for an upper management position, you go to people who've worked in reputable firms. If the person performed successfully in Firm X, which you respect, you may believe that person has the technical skills needed to perform in your company. Of course, you may be wrong, and without the benefit of candid reference information, you may never really know how a person performed in Firm X. You may hire someone you assume has the technical skills because the person graduated from a college or university you respect or worked for a period of time at a major company you respect. Later you may learn the person lacks the skills to do the job. Most organizations test a person's strategic skills during probationary periods. During that period, usually three months, a person who lacks the basic technical skills will become obvious. Human resource managers should remove that person quickly or make the decision to invest in expensive training. In addition you may run into candidates who falsify their résumés or applications; however, the frequency of such fraudulent behaviors happens less often than hiring someone who lacks the soft skills to do the job—communication, teamwork, leadership, initiative, and so forth. Nonetheless, human resource managers who have been burned feel betrayed and frustrated. These instances, however, are the exception to the rule and you should not base your entire recruiting program on one or two unprepared candidates.

In addition to the unreliability of testing methods is the unavailability of references. As we noted in Chapter 1, fewer and fewer human resource managers candidly share information about former or current employees.

The fear of lawsuits keeps their mouths firmly shut. We used to depend on reference information as the one reliable source—the source that could tell us how someone actually performed in a job. No more.

In today's world reference information has for all intents and purposes vanished.

So without tests and without references, how can we tell if someone fits the job we have open?

THE INTERVIEW TAKES ON NEW IMPORTANCE

As we move through this uncertain time, where we must make hiring decisions without valid tests and without candid references, interviews take on a new and all important role. In the past the interview might have been the tweaking place. With references in hand, we'd interview to confirm or deny what we learned by checking references. Today, the interview is the be all and the end all.

What the Interview Can and Cannot Tell Us

Interviews tell us less than we may like. One common mistake among managers is to believe interviews tell us more than they actually do. As we examine the interview, we must look at it realistically. What does the interview actually tell us?

Practice Exercise

Read the list below and check those factors you feel you can easily determine during the interview:

1. _____ *The candidate's philosophy and objectives*
2. _____ *Reason for choosing your organization*
3. _____ *General career aspirations*
4. _____ *Background*
5. _____ *Interests and hobbies*
6. _____ *Attitude*
7. _____ *Enthusiasm*
8. _____ *Willingness to accept criticism*
9. _____ *Loyalty*
10. _____ *Ability to solve problems*
11. _____ *The candidate's job performance*
12. _____ *Missing information*
13. _____ *Physical appearance*

14. _____Ability to appraise strengths and weaknesses

15. _____Intelligence

16. _____Poise under pressure

Interviews tell us only what we observe during the interview. Often we make judgments beyond these observables, but we need to recognize when we do so and know those judgments carry a high degree of risk. In Chapter 1 we saw the difference between inference and observation. We saw how we might take an inference and believe it to be a fact. Strategic interviewers know the limitations of the interview and search for ways to ascertain facts through the interview process.

The above list contains only six observable items:

- Reason for choosing our organization
- General career aspirations
- Interests and hobbies
- Missing information
- Physical appearance
- Ability to appraise strengths and weaknesses

The remaining items cannot be **absolutely** determined during an interview. Once managers recognize the limitations of the interview, they make more realistic hiring decisions. As Rosse and Levin suggest, the best we can do is **predict** whether or not a person can do the job effectively. Even so, interviews cannot predict job success in all instances. That's why we've turned to strategic interviewing.

Strategic interviews get us closer to that magic success by targeting our questions and probing beyond the superficial.

The Limitations of References

Because reference information has become evasive at best, the interview ends up being our most valuable resource for determining job performance. In the past we picked up the telephone, called the former employer, and that person shared what he or she experienced working with the candidate. Litigation has changed all that. Human resource managers no longer provide reference information. Instead they merely confirm that a prospective employee worked in their company for a certain number of years. Some candidates bring glowing reference letters. Beware! Think about the last time you wrote a reference letter. Perhaps the employee was mediocre at best. What did you say in that letter? Most employers strive to put a positive spin on the reference letter. Again, they don't want that letter coming back to haunt them during some later lawsuit. While reading this, you may feel your frustration mounting. My goodness, you say, why can't we be honest and straightforward with one another? Why can't we tell it like it is? There are some good reasons.

- In the past if you didn't like someone, regardless of his/her work performance, you could blackball that person through your reference. In other words, our unprofessional behavior in the past put us in the position we now find ourselves.
- Sometimes a person isn't successful in one type of job but could perform with success in another. If you give this person a poor reference, he/she may not be given another chance.

Some human resource managers have strong ties with their counterparts in the industry. These managers sometimes share information about former employees "off the record." But, as many of you know, nothing is really off the record anymore. The interview, therefore, takes a much more dominant role in the recruiting process. For that reason we cannot take the interview lightly.

Evaluating the Candidate's Interview Performance

The rigors of strategic interviewing enable us to get the most out of an interview that we possibly can.

In *The Right Choice* (1993), R. Cleve Folger says that the basic philosophy of testing is that past performance and learned skills are the best predictor of future performance.[3] Our goal in the interview is to develop a trusting relationship in order to determine how candidates describe their past performance and how they interpret their skill level.

Practice Exercise

The following is an example of a poor interview. List the reasons this interview was not strategic and will not help us determine the candidate's prediction of past performance and learned skills:

Interviewer: *"I see you went to Rutgers University."*

Candidate: *"Yes, I got my bachelor's there last year."*

Interviewer: *"How did you like Rutgers?"*

Candidate: *"Oh, it was fine. It's a good school, and it prepared me for graduate work."*

Interviewer: *"Yes, I see here you went to Columbia University. That was while you were working for Peter's Company. Did you go in the evenings?"*

Candidate: *"Yes, I went to school in the evenings."*

Let's examine this interview. The first question, "I see you went to Rutgers University," exemplifies asking a question you know the answer to.

Why ask this question? What is the strategic reason? The interviewer formed a nice open-ended question in his second response. That question led the candidate to respond openly about graduate work. But the interviewer completely ignored the response. Instead of listening with INtentionality as we saw in Chapter 8, the interviewer responded, "Yes, I see here you went to Columbia University . . ." The interviewer did not hear what the candidate said, react, and then give feedback. Instead the interviewer simply made another obvious observation and then asked a closed leading question, "Did you go in the evenings?"

Looking at that interview, we cannot guess the interviewer's strategy. Perhaps the interviewer saw a discrepancy when he noted the candidate went to school and worked at the same time. If so, the interview led only to the interviewer's explanation of that discrepancy. We heard nothing from the candidate except a confirmation of what the interviewer believed to be true. But was it indeed true? Who knows? This interview won't help us Test the candidate's interpretation of past performance or skill level.

Let's see if we can conduct a more strategic interview using the situation above.

Interviewer: "I'm confused about something on your résumé. You went to Columbia University while you worked full time with Peter's Company?"

Candidate: "That's right, actually. I attended Columbia at night."

Interviewer: "What was it like going to school and working?"

Candidate: "It wasn't easy. I seemed to either be working or studying all the time. I had no time to myself. But I knew it would be hard when I began the program at Columbia."

Interviewer: "What program?"

Candidate: "I entered the graduate program in clinical psychology."

Interviewer: "What is your current status in that program?"

Candidate: "Well, I'm still working for Peter's, but I dropped out of the graduate program last semester. I needed a break."

Interviewer: "How long a break?"

Candidate: "I hope to complete my degree at some point. I've still got quite a bit left, including an internship. But right now I'm more interested in finding a job that will give me more variety than what I currently have."

In this interview example the interviewer immediately addressed the question that bothered him, i.e., the fact that the candidate worked full time and went to school. The interviewer persisted until he learned that the candidate didn't finish school but wants to. Depending on the job you have open that ambition may or may not be possible.

Olson, in *Managing the Interview*, describes the Belly Button Method of Evaluation.[4] Olson, as well as Rosse and Levin, introduces a number system for objectifying gut feelings. The numbers help you clarify your feelings from one candidate to another. The numbers carry no meaning beyond your arbitrary association to them. For example, Olson says when a candidate leaves the room, we should circle a number that helps us identify the way we feel about that candidate (overall feeling) at that moment. The scale he uses is as follows:

1 _____ 2 _____ 3 _____ 4 _____ 5
Accept   Reject

Many organizations use other types of rating scales, but again, the numbers are arbitrary decision points to help individuals codify their reaction to a candidate. These numbers are meaningless to another person. If someone asks you what number you gave a candidate, you might respond, "3." That person might say, "Well, you didn't like that candidate very much, did you?" Actually "3" might represent a high rating for you. Perhaps you've never given someone a "4."

The following sample form attaches numbers to the specific skill areas.

Sample Form
Candidate Evaluation

Rate the candidate with a number on each of the six attributes below.
1–5 Scale: 1 = Highest, 5 = Lowest

1. Communication:	Expressive/ listens	True empathy	Confident in speech	_____
2. Organization:	Plans well	Takes initiative	Systematic	_____
3. Leadership:	Directs	Takes an active role	Inspires	_____
4. Decision Making:	Decisive	Gets results	Implements ideas	_____
5. Responsibility/ Maturity:	Self-confident	Dependable	Sets priorities	_____
6. Assertiveness:	Fair but firm	Takes action	Shows empathy	_____

Using the scale above, how would the candidate fit in our organization? _____

In order to use this form, the interview team needs to identify six attributes needed to perform the job, and each interviewer designs strategic questions to determine the candidate's ability in each attribute. Not all the interviewers focus on all six attributes. The team decides who will focus on an attribute. If you focused on leadership and assertiveness, but not the candidate's ability to make decisions, you would not rate the candidate on that attribute. Again, it doesn't matter that you didn't rate all attributes because this form compares candidates to each other. The form has no meaning from one interviewer to another.

TESTS, ASSESSMENTS, INTERNSHIPS

Performance Tests

We've talked about the value of tests to help employers screen candidates. I spoke to the owner of Pinebush Farm and Nurseries—a family owned business. Apparently in the landscape and horticulture field, candidates often exaggerate their plant knowledge. For the purposes of determining if someone has sufficient understanding of plants to work in the retail area of the nursery, Pinebush Farm designed a short, ten-question test. The purpose of this test was to screen out candidates who lacked basic skills. By so doing, the employer only interviewed those who passed the test. Recognizing that some tests might eliminate quality candidates, Pinebush Farm designed a test with sufficient simplicity to eliminate only those with no knowledge of plants.

Some organizations use performance tests to determine whether candidates can do the job. These tests include typing, literacy, and other skill-related tests. As we noted with Pinebush Farm, performance tests work best when combined with a comprehensive selection process. Furthermore performance tests must be job-specific. Why give a literacy test to a candidate who graduated with a 3.8 GPA from a reputable college or university? Why give a typing test to someone who will never type?

Assessment Centers

Law enforcement organizations routinely depend on assessment centers to determine a candidate's ability to handle job complexity.

Assessment centers are elaborate selection systems that measure anything from basic performance skills to psychological ability to handle certain jobs.

Assessment centers usually include exercises designed to measure delegation, planning, leadership, teamwork, crisis management, problem solving, decision making, communication, and other "soft" skills. Trained psychologists observe people in action.

For assessment centers to work, the behaviors must be measurable. But often assessment centers measure unmeasurable behaviors. How do you measure leadership? How do you measure teamwork? Much of what we look for in assessment centers defies structured scale analysis. Once again we're trying to impose structure in the interview process. By doing so, we eliminate creative candidates and perhaps hire those who simply know how to manipulate the system. We must recognize the limitations of assessment centers. They are tools or add-ons to the interview process and not the sole criterion that drives our decisions.

Internships

Many organizations hire interns or co-ops for periods of three months to six months. During these internships the manager observes candidates actually doing the job. Of course, for jobs that require months of on-the-job training, internships are impractical and do not provide adequate performance information.

Some companies adopt a policy never to hire their interns. Why have interns unless you're trying to groom people to work for your organization? Such policies need revisiting.

The bottom line, however, is the interview. We use assessment centers, internships, co-op programs, or performance tests as **added information** to help us determine the candidate's suitability.

The interview enables us to see the candidate in action, responding to questions, and thinking spontaneously.

Let's look at an interview with Sonya Ruth, who is applying for a management information position with ABC Company. The job Sonya Ruth wants is an upper-level position in which she would supervise five programmers. To perform adequately she must demonstrate technical competence as well as an ability to supervise others.

Sonya Ruth Potter
1212 S. Milledge Ave., Apt 11 Athens, GA 30605
706–549–2123
srpotter@negia.net

EDUCATION	UNIVERSITY OF GEORGIA
	Master of Business Administration, *June 1998*
	GPA: 3.4/4.0
	Specialization: Management Information Systems
	Strategic Marketing
	Additional classes: Data Communications & Networking, Electronic Commerce, Executive & Group Information Systems, Conflict Resolution
	Bachelor of Arts in Journalism, *March 1992*
	GPA: 3.6/4.0
	Major: Public Relations; Minor: Business/English
PROFESSIONAL EXPERIENCE	UNIVERSITY OF GEORGIA TERRY COLLEGE OF BUSINESS

Graduate Assistant

Management Department, *September 1997–present*
- Maintain web pages

MBA Placement Office, *September 1996–June 1997*
- Updated and maintained student resume database
- Facilitated on-campus interview process

DELTA AIR LINES, INC.
Summer Intern, *June 1997–August 1997*
Corporate Communications Office
- Wrote news releases concerning various areas of Delta
- Coordinated communications with Delta Express business unit.

UNIVERSITY OF GEORGIA COLLEGE OF VETERINARY MEDICINE
Director of Public Relations, *August 1994–August 1996*
- Planned, wrote, and edited alumni and staff newsletters
- Coordinated relations with university Public Information and external media
- Developed a new fundraising information system (Programming liaison for committee)

Information Specialist, *June 1993–August 1994*
- Assisted Director of Public Relations and Development with communications and fundraising
- Developed system for tracking fundraising statistics

Sr. Administrative Secretary, *January 1993–May 1993*
- Developed database application for responding to donors and their clients
- Tracked direct mail response statistics

COMPUTER SKILLS

- Experienced with Macintosh, DOS, Windows operating systems
- Database: MS Access, Dbase, FoxPro
- Word Processing: WordPerfect (Mac and DOS), MS Word
- Internet; ftp, goper, world wide web, html
- Other programs: Visual Basic, JavaScript, PageMaker, Excel

ACTIVITIES

Graduate Business Association
- Public Relations Committee
- Philanthropy Committee

Interviewer: "It looks as though you had an interesting and strong career in public relations before you returned to school. What made you decide to make a career change?"

Candidate: "I had been working in public relations for three years. I enjoyed the work very much, but it seemed so hit and miss."

Interviewer: "What do you mean by hit and miss?"

Candidate: "There was no data that supported what we did or didn't do. We talked about marketing research, particularly in my job as director of public relations, but I couldn't get too much support. So on my own time I developed a new fundraising information system. I did it just for me because I wanted to know more about the people who gave money to the Vet School. I thought we could tailor and target better that way. That experience led me into management information."

Interviewer: "So, are you saying the rather gray nature of public relations troubled you and led you into a new career?"

Candidate: "Not actually. Yes, public relations has miles to go in order to make the best use of information. But, I don't see that I've moved into a totally new career."

Interviewer: "If you didn't intend to move from public relations to management information, what did you intend?"

Candidate: "I intended to strengthen my skills. I bring certain skills to the field of public relations. I went into the job with Delta and the Vet School with no knowledge about management information, but I felt systems analysis was the wave of the future. I wanted to be more adept. I had to really struggle and learn what I could when I developed the system for the Vet School. It taught me how much I didn't know. Actually, I see myself lending my public relations skills and my management systems skills to any job I accept."

Interviewer: "Tell me how you see yourself bringing those two sets of skills to the job at ABC Company."

Candidate: "I noticed when I applied for this job that ABC Company doesn't have a website. Your company also doesn't have a strong information source that relates to internal operations such as recruiting or promotions. I found some databases related to the clients, but that could be strengthened. ABC Company sells products to customers. I know a lot about sales and marketing from my public relations experience and my degree. I would propose marrying that knowledge with my interest and ability in management systems."

Interviewer: "So you're interested in more than the nuts and bolts of programming?"

Candidate: "I can do the nuts and bolts programming, and I enjoy doing that, but it is not something I want to spend the rest of my life doing."

Interviewer: "What do you want to spend the rest of your life doing?"

Candidate: (*laughs*) "That used to be a very difficult question to answer. But, when I made the decision to leave my job and go back to school, I knew what I wanted in my career. I want to apply my knowledge of public relations and my ability to work with people within a framework of management information."

Interviewer: "You mentioned your ability to work with people. How have you worked with people in the past?"

Candidate: "While at the Vet School, I supervised three other people, two student interns and one assistant."

Interviewer: "What was it like to supervise others?"

Candidate: "It had its pros and cons. My assistant was great. She knew as much or more than I did about the job. She never let me down when we had deadlines to complete. The student workers, on the other hand, proved more difficult."

Interviewer: "In what ways were the students difficult?"

Candidate: "They weren't as committed to the job. They often didn't show up for work, and we couldn't depend on them to complete tasks. They lacked motivation."

Interviewer: "It is frustrating when people don't have the drive we have. How did you handle the students' lack of motivation?"

Candidate: "My assistant and I worked with them—tried to help them understand the big picture. We gave them more interesting tasks instead of just the grunt work. With some students that worked. With other students we had no choice but to replace them or not to depend on them for the important jobs."

Interviewer: "So you're saying when people lack motivation you try to help them understand the 'why' behind their work and get them more involved in more meaningful tasks. But when all fails, you either replace them or cope with their behavior?"

Candidate: "That's how I tended to handle the students."

Practice Exercise

You want to Test this candidate for the management information position you have open.

1. *From the interview, what skills does this candidate bring to the job?*
2. *From the interview, what skills are lacking or what skills would you like to find out more about?*
3. *From the interview, what did you like about Sonya?*
4. *From the interview, what reservations do you have about Sonya?*
5. *Would you recommend Sonya for hire?*

The example with Sonya shows how much you can learn from an interview. Sonya has tremendous initiative. She seems creative as well as a person who enjoys working with people. As for her supervising skills, she had trouble with student workers, but she looked for ways to motivate them.

As for reservations, our chief concern is the strong interest in public relations. Even though Sonya says she would find ways to adapt her PR experience in our company, we wonder how long she will enjoy doing that. We suspect she will learn from us and after a few years develop her own public relations firm. From what she told us, she returned to school in order to strengthen her skills, not change careers. She remains tied to public relations. That's where her passion lies.

No, we would not recommend her for hire if we're looking for an employee to remain more than two years. If we're willing to accept a short-term tenure, yes, we would consider her for hire.

In this section we examined the POINT process with the candidate in mind. We Planned for the particular candidate through résumé screening; we conducted an Open interview by sharing information about ourselves to create trust; we INtentionally listened and heard what candidates said before we gave feedback or responded; and finally we Tested the candidate's performance in the interview and rated the candidate based on that performance.

The next section will apply the POINT process to the interview itself. In Chapter 10 we will set the stage for the interview and plan the overall process.

NOTES

1. Joseph Rosse and Robert Levin, *High Impact Hiring: A Comprehensive Guide to Performance Based Hiring*, (San Francisco: Jossey-Bass Publishers, 1997) p. 259.

2. Joseph Rosse and Robert Levin, *High Impact Hiring: A Comprehensive Guide to Performance Based Hiring*, p. 259.

3. R. Cleve Folger, *The Right Choice: Hires That Meet Your Agency Needs.* (Indianapolis, Indiana: The Rough Notes Co., Inc., 1993) p. 39.

4. Richard Olsen, *Managing the Interview*, pp. 92–93.

10

Planning for the Interview

In this chapter we will Plan for the actual interview. Where will you conduct the interview? Your office environment sends messages; what are those messages saying? Will the candidate tour the facility? How will you prepare the candidate for your note taking?

You also need to prepare for the interview process within your organization. Your interviewing team must meet and design step-by-step what will happen when the candidate enters the front door. Who will interview the candidate? Strategically what will the focus of each interview be? To avoid interviewing on a superficial level each interviewer must pursue a different area and ask different questions. Will you conduct team interviews and if so, how many? This chapter will give you tips for determining when and how to conduct team interviews as well as tips for an interview process that works.

Often human resource managers face a situation where the rest of the management team in the company sees interviewing as a necessary evil but less important than the rest of the daily duties. The schedule for a candidate often becomes the task of the human resource manager, often without team support; sometimes a manager snags whomever is available to interview the waiting candidate. Communication upward is one of the most critical jobs all human resource managers face. In that communication they must emphasize the importance of strategic interviewing and how the manner in which we interview each candidate affects the strategy. With careful planning for the interview itself organizations could save untold dollars, both in time and in better hiring decisions. Human resource managers should solicit the support of top managers in order to assure quality interviewing, on-time interviewing, and careful consideration of each candidate. Just like anything else we do, strategic interviewing demands an efficient, thought-out plan.

You've identified the skills needed to fill this job and have thoroughly examined the résumé. Now you're ready to begin the interview. Wait! There's more to think about before you call the candidate in. First, where will you talk to this person? What nonverbal messages are you sending? Will you take notes during the interview? Who else will interview the candidate? Will you conduct a team interview or do it solo?

SET THE INTERVIEW STAGE

In Chapter 1 we looked at the communication process. We learned that 92 percent of the power of communication comes through nonverbal messages. We also learned that those messages are **interactive**. In other words while you receive nonverbal messages from the candidate, you send messages as well.

Part of strategic interviewing is planning and controlling the nonverbal messages you send.

One powerful visual nonverbal message is the environment. If you work in a busy, hectic atmosphere, but choose to interview the candidate in a quiet room isolated from the busy work world, what message are you sending? At the same time, no one wants to interview in an environment fraught with interruptions. We learned also in Chapter 4 that first impressions and perceptions play an important role in the interview process. First impressions imprint themselves in the mind of candidates as soon as they set foot into your workplace. You have some control over those impressions when you carefully consider and plan the interview environment.

As a manager there are several things you need to consider as you examine your interview environment:

Candidates enter interviews nervous. There is probably no more humiliating task in our lives than placing ourselves in a position to "sell" ourselves to someone we've never met. We make every effort to put our best foot forward in the hopes of being selected. The interviewer must set a stage that will reduce or ease the candidate's tension. Should you interview from behind your desk or at a neutral round table? Some managers prefer the neutral round table so as to convey less authority and to give the impression of informality. The desk, however, serves as a barrier. When candidates walk into your office, they are strangers. Many haven't met you or if they have, they've met you briefly. During this initial meeting we can easily predict that the candidate's Johari Window is closed (See Chapter 3). Some people relax quicker than others, but everyone experiences those first few jittery moments. A desk or physical barrier feels safer for the candidate. Yes, it removes some of the intimacy, but intimacy may not be appropriate at this stage in the interviewer-candidate relationship. Strategically you want the candidate to relax and trust you. The sooner you establish trust the more information the candidate will share and the larger the Johari Window will become. To set a stage that is safe, put yourself in the candidate's shoes—an informal round-table environment communicates a message that is a little too intimate for this initial meeting.

Although you want to convey a busy, hectic environment, you must manage the interruptions. Once I interviewed with someone whose telephone constantly rang. He answered it, conducted business, then returned to the interview. His attention wasn't with me. I felt he wanted to end the interview as quickly as possible so as to return to his other duties. My interview was an annoying diversion for him—an interruption in his day. It's not possible to conduct a strategic interview with constant interruptions. To intentionally listen to the candidate, stay open yourself, and keep your focus. This will take every bit of your concentration; one interruption destroys the flow. Before you commence the interview, stop telephone calls and curtail other interruptions. Afterwards, take the candidate on a tour so he can experience the hectic life of the organization.

Human resource managers must convey to others in the organization the supreme importance of the interview. Those who interview must see it as not only part of their jobs but carrying equal importance with the other tasks for which they are held accountable. Human resource managers, who provide in-depth training for the other manager-interviewers in their organization, have more success in convincing the powers-that-be of the importance of the interview. This book along with the other tools will give the human resource manager leverage to support that training.

Study your office with a detached eye. As you look around at the papers scattered on your desk, the books on your shelves, the photos of your family, the message slips covering your telephone, the dying plant by your sunless window, your college diploma hanging over your desk, imagine what messages you're sending. We are so close to our environment, we no longer see the shadows. Our visual world sends thousands of messages about us. Once my husband and I visited a newly refurbished bed-and-breakfast. Ten minutes after our arrival, my husband startled the host when he asked, "So, who is the pediatrician?" How did my husband discern the host's profession? The books in the library gave him away. What do you want to convey about yourself and your organization and how can your environment help you? You have some control over your environment. You can alter the things the candidate sees. You don't want to give a false impression of the job, but you do want to send visual messages that inform the candidate about working in this organization. The candidate will believe what he sees more readily than what you say. For example, if your office is in great need of a paint job, and you say, "At ABC Company, we value our work environment. You will have a beautiful office overlooking the lake." What do you think the candidate will believe?

By recognizing the power of the nonverbal message conveyed through the environment, you make your communication more efficient and more consistent.

Do You Take Notes or Not?

As soon as you look down to jot a note, what do you miss? Remember the power of nonverbal messages sent through the eyes. Furthermore, you will be thinking about the note you're writing, rather than listening to the candidate's words. Note taking can cause you to miss an important probe point or an important nonverbal cue. People who depend on note taking don't just write a few little notes to themselves; they often use note taking as a crutch. They end up writing down much more than they need and spend more than 50 percent of the interview with their eyes on the note-paper rather than the candidate.

Nonetheless, some people insist they cannot interview effectively without writing down a few things the candidate says. If you *must* take notes, the following tips will ease the candidate into your need for note taking:

- Tell the candidate you're going to take a few notes. Assure the candidate that what you are writing is for your use only and will help you recall the interview.
- Do not write down everything the candidate says.
- When you are not writing, put the pen or pencil down in front of you. Do not fiddle with it.
- While writing a note, do not ask a question. Use your pauses for note taking.

For example:

Interviewer: "Tell me what you did while you sorted computer data at XYZ Company."

Candidate: "I was in charge of six people. We separated the data according to batch needs. Each afternoon I looked over the work of the other six to make sure we finished our job and nothing was left out."

Interviewer: "So, you handled the batch needs with six others, and you checked on the work of the others after they left for the day?"

Candidate: "Yes, I usually didn't get started with the spot check until 5:30 or so."

Interviewer: (*Looks down, jots a note on the paper in front of him. After completing the note, the interviewer looks up and continues.*) "How did the others feel about the spot check system?"

CONDUCTING TEAM INTERVIEWS

In Chapter 4 we learned that the interview process should be done as a team. To determine who sees the candidate, when, and under what circumstances falls to the team—a group of managers involved in the selection of candidates. Usually interviews happen one-on-one. There are times, however, when the team decides to conduct team interviews, i.e., two on one.

Let's look at what a team interview is and when it is effective.

What Is a Team Interview?

A team interview involves two or more people interviewing one candidate at the same time. I recommend no more than two interviewers to one candidate. More than two people facing a candidate threatens to overpower and intimidate the individual.

What Effective Team Interviews Look Like

- Two interviewers need to balance one another. One may be new to the organization; the other may be a more seasoned employee. One may be a line employee while the other is in management. One may be a nurse or doctor, and the other may be a human resources manager. You wouldn't pair two vice presidents, the president and vice president, or the hospital administrator and the medical director. Each interviewer brings a different focus to the team interview.

- The individual interviewer introduces himself or herself, rather than one interviewer introducing them both. You want to set a tone that says both interviewers will talk and both are equal.

- Although the interview is well planned, it appears conversational. One interviewer asks a question; the other follows up and tags with another question. The interviewers pause after each statement in order to allow the other interviewer to chime in. It's perfectly appropriate for one to ask of the other, "Do you have anything to add?" If, on the other hand, one interviewer finishes his or her questions or comments before the other has a chance to participate there's no point in the team interview.

- The team interview strategy must be planned by both interviewers. Knowing the overall plan keeps the interviewers clear and on target no matter who is asking the questions. During the interview, however, both respond to the candidate with flexibility.

An Example of a Team Interview

Interviewer 1: "Good morning, I'm Patrick Hayes. I am a shift supervisor with XYZ Company."

Interviewer 2: "I'm Lucy Cobb. I work in human resources. We're going to ask you a few questions just to get to know you."

Interviewer 1: "And allow you to get to know us. Tell me, Mary, how do you like living in Bainbridge?"

Mary: "I've enjoyed it okay. But the town is one of the reasons I want to leave. I've lived in Bainbridge for almost ten years. The town is really drying up. There wasn't much there ten years ago, but since the Ford plant closed, the place is really dead."

Interviewer 2: "You say the community is one reason you want to leave. What other reasons are driving you from your present job?"

Mary: "There are things I really like about my work. I love working independently and being creative. My boss gives me lots of leeway. But I've gone about as far as I can go. There's no room for advancement in the company, and there's really nothing else available in the community."

Interviewer 2: "I had a similar situation early in my career. That's one reason I moved to human resources. What sorts of career paths are you looking for?"

Mary: "I studied industrial engineering at school but never really had a chance to use it. During the last few years, I took refresher courses. I hope to get back into my field."

Interviewer 1: "By 'back into your field,' what do you mean?"

Mary: "I know I won't be able to make as much money as I do in my current job because beginning positions in engineering start out less. But, I'm willing to take the cut to get into engineering."

Interviewer 2: "So you're saying you don't mind taking less money to change career paths?"

Mary: "That's right."

Interviewer 1: "Mary, you told us you took some refresher courses. Tell me about those courses."

Mary: "Since I'd been out of engineering for ten years, I took courses at the community college on analysis of technical data, and project planning and control. Then I took three computer courses to bring me up to speed on the software currently used by industrial engineers."

Interviewer 1: "What computer courses did you take?"

Mary: "I took introduction to C programming, a course on computer aided design and two on Wordperfect and one on Microsoft Word."

Interviewer 1: "What languages do you feel proficient in?"

Mary: "Lotus, QI-Analyst, SIMAN."

Interviewer 2: "It sounds as though you dedicated a good deal of your time to studying. What else do you like doing in your spare time?"

Notice how the interviewers went back and forth with their questions. Interviewer 1 focused on the particulars of Mary's education and Interviewer 2 focused on Mary's aspirations regarding her life in the small town, her special interests, and her reasons for changing jobs. The interview contained balance and one interviewer didn't overwhelm the other.

When to Choose Team Interviewing

Team interviews work best when you have quite a few people who need to see the candidate. Some of the reasons to consider team interviews:

- Two interviewers bring a broader perspective to the interview process. Two people limit the influence of biases and perceptions.
- Two interviewers working together in the planning phases of POINT spin ideas off each other and do a more thorough job than one person working alone.
- What one interviewer misses in a strategic interview the other catches. As we've said, strategic interviewing requires us to stay alert and listen with our full antennae. No matter how hard we try, we'll miss something. Two interviewers are less likely to allow an important piece of information to slip by.
- Two interviewers represent a cross section of the organization and thereby give the candidate a broader picture of the company.
- Team interviewing shows the candidate that teams and teamwork are important values in the organization.

What works against team interviews?

- The two interviewers don't balance each other; both want control or neither takes control.
- Two interviewers tend to intimidate the candidate.
- The interviewers don't plan together and go into the interview unfocused.
- The organization doesn't value teams and teamwork.

In one of my classes after we practiced team interviews, someone asked, "While one interviewer is questioning the candidate, is it okay for the other interviewer not to listen?" What this question suggests is that while one person is talking to the candidate, we can relax, formulate our questions, and not be as much "on our toes" as we must be during a single interview. The entire class answered with a resounding No! For the team interview to work effectively and efficiently, both interviewers must listen to the candidate's responses and jump in with probes, paraphrases, reflections, flipsides, and reality tests whenever an opportunity presents itself. The non-talking interviewer positions himself or herself to study the nonverbals and might readily jump in with a reflecting response or with a probe to dig deeper. Unfortunately team interviews do not give us a chance to relax. In fact, we need to stay even more alert; we not only must watch the candidate, but we must also watch our partner and take cues from him or her.

Practice Exercise

Mark Smith is the human resources manager for XYZ Company. He has three candidates coming for interviews in the next two weeks. Five people in his company conduct the interviews. Those five people represent the five major divisions of the organization. Each has been with XYZ Company for over ten years and each is a company vice president.

In recent years turnover at XYZ Company has been high. Mark has suggested a change in the interviewing process in order to help cut down on people leaving. The average length of stay for management hires is less than one year. When Mark suggested to the CEO a need for more people to interview candidates, the CEO said, "We don't have the time. If we allow others to interview, all our staff time will be consumed with interviewing. As it is the vice presidents and myself spend more than 50 percent of our time interviewing."

1. *What would you recommend Mark do to improve the interview process?*
2. *How might Mark respond to the CEO's concerns?*
3. *If you were Mark, what first steps would you take?*

Let's look at some things Mark might do to improve the interview process at XYZ Company. First, he must win the support of the CEO.

Mark: "To improve our interview process, we must expand the number of people in the company involved in interviewing."

CEO: "We don't have the time. If we allow others to interview, all our staff time will be consumed with interviewing. As it is the vice presidents and myself spend more than 50 percent of our time interviewing."

Mark: "One reason we spend so much time interviewing is that we haven't given the interview process any thought. We interview anyone who wanders in or has been sent over here. Another reason we've spent so much time interviewing relates to our high turnover. I've talked to people who have left, and I have ideas that will help us retain employees."

CEO: "What do you propose doing?"

Mark: "We must create an interview team—a group of managers and others throughout the company that will be responsible for interviewing. I've put together a list of twelve people who represent a cross section of the company and include different levels of expertise and tenure."

CEO: "Twelve people! That's entirely too many people to interview."

Mark: "I agree. Twelve people won't interview all candidates. Some of the twelve will interview each time. We'll also conduct team interviews using two interviewers. Most of the people who left us say they didn't really understand the job and all it entailed when they were hired. By involving more people in the recruiting, we can show candidates what it's like working here."

CEO: "Mark, I'm not sure how your process will work, but if it will help us keep people on board, I'm all for it. What do you need from me?"

Mark clearly stated what he thought needed to be done to improve the interview process, and he responded honestly to the CEO's concerns. What Mark sees as essential to a successful recruiting effort is greater company commitment to the hiring process. He wants to expand the interview and selection program and create a team.

The bottom line for most human resource managers is commitment. How committed is your company to hiring and selection? Usually things have to reach dire circumstances before upper management recognizes a need to streamline recruiting. Things need not get so bad. As a trouble-shooter for human resources, it's your job to look at your own interviewing and selection process and diagnose its chance for ongoing success.

TIPS FOR AN EFFECTIVE INTERVIEW PROCESS

Organizations use many interview processes. Some work and some don't. Even the best strategic interviewer will fail if the process is ineffective.

Practice Exercise

Let's look at an organization and attempt to diagnose its interviewing process.

Sandra is the human resources manager for the Mental Health Department at the Community Hospital. When she came into the job, she learned that a recruiting process was in place. It consisted of the following:

- *The human resources manager visits four major universities where graduates study in the field of mental health, including social work, psychology, and marriage counseling as well as one major medical school where graduates study psychiatry. The manager visits these schools twice a year and returns with two or three candidates to fill the various jobs that are open. These candidates are interviewed on site.*

- *The human resources manager takes the candidate to dinner the night before the interviews and gives the person a schedule of interviews for the next day. When the candidate comes into the department on the morning of the interviews, he or she has breakfast with the chief of psychiatry and the hospital administrator before meeting with the rest of the staff.*

- *After the breakfast interview, the candidate visits with the chief nurse. Then the nurse in charge of the records takes the candidate on a tour of the hospital.*

- *The human resources manager takes the candidate to lunch and interviews him or her after lunch. During that interview, the human resources manager tells the candidate about the hospital benefits.*

- *The candidate visits with the nurse in charge of reception and with a mental health professional who has been on staff for fifteen years.*

- *At the end of the day the candidate talks with the human resources manager who answers his or her questions.*

If you were Sandra, coming into this process, what, if anything, would you change?

What do you like about the recruiting process in the Mental Health Department?

- The human resources manager searches for candidates in reputable schools. She visits those schools twice a year. We assume the manager develops a rapport with the career planning people and with the faculty. By doing so, the human resources manager gets the information she needs to conduct quality interviews at the school. Usually colleges provide a room and the students sign up for interviews. As the interviewer, you must get the résumés in advance of the interview and students must show up for interviews without a lot of substitution. The college placement people can assure a smooth flowing interview process on their campuses when the human resource managers work with them.
- It looks as if the candidate sees people at different levels in the department.
- The human resources manager greets the candidate the night before and explains the interviewing process.
- The human resources manager talks to the candidate at the end of the day to answer questions.
- The candidate meets with people from the hospital administration as well as people within the department.
- The candidate gets a tour of the facility.

What don't you like about the recruiting process at the Mental Health Department?

- Interviews are conducted during meals. It's hard enough for a candidate to respond to questions without having to eat and respond. If you take a candidate to breakfast or lunch, refrain from interviewing. Instead visit with the candidate as you would visit with anyone during a meal.
- There doesn't appear to be any teamwork. In other words no one seems to know what the other interviewer is doing. Each could be asking the candidate the same questions.
- When did the human resources manager actually interview the candidate? At dinner the night before? If so, that is not a good time to conduct an interview. During the session after lunch? It seems the HR person spent time talking about benefits rather than conducting a strategic interview.
- A breakfast meeting with the chief of psychiatry and the hospital administrator could be daunting to the candidate. The candidate should meet with these people but separately and not during a meal. By scheduling this interview during breakfast, it might appear to the candidate that upper management sees interviewing as a secondary function that must be worked in at odd times.

- The human resources manager should not give the candidate the complete schedule for the day at the outset. What if the HR manager realizes this candidate is not going to work out? During the short interview on campus, major problems might go undetected, but now they surface. Maybe you learn the salary is too low for this individual or the person is looking for a job vastly different from the one you have open. What will the HR manager do? Allow everyone to interview as planned? The best course is to give the candidate a brief overview of the day, saying generally, "You'll meet with me and then several people in the department. We'll give you a tour and later take you to lunch."

- There seems to be no team decision making on the candidate. People interview solo and pass their individual decisions on to the human resources manager. Too much is being placed on the human resources manager, suggesting a lack of commitment to the hiring process within the department.

- Although several key people interviewed the candidate, peers or newly hired staff did not interview. Allow candidates to talk to people just hired so they get a fresh reaction to the organization. It also helps for candidates to talk to people doing the kind of work they'll be doing.

Sandra's recommended process for recruiting:

- Put together a team of ten to twelve staff who represent a cross section of the department to oversee the hiring and recruitment. Not all ten or twelve people will interview; it will depend on the nature of the vacant position.

- Set up visits to the colleges. Take at least one team member to help with the screening of college candidates. Different team members may visit the colleges at different times, but Sandra participates in all the campus recruiting.

- Once site interviews are arranged, review the résumés as a team. Determine who will interview and what focus each interview will take. No more than five people (or seven if a team interview is included), including Sandra, should interview the candidate. These people constitute the interview team for all candidates for this particular position.

- Greet the candidate the evening before the interview and share a general overview of the plan for the next day. Invite the candidate to dinner, but do not interview the candidate during dinner.

- Sandra greets the candidate the morning of the interview and conducts an interview first.

- Following Sandra's interview, the remaining team members interview the candidate either solo or in teams, depending on what the team decided would work best for this candidate and this position. Each interviewer tags the next by telling them if they accomplished their interviewer goals or if certain other items need probing. **An interviewer should not reveal his or her hiring decision before the next interviewer sees the candidate.**

- A team member takes the candidate on a complete tour of the facility.

- A team member takes the candidate to lunch and shows him or her the community.

- The hospital administrator and other staff members, including the director of benefits, talk to the candidate.
- Sandra ends the day and answers any questions the candidate has. She specifies when the candidate can expect a decision.
- All other candidates for the same position are interviewed with the same process.
- Once all the candidates have been interviewed (and this should be completed in no less than a week), the team meets to share observations and to make a hiring decision.
- Sandra contacts all the candidates.

In summary a process that works contains the following elements:

- Screen candidates thoroughly before inviting them to come for an interview at your facility.
- Develop a team approach to the Planning phases of the interview process. A group of managers or the interviewing team determines the qualifications needed and screens the résumés. Don't leave all decisions up to the human resources manager.
- Give the candidates a general schedule when they visit your site. Make sure managers have a detailed schedule and stay on time.
- Prior to the interview the team discusses the attributes and decides who will focus on what areas. The team determines whether or not to conduct team interviews and pairs up the teams.
- Do not plan interviews around meals. Candidates cannot respond and eat at the same time; interviewers cannot apply the POINT process and eat, too.
- Give the candidate a thorough tour of your facility.
- After one interviewer finishes with a candidate, he or she tags the next interviewer. This means the next interviewer is told what was covered and what was omitted. Feelings about the candidate's suitability should not be shared at this time.
- When all of the interviews have been completed, the team meets to select the best suited person. They examine the pros and cons for selecting one person over another. They should not discuss candidates until this final meeting.

In this chapter we Planned for the actual interview. We examined the environment in which the interview will take place. We looked at our non-verbal cues to strategically determine what messages we wish to send. In addition we determined whether to opt for a solo interview or a team interview. Finally we examined our interview process to make sure it fits the hiring strategy of the organization. In Chapter 11 we will look at how to actually Open the interview.

11

Opening the Interview

How do you begin the interview? From your handshake to the first words you say, images form. And those images affect the success or failure of the interview. As the interviewer you can control those initial images and first impressions. In those early moments you create the tone for the entire interview. Just like with candidates who immediately turn you off or on, you do the same with them. Let's reiterate the definition of interviewing:

A set of verbal and nonverbal interactions between two or more people focused on gathering information to decide a course of action.[1]

Interactions is a key word in this definition. What happens to the candidate happens to you. As candidates transmit nonverbal messages that you interpret, you do the same to them. The important thing to remember is that you're in control of the interview. You set the stage and maintain the focus throughout. That's the edge the interviewer has over the candidate.

Tony Alessandra in his book *Charisma* (1998) talks about the ability to relate to people on their level. He defines charisma as "the ability to influence others positively by connecting with them physically, emotionally, and intellectually."[2] He tells us charismatic people can see things from other people's perspective and they are constantly searching for common ground. What Alessandra is describing is the ability to empathize (see Chapter 9). During the opening of a strategic interview, we strive to create trust and develop rapport with the candidate; we strive for that charismatic state.

In this chapter we'll look at setting the stage, that is, beginning the interview in ways that enable the candidate to relax and open up. Remember we strive in strategic interviewing to create enough comfort that the candidate will tell us things he or she didn't intend to say. We're trying to peel away the superficial and learn what's underneath. The opening is critical to achieving this goal. One thing that makes people charismatic is their ability to create immediate rapport with others. In the first few seconds when a charismatic person greets you, you feel as if you're the most important person around. Why? They've given you their full attention; they've shared with you; they've shown you respect and trust; they've listened to your feelings and responded to you as if you really matter.

HOW TO BEGIN THE INTERVIEW

Most human resource managers spend the first few moments of the interview talking. They share information about the company, about the vacant position, and about themselves. There is nothing wrong with this approach except you must consider how much the candidate can actually **hear**. Consider, for example, when you introduce yourself to someone. What is the first thing you say? Your name. What is the first thing we all forget? Your name. Why do all of us forget names so easily?

Communication consists of a bombardment of stimuli. When you initially meet someone, you're hit with millions of pieces of information, and that information goes bit by bit through your brain's processing or filing system. At the same time, your mind is busy with your internal thoughts, such as, Will this person approve of me? Is my tie too long or my zipper zipped? What kind of impression am I making? Between the outside bombardment and your internal dialogue, it's a miracle we ever recall someone's name!

When you open the interview you must consider several factors:

- The candidate is nervous and probably closed.
- The candidate cannot absorb too much information right away.
- You are probably more nervous at this stage of the interview than at any other stage.

Given these factors the best you can accomplish in the opening moments is to orient the candidate to you and to the process. In other words, you let the candidate learn more about you and about what will happen to him or her during this interview.

Your goal for the first few moments of the interview is orientation.

In the 1950s William Schultz studied human interaction and group behavior. As he discovered similarities from person to person, he began to test those similarities through an instrument called FIRO-B (Fundamental Interpersonal Relationship Orientation-Behavior).[3] Schultz studied basic human needs. His premise relied on the assumption **people need people** to survive.

From here he isolated three basic needs: inclusion, control, and affection. He looked at these needs from the standpoint of what people **express to others** and what people **want from others**. Given these data, Schultz extended his research to human interaction in groups. After all, groups are merely conglomerates of people. What an individual desires in an interaction with another individual mirrors what individuals desire in groups. The definition of a group is two or more people with interlocking needs, common values, and shared norms. If two or more people make up a group, then the interviewer-candidate relationship is a group relationship. From Schultz's research came the stages of group development:

- Approach/Avoidance. Individuals struggle with themselves to find a place where they fit in relation to others. Here individuals look for similarities to which they can relate.
- Power/Control. Individuals no longer look for similarities but want to distinguish themselves from others. Here individuals look for ways they differ from others.
- Intimacy. Individuals no longer struggle but relate cohesively with one another. Here individuals express openly without fear of rejection or rebuke.

The group process relates to the interview, particularly in the first stage. Most interviewers are not with a candidate long enough to leave the first stage of group development—the approach/avoidance stage. The only task people can accomplish in that first stage of human interaction is orientation. We strive to get to know one another and to find places where we can relate. If one person strives to get to know the other, but the other person remains closed, the interaction fails. For this basic reason, interviewers must do more than probe the candidate in the first few moments. They must relate to the candidate openly.

Interviewer: (*shakes candidate's hand*) "Hello, my name is Mark Edwards. I'm the human resources manager for XYZ Company. Thank you for taking the time to visit our facility today."

Candidate: "I'm delighted to be here."

Interviewer: "Good. I'm going to talk to you for a few minutes, just to get to know you and understand what you're looking for. Then you'll visit with Jane Reece, our production manager."

This example shows us the basic opening. The interviewer introduced himself with his name and title, no more. He explained the process—talk first to him, then to the production manager. At this stage rapport isn't yet established. We want to make sure we don't overload the candidate. Later and throughout the interview you will sprinkle in information about the position itself and about the company. This example illustrates the first step in the opening.

Practice Exercise

Interviewer: (Shaking the candidate's hand) "Please have a seat. My name is Jamie Lewis. I've worked for XYZ Company for five years as the employment manager. We're looking for a senior vice president for finance. This person is responsible for the budget and for all the financial decisions in the company. He or she reports directly to the president and has about two hundred people reporting to him or her. We've reorganized in recent months. In the past all the unit managers handled the financial aspects of their units. That worked well when we were a small company, but we've tripled our size over the last ten years and now it's time to change. Part of the reorganization was to create a new position for the senior vice president for finance and that's the position we're interviewing you for today. As you can well imagine this person will be up against some resistance. The unit managers are used to getting their own budgets and working within them. They won't like someone telling them what they can and can't do. How does all this sound to you?"

Candidate: "It sounds great."

What is wrong with the opening above?
Rewrite the opening.

In the above example the interviewer shared too much information. Perhaps it was important information, but the candidate couldn't possibly absorb it all in the first few moments. Furthermore, the interviewer may not wish to show all the cards so early. Indeed, strategically, this interviewer needs to discover how the candidate handles resentment and conflict. By sharing all this information at the outset, the candidate discovers what the interviewer wants in response. This interviewer gave the candidate the edge. A better opening for this interview might be something like:

"Good morning, Mr. X, my name is Jamie Lewis. I'm the director of employment. I'd like to talk to you for a few minutes before you visit with others in the company. Tell me what you know about our firm."

This opening immediately directs the interview. The interviewer decided not to conduct a typical icebreaker and proceeded with the first probe. Whether or not to conduct an icebreaker is one of the first decisions an interviewer makes. As we learned in Chapter 1, that decision is based on the nonverbal information you pick up from the candidate. If the candidate appears relaxed—good eye contact, firm handshake, no fidgeting, smiles, clear voice modulation—you might choose to skip the icebreaker. If the candidate appears tense—eyes jump around, clears throat, straightens self or clothing, blinks fast—you should select an icebreaker before you delve into the interview.

If you select to skip the icebreaker, you must still orient the candidate to yourself. You need to find places throughout the interview where you can share information about who you are. Remember, the candidate is searching for similarities. If you don't give him or her any information, the candidate will give up and stop trying to relate. From the example above, we learn nothing about the interviewer. A more appropriate opening might be: "Good morning, Mrs. Y, my name is Jamie Lewis. I'm the employment manager. From your résumé I see you and I have something in common. We both worked for McDonalds when we were in college. How was that experience for you?"

WHAT IS AN ICEBREAKER?

Icebreakers do exactly what the name suggests: they break down the barriers. In order to erase that awkward and uncomfortable time at the beginning of the interview, we must plan for some type of icebreaker.

Many action-oriented managers ignore the icebreakers. They wish to get to the meat of the interview right away. If the person left something off their résumé, these managers jump in with "So, what did you do when you stopped working for XYZ Company?" If the person lists a desirable salary above what you can offer, these managers might begin with, "You say you want to work for a company that pays at least $100,000 per year. What brings you to apply with us?" If the candidate lists a salary much higher than you can offer, why go any further, you might ask. Why waste time talking about irrelevant topics, especially when you only have a few moments with the candidate? In reality if you skip the icebreaker and jump full steam into the interview, the candidate will never open up to you. You will never accomplish the fundamental goal of a strategic interview. You will only discover the surface items the candidate wishes you to discover. Icebreakers ease the tension in the interview environment to help you develop a rapport with the candidate.

So, you say, why develop a rapport with someone who clearly isn't in contention for the job you have open? Mitigating factors might be at work. For example, the candidate may no longer want to limit himself to the salary requirement or the candidate likes the sound of your job so much, salary is no longer a top priority. What often happens is the candidate believes salary can be negotiated. If you begin with such bluntness, your job may lose some of its appeal. You may turn a good candidate off.

According to Webster's, rapport means "relation marked by harmony, conformity, accord or affinity."[4]

If an icebreaker helps bring harmony, conformity, accord, and affinity to a relationship, the interviewer must reveal information about himself. Remember the definition of interviewing tells us interactions occur. The only way for harmony, conformity, accord, and affinity, i.e., rapport, to happen is through self-disclosure. Most interviewers forget this essential part of the icebreaker.

We've learned already why self-disclosure is critical in the strategic interview. We've seen how the Johari Window affects a candidate's ability to respond. People won't open their Johari Window when the interviewers keep theirs firmly shut. We've also learned how self-disclosure sets the tone for the interview. It says to the candidate, this interview will not be an interrogation. While I learn about you, you'll learn about me. We will interview each other; we will interact with each other.

Wilson describes the first few moments of the interview in *Conducting Better Job Interviews* as follows:

- Warmly welcome the candidate. An interviewee who is at ease will be more likely to answer questions spontaneously.
- Introduce yourself by name and title.
- Sustain a relaxed atmosphere by initiating a brief conversation unrelated to the interview.[5]

Wilson's last step constitutes the icebreaker. In a strategic interview, however, nothing you do is "unrelated to the interview." **Everything you do in a strategic interview has a purpose and is related to the interview, including the icebreaker.** What, then, do you talk about in that brief conversation that we call the icebreaker? And how long does an icebreaker last?

What Do You Talk About During the Icebreaker?

Because the icebreaker sets the tone for the interview, it is critical to the process. If you falter on the icebreaker, you've lost the opportunity to succeed during the interview. You can recover, but it takes a lot of time and energy to do so. The icebreaker reveals something about you while it allows the candidate to respond to an "easy" question. For example: "I noticed on your résumé that you play tennis. I play recreational tennis and find it helps me unwind. How long have you played tennis?" The candidate learns that you play tennis and that you need something to help you unwind.

This icebreaker works for people who indeed play tennis. It doesn't work if you don't play tennis. You must reveal something about yourself as you attempt to get the candidate talking.

Candidate: "I've played tennis all my life."

Interviewer: "Wow, all your life? I just started playing a few years ago. I find the sport challenging in many ways, physically as well as mentally. So often I lose a match because of what I do to myself mentally. How have you dealt with the mental aspects of the game?"

Candidate: "I'm still working on it. Even though I've played all my life, I sometimes hurt my game when I lose confidence. If a guy walks on the court and looks big, I get scared. It's taken me years to realize that size and skill are two different things."

Interviewer: "So that mental stuff never goes away?"

Candidate: "Not with me, especially if you're constantly trying to improve."

Notice how this icebreaker (supposedly an irrelevant topic), brings us deeper into the mind of the candidate. We began by sharing our own experiences with the game of tennis. When we shared our frustrations, the candidate felt free to share similar frustrations. The interviewer might stay with this line of inquiry for a while or move on with something like, "How have you noticed your experiences with tennis helped you deal with difficult situations in the workplace?"

Here's another example of an icebreaker:

Interviewer: "I see on your résumé you're originally from Kings Mountain, North Carolina. I have family from Bessemer City."

Candidate: "That's amazing! My grandparents live in Bessemer City."

Interviewer: "I've been away from North Carolina for a long time so I no longer have relatives there, but I know the area quite well. It was a great place to grow up."

Candidate: "Yes, it certainly was. I go back frequently. Not much has changed."

Interviewer: "That's the beauty of a small town. Usually you can leave and come back and everything you remember is still there."

Candidate: "You're so right. I've lived in Detroit for five years now and I swear the place I first lived in doesn't look the same anymore. They're tearing down buildings and putting up new ones all the time."

Interviewer: "So, you've lived in both large and small communities?"

Candidate: "I've lived here, there, and everywhere over the last fifteen years. My jobs took me from Detroit, which was where our company was based, to Carlsbad, California for a year and on to San Diego."

Interviewer: "What have you enjoyed about living in these different places?"

Notice how this icebreaker told the candidate about the interviewer. The candidate knows he grew up in a town very close to the interviewer's hometown. Suddenly there's affinity, accord, harmony, and conformity. Suddenly the candidate and the interviewer have something in common. Notice also how the interviewer used the icebreaker to transition into an area of questions he planned to explore. In a strategic interview the interviewer searches the résumé for something that will not only build rapport but will also help transition into the interview. You wouldn't want to spend an entire twenty minutes talking about tennis or about your friends and acquaintances from Kings Mountain.

Let's examine a résumé and develop meaningful icebreakers. Imagine you're the human resources manager for an established company. The position you're recruiting for is the manager of sales. You've established the following strategic points for the interview: team player, high energy, supervising skills, strong communication skills, successes in sales, risk taker, willing to relocate. Smith Saunders's résumé looks promising. You spoke with Saunders on the telephone and arranged for the site interview.

SMITH W. SAUNDERS
12321 Hardy Street
Overland Park, Kansas 66223
(913) 851–2300

SUMMARY: Educational background in business communication with work experience in sales and marketing.
• Excellent conceptual and analytical abilities
• Aggressive, hard-working, and goal oriented
• Strong self-motivational skills
• Excellent verbal and written communication skills

EXPERIENCE: **Midwest Sales Manager** (January 1998 to Present)
P & W Industrial Services, Inc.- Detroit, MI
• Promoted to sales manager of a 3.5 million dollar territory.
• Responsible for hiring, training, developing, and managing 7 employees throughout a seven-state region.
• Utilize ability to develop major accounts while establishing customer loyalty through long-term business relationships.

Sales Representative (June 1994 to December 1997)
P & W Industrial Services, Inc.- Detroit, MI
• Increased regional sales from $250,000 to $1.3 million annually.
• Responsible for self-managing Kansas City office and performing all sales/marketing functions including prospecting, client analysis, proposal preparation, and client support.
• Achieved one million dollars in sales within first year—*first time in company history.*

Customer Service Representative (September 1993 to May 1994)
Service Corporation- Overland Park, KS
• Responsible for prospecting, negotiating, and retraining accountants nationwide for representation of over 40,000 clients.
• Negotiated reduced accounting fees resulting in $360,000 annual savings.

Sales Representative (March 1993 to September 1993)
Precision-net Communications- Detroit, MI
• Generated new business and built successful relationships with customers through networking and cold calling.

- Researched and analyzed corporations' business communications needs and proposed the most cost effective and technologically advanced plans available.

EDUCATION:	Bachelor of Arts Degree- BA
	University of Michigan, December 1992—*Financed 75% of college education.*
	Major: Communications Emphasis: Business
HONORS:	Member of the Million Dollar Sales Club – 1995, 1996, 1997
	"Hunter of the Year" Award – 1997
	P & W Industrial Services – Employee of the Month – November 1995
HOBBIES:	Golf, Softball, Exercising, Traveling

Interviewer: (*stands, shakes hands*) "Welcome to XYZ Company. Please have a seat. As I told you on the telephone, I'm the director of human resources for XYZ and your liaison for the day. How was your flight in?"

Saunders: "The weather caused a delay in Kansas City. We didn't get out until midnight. Otherwise it was smooth sailing."

Interviewer: "That's one thing I hate about traveling, the unknown. It's maddening thinking you're going somewhere and getting no further than the airport."

Saunders: "My career over the years has entailed so much travel, I suppose I've gotten used to it. I realize there's nothing I can do. Usually I bring something to read or work on, knowing there'll be delays."

Interviewer: "So your job with P & W requires a good bit of travel?"

Saunders: "Not so much anymore but still quite a bit. I used to be on the road five days a week. Home only on the weekends. Now it's more like ten to twelve days a month."

Interviewer: "When I first started working for XYZ, I, too, traveled as much as five days a week. It nearly drove me crazy. How have you managed to keep your sanity?"

Saunders: (*laughs*) "I'm not sure I've done that. But one thing I've learned is to get to know the place I'm in. I sorta make each new city my home. Rather than hole up in the hotel, I get out and do things as if I lived there."

Interviewer: "Like what sorts of things?"

Saunders: "I love golf. I often find a driving range or a place where I can play nine holes. I like to find a small course and someone to play with. That makes it much more fun than just practicing on the driving range."

Interviewer: "I enjoy golf, too. And I have to keep up with it to play a decent game. So, you play even when you're on the road?"

Saunders: "My wife says I'll play anywhere. My clubs go wherever I go."

Look at what we've learned about Saunders in this brief, early interchange:

- He travels in his job and has done so his entire career. Rather than bemoan the time away from home, he makes the best of it. He seems to be a person who looks for the best in whatever he does. Going to a new city and trying to fit into that city—becoming a part of it helps him adjust to the strain of travel.
- Saunders appears to be a people person. He prefers to play golf with someone, even a stranger, than to hit balls alone on the driving range.
- He's driven. Even his hobby is a passion for him. He plays golf wherever he goes and finds opportunities to play.
- Saunders appears to be a person who accepts what he cannot change and makes the best of it. When travel plans are diverted, rather than pace and curse, he accepts it and brings work along. He realizes there are some things in life he cannot control.

These first few moments helped the interviewer learn a lot about Saunders, but what did Saunders learn about the interviewer?

- The interviewer has had experience with extensive travel in his or her career and is sensitive to the difficulties posed by being away from home.
- Having to be away from home as much as five days a week was not something the interviewer could adjust to and yet, he/she experienced the frustration of an extensive travel schedule. The interviewer knows what it's like to live in a hotel for extended periods of time.
- The interviewer loves to play golf, too, and must play often to keep up. The interviewer shares Saunders's passion for his hobby.

As this interview continues the candidate and the interviewer learn more and more about each other—that tone was set at the outset. The candidate knows this interview will not be an interrogation but an interchange and a two-way conversation.

Notice the interviewer did not begin with a light question from the résumé. Because this interviewer traveled extensively in the past, he/she knew to ask about the flight. That first question showed sensitivity to the candidate and what the candidate had recently experienced. Later more similarities emerged.

Icebreakers begin with "getting to know you" conversation. Some people call this conversation "small-talk." I don't like that term because it appears as if the conversation were small or less important.

Practice Exercise

List some other icebreakers interviewers might use with Saunders.

What area might the interviewer transition to with this icebreaker?

Some potential icebreakers you might include in the above practice exercise include:

- I see you financed 75 percent of your college education. I had to work my way through college, too. That gave me a different college experience than many of my friends. How was your experience different from others?" (Areas to transition to: time management, organizational skills, dealing with others when your experiences are different.)
- I noticed you listed exercising and traveling as a hobby. I try to exercise when I travel for pleasure, but most of the time I end up with good intentions and nothing more. How do you manage both? (Areas to transition to: how industrious or conscientious the candidate is, the importance of outside activities to the candidate, and what kind of outside activities the candidate enjoys.)
- I started out in sales, like you, and then moved into training. One thing I had trouble with was the cold calls. How did you manage to get your foot in the door? (Areas to transition to: ability to exercise leadership, ability to communicate persuasively.)

All of these examples share something about the interviewer while they prompt the candidate to talk about something "easy."

What do you do when there's nothing you can relate to on the résumé? Suppose you have a candidate who didn't list any recreational activities and whose job history, places the candidate lived, the candidate's interests have nothing in common with you. Human resource managers face this dilemma frequently. When nothing strikes you from the résumé, try the following icebreakers:

- Talk about a current sports event that's on everyone's mind: "Wasn't the Ryder's Cup exciting? I don't play golf, but even I got hooked on watching the Americans come from behind. That was teamwork at its best." Or "Being from New York, I suspect you're following the World Series. My southern roots put me on the side of the Braves. But either way, they are both outstanding teams." Or "Wasn't the Women's World Cup Soccer finish a heart stopper? My kids play soccer so I've learned quite a lot about the sport over the years. I loved the way all the players pulled together to win." Each of these examples would focus the early part of the interview on teamwork.
- If the candidate looks totally un-sportslike, you might talk about current weather related news, such as the approach of a hurricane or flooding or extreme heat or cold. If the weather is perfectly gorgeous, you might say, "Don't you love days like this? When I look out my window and see the mountains framed in that sunshine and blue sky, it reminds me why I live in Colorado." This icebreaker might focus the early part of the interview on location preferences.
- If there are no sports or weather issues, you might start with a general, easy-to-answer question that gets you into the interview but also shares something about

yourself. For example, "I'm curious about how you found out about our company. When I came here five years ago, there was no information out there. I had to really scratch to learn the basics." In this instance the interviewer learns what the candidate actually knows about the company and what initiative he or she took to discover that information.

In this chapter we discovered that the icebreaker and the opening of the interview are important. In fact, they are the most important part of the interview. If we don't start off right, we've destroyed our chances for a successful interview. What we're trying to do when we attempt to establish rapport is develop trust. Most managers know if they cannot develop trust or if they've violated trust, getting it back is next to impossible. That's why we place so much emphasis on the first few moments of the interview. Establishing a firm relationship with the candidate in the first few moments will make the rest of the strategic interview easier.

After you've developed trust in your opening, you must keep it throughout the interview. As you probe deeper into the background of the individual, you must prove yourself a trustworthy confidant. In the next chapter we'll discover how to keep the trust we created by continuing to INtentionally listen throughout the interview.

NOTES

1. Olson, *Managing the Interview*, p. 8.

2. Tony Alessandra, *Charisma: Seven Keys to Developing the Magnetism that Leads to Success* (New York: Warner Books, Inc., 1998), pp. 11, 14–16.

3. William C. Schultz. 1958. The Interpersonal Underworld. *Harvard Business Review* 36: 123–135.

4. *Webster's Seventh New Collegiate Dictionary* (1972), p. 709.

5. Wilson, *Conducting Better Job Interviews*, p. 45.

12

INtentional Listening During the Interview

Throughout this book we've examined the strategic interview within the framework of the POINT process. We looked at the POINT process in relation to the job and all aspects of job analysis. We applied the POINT process to the candidate and all aspects of an individual's skills and abilities, and now we're ready to incorporate the POINT process directly to the interview by INtentional listening.

In Chapter 8 we looked at the skills to intentionally listen. They include:

- Probe
- Paraphrase
- Summarize
- Reflect
- Reality Test
- Flip Sides

These listening skills show the candidate we've heard what they said. It's the way we **react** to what someone has just told us. When we suddenly ask an unrelated question, it seems as if we didn't hear what the candidate said. Asking a new, unrelated question gives the impression we didn't pay attention, even if we did. When we decide to pursue another area, we still must make a smooth transition; that means we must move to that new area with a paraphrase or summary. For example:

Interviewer: "You seem to have a lot of experience working with people. What was the most difficult encounter you had when you worked in customer relations at the bank?"

Candidate: "The one incident I remember was when an elderly lady came in with her bank statements covering at least five years. She couldn't get her accounts in order and accused the bank of stealing her money. She was very loud and insistent. I took her to a quiet corner of the bank, offered her a seat, and told her I'd go over her statements with her. She got all nervous and paranoid about my looking at her statements. I decided to just talk with her, ask her questions about living in the community, about her church, and her family. She began talking. As I questioned her, we began to laugh and soon she softened up. But that situation was certainly touch and go."

Interviewer: "It sounds as though you didn't panic when the lady got loud and demanding. I'm sure your demeanor and willingness to take time with her helped ease the situation. Your experience with people must have also come in handy when you worked for the insurance company. Tell me about what you did there."

The interviewer didn't just jump into the line of questioning about the insurance company. Instead the interviewer summarized what was just said and made a smooth transition to the next line of questioning.

According to Tony Alessandra in his book on charisma, listening is one of the seven qualities that comprise the core of charisma. He says, "listening is a key to communicating and making others feel special in your presence."[1]

In this chapter we will review the listening skills we learned in Chapter 8. We will also look at the nonverbal messages that demonstrate to candidates we've heard them. Then we will apply those skills in an interview example. We'll discover how those listening skills strategically take us where we intended to go and how we can direct the interview to hit our probe points.

INTENTIONAL LISTENING SKILLS

Probe. Ask a question related to what the candidate just said. For example:

Candidate: "I love jobs that keep me busy."

Interviewer: "Describe a job you've had that kept you busy."

Probes should be open, not closed. As we noted in Chapter 8, there are strategic times when an interviewer selects a closed question, but not during probes. The point of a probe is to get people talking. In Chapter 8, we learned one reason we might ask a closed question is to stop the flow of conversation. Probes, by their very nature, cannot be closed because probes are designed to encourage conversation.

Paraphrase. Ask a question that repeats in your words what the candidate just said. Paraphrases need not be in question form, but must have an understood question mark at the end. Paraphrases show candidates you heard what they said and you want to clarify the meaning. For example:

Candidate: "I like working at my computer."

Interviewer: *(paraphrase)* "So you prefer working at your computer versus working with the public?" *(Notice, by adding "versus working with the public," the interviewer doesn't just paraphrase but directs the response.)*

Candidate: "Actually, I like doing lots of things, including working with people, but I don't mind spending the whole day at my computer either."

Interviewer: *(paraphrase)* "If I'm understanding what you're saying, you feel you're skilled at many different things that include working with people, but you enjoy working at your computer and don't find computer work tedious."

Candidate: "That's correct."

Interviewer: *(probe)* "What skills do you bring to instances when you must work with people?"

Summarize. When you want to clarify a series of comments the candidate made, you use several paraphrases to summarize. Interviewers often summarize to make sure they've completed their questions in a certain area before moving to other areas.

Interviewer: "Let me see if I understand everything you've said so far. You enjoy working with figures, but you also like working with people. It doesn't bother you to be interrupted while doing detailed work, but you'd prefer to work in a quiet place when working with figures."

Candidate: "That's right."

Interviewer: "If it doesn't bother you to be interrupted while doing detailed work, how do you manage to maintain your focus?"

Here the interviewer summarized a rather ambivalent response. The interviewer used the "summary" to get the candidate to agree to what was said and then followed with a probe to help clarify the ambiguity.

Reality Test. Often candidates will say something that seems unrealistic to you. Interviewers pounce on these lofty statements and give them the "reality test." For example:

Candidate: "I'm very flexible. I can work with all kinds of people."

Interviewer: *(paraphrase)* "So, you're saying you've worked with all sorts of people in your career?"

Candidate: "My philosophy is to get the job done no matter what it takes. If some people don't pull their load, I do it for them. There's no sense in standing around and complaining when a job needs doing."

Interviewer: (*probe*) "Looking back over your career, when have you had to jump in and do someone else's job because they didn't do it?"

Candidate: "I can't think of a particular situation, but I would do it if necessary because I believe getting the job done is the first priority."

Interviewer: (*paraphrase and reality test*) "What you're saying is you would jump in if necessary, but you've never had to do that. What makes you believe you would actually jump in when you've never had to do that in your career?"

Candidate: "I suppose I just believe I would. But I've never needed to do so. My last job wasn't as challenging as this job is. I suspect the demands of this job would require everyone to jump in wherever necessary. I'm sure I'd be willing to do that."

Interviewer: (*probe*) "Most jobs should not require everyone to jump in to complete tasks if they're properly staffed. How do you perceive the responsibilities of this job that make it more demanding than your previous job?"

In this interview the candidate is saying he or she will do something the person has never done. It's important for the interviewer to test the reality of that position and to determine what makes the candidate believe those behaviors are necessary in this job. Reality testing keeps you from falling into the trap of allowing candidates to say things they believe you want them to say—or glossing over the truth.

Flip Sides. Strategic interviewing requires you to look at things from every angle. When you've asked questions with a positive spin, for example, when you ask what someone liked in a previous job, it's important for you to also examine the negative (or flip side), what the candidate found challenging in the previous job.

Interviewer: (*flip side*) "You've shared a number of things you liked when you worked in the grocery store—the interaction with people, the ability to make your own decisions, the emphasis on quality—what things in that job did you find difficult?"

Reflecting. To reflect is one of the most difficult communication skills we use. One reason for the difficulty is our reluctance to identify feelings. Many people struggle to identify their own feelings, much less helping someone else identify theirs. But the power of reflecting will enable you to produce the openness you need in the interview. Reflecting requires you to hear more than the words. It requires you to reflect (as a mirror reflects) the feelings you hear behind the words. For example:

Candidate: "I can't seem to get everything straight with so many bosses."

Interviewer: (*reflect*) "It sounds as if you're frustrated with the line of command in your current job."

As with the paraphrase, when you reflect, a question is always understood. You mirror back the feelings you believe you heard. In this case that feeling is frustration. The person must affirm that feeling for it to be real.

Candidate: "I'm not actually frustrated. I'm worn out. It's hard keeping up with so many people."

The candidate's response makes clear what was said earlier and helps the interviewer move closer to understanding what the candidate means.

MANAGE YOUR NONVERBAL CUES

Throughout this book we've discussed the power of the nonverbal message. We learned the importance of reading those messages as we interview candidates. In the last chapter, we noted that strategic interviewing requires you to manage your own nonverbal cues. Interviewing is an interaction—it is two-way. What are your nonverbals saying?

Nonverbal messages are all the physical cues we use to express ourselves.[2]

Eye contact. This may be our most powerful nonverbal cue. In many cultures whether or not a person looks at you determines that person's credibility. Some say the eyes mirror the soul. Direct eye contact sets the stage for trust. As candidate Mary walks into your office, you look at her, reach for her hand, and continue your direct eye contact as you shake hands. If you maintain intense eye contact, without occasionally glancing away, Mary may stiffen and feel uncomfortable. For the interviewer, there's a fine balance between direct eye contact that conveys warmth and interest and intense eye contact that invades. Unlike negotiators who count blinks and avoid breaking the stare, the interviewer looks away naturally, but the eyes come back, particularly during someone's response. I've seen interviewers studying the résumé when a candidate walks in; their eyes stay glued to the page as their hand reaches up for the perfunctory handshake. The message sent is not one of warmth and trust, but one of lack of preparation.

Pamela Butler, in *Self-Assertion for Women* (1981), says that one value of good eye contact is that it helps us focus less on ourselves and more on others. She talks about women with downcast eyes who worry about their appearance or their behavior.[3] This premise holds for interviewers. When we look down, our thoughts wander to our next question instead of staying with the candidate. **When we talk without looking at the candidate, we tend to talk about ourselves rather than focus on the person in front of us.**

Note Taking. Should you take notes during the interview? This question comes up in each of my workshops. As we saw in the last chapter, many people feel uncomfortable without taking notes. They say they cannot recall everything the candidate said without writing things down as the interview progresses. Note taking has its pros and cons. **The pros:** You have an excuse to break eye contact. You are better able to keep track of what was said. **The cons:** Whenever you look down to write, you lose the power of eye contact. You risk missing some nonverbal cues. Furthermore, the candidate wonders what you wrote. *Why did you make a note about my dissatisfaction with my boss, but not about the award I got in high school?* In reality, interviewers who take notes tend to spend much more time looking down than looking up. Furthermore, note taking serves more as a crutch than a useful tool. I jot down a note to give me something to do with my hands or to give me some time to think about what to say next.

In my view, note taking carries too many risks. The power of the nonverbal cues are too strong to miss. I suggest learning to interview without taking notes. Strategic interviewing requires you to focus on the candidate. You can't do that and write, too. You should write down your impressions and everything you recall from the interview as soon as the candidate departs. By the way, **you don't have to remember everything the candidate said!**

What about taping the interview? Absolutely not! Remember you're trying to establish trust. Candidates will never open their Johari Windows if you've got a tape recorder going. Tape recorders stifle conversation. They're too intimidating. Reporters use tape recorders; you're not a reporter; you're an interviewer.

Facial Expression. Our faces convey all kinds of signals. We smile; we frown; we squint; our mouths droop; our noses twitch. All these physical cues mean something to an observer. To convey warmth, we smile. When we greet candidate Mary with a smile, direct eye contact, and a handshake, she feels welcomed. She relaxes. When she says she left her last job because she couldn't handle the pressure, we frown, and Mary tenses. Throughout the interview, we must monitor our facial expressions. By monitoring our facial expression we do not mean becoming deadpan. We mean being aware of what our face says to the candidate. We don't want to plaster a smile on our faces throughout the interview. False smiles make candidates as nervous as frowns. Our goal is to be natural and relaxed, but aware of our facial expressions. I once had a student in my class who frowned the entire session. I worried I wasn't meeting his needs. I focused on him and tried to say something to make him smile or at least stop frowning. I failed. At the end of the day the student came up to me and said, "That was the best class I've ever attended." He was still frowning! Awareness of our facial expressions and how others might interpret their meaning is half the battle.

Another lesson I learned from the frowning student is the fallacy of the feedback we get from a nonverbal cue. If a candidate frowns throughout the interview, it doesn't necessarily mean he or she is unhappy or distressed. If you respond to the nonverbal cue in different ways, and nothing changes, you might consider the nonverbal cue has no meaning in relation to your behavior. That nonverbal cue may just be the way that person looks. **With regard to human interaction and interviews, we look for changes in the nonverbal expression.**

Body Stance. How you sit or stand conveys messages about you. People who slump or wrap their arms about themselves appear less confident than those who stand erect with arms by their sides. In an interview, whether you lean toward the candidate or lean away suggests more or less interest. Of course interviewers become too intense when they hover over the candidate during the entire interview. As with eye contact, the candidate needs some space. When you begin the interview, lean toward candidate Mary to show her you're listening to her. As the interview progresses, lean back now and then. If you slump down in your chair, you tell candidates you're tired and not really interested in talking to them. In one of my classes a seasoned interviewer was stretched out under the desk so far he looked as if he were lying down. His demeanor sent a message of being too relaxed. Strategic interviewing by its nature requires you to stay on the edge. That's the message you want to send to the candidate. "I'm here, ready, listening, and responding." If you are a large person, you don't want to overpower the candidate. You may wish to lean away more frequently than might a smaller person, but you needn't slump down to compensate for your size.

Silence. Interviewers worry about periods of silence. They feel they must fill the space with talk. Silence conveys nonverbal messages. When you ask a solid open-ended question, and the candidate pauses in a period of silence, the candidate is thinking. Your mind is empty; their mind is full and busy. If their mind is empty, that is, wondering what you're going to ask next, and yours is full (probably wondering the same thing!), then silence becomes uncomfortable. **Silence works when the interviewer asks an open-ended, thought-provoking question and waits**. If candidate Mary has not responded in ten seconds and her nonverbals suggest discomfort (shifts in her seat, sighs, looks away, bites her lower lip), the interviewer might ask "Can I clarify the question for you?" Be sure to count to ten slowly, however, before you break the silence.

INtentional Listening During the Interview

In the following example, you are interviewing Sharon Seymour. You are looking to fill a position for a fund-raising manager to run a large capital fund drive for your nonprofit organization. Your goals are to find someone who takes initiative, is willing to take risks, makes decisions independently, is creative, works well with people, and manages large budgets.

Sharon Seymour
321 Peterson Court, Decatur, GA 30030 404–377–3312 sseymour@aol.com

PROFESSIONAL EXPERIENCE
Telenet Corporation, Atlanta, GA   October 1997–present
Marketing Representative

- Planned seminars and events focusing on needs in the marketplace
- Worked with Microsoft marketing representatives for coverage in the Southeast
- Identified cast study projects, gathered information, gained clients
- Organized direct mail campaigns

Assistant Marketing Representative
- Maintained relationships with four sales managers and three sales teams
- Performed sales calls to clients
- Sold consulting and services, provided contract follow-up for clients
- Identified new sales leads

Holy Methodist Church of Atlanta, Atlanta, GA   May 1995–October 1997
Planned Giving Manager
- Developed a program of planned giving
- Raised over $5 million in less than one year
- Managed a committee of twenty volunteers, representing leading financial institutions
- Coordinated the solicitation of donors
- Database coordinator

Campaign Manager
- Managed capital campaign which raised over $10 million for capital projects
- Organized and managed volunteer committee of business, church, and civic leaders
- Wrote funding proposals
- Created marketing materials
- Managed the events for campaign donors, volunteers, dedications, and openings.

EDUCATION
        Bachelor of Arts, May, 1995, Journalism and Communication
        University of Georgia, Athens, GA

HOBBIES AND INTERESTS
        Traveling, Teaching, Reading, Internet surfing, Rollerblading

Interviewer: (*icebreaker*) "Good morning, Miss Seymour. Thank you for coming today. I'm Janice Welch, the director of human resources. I see you majored in journalism at the University of Georgia. I did, too."

Seymour: (*eyes brighten*) "That's amazing. Didn't you love going to school there?"

Interviewer: "I did. Dr. Russell was dean while you were there, wasn't he?"

Seymour: "Oh, yes. I also had him for a course on media relations."

Interviewer: "So did I! I didn't know he still taught. When I went to school, he wasn't dean, but I really enjoyed his class. I was delighted when he was appointed."

Seymour: "I loved all my classes, including that one. Going to school was one of the best experiences in my life."

Interviewer: "Yes, too bad we don't usually realize that while we're there. I had an unusual college experience. I worked full time and went to school part time. So I didn't benefit from a true college experience."

Seymour: "I worked, too, but only part time. School was my full time work, and I actually loved every minute of it while I was there."

Interviewer: (*probe*) "What did you enjoy about school?"

Seymour: "Mainly the classes. The entire journalism curriculum was such fun. Taking classes in public relations and marketing and graphics. It seemed so much more relevant than the courses I took in high school."

Interviewer: (*transition*) "I see you used much of your college experience at work. You've had some interesting jobs. I'm particularly interested in the position you had with the Holy Methodist Church."

Seymour: "That was a great experience, especially for my first job out of college. I came to work all excited and ready to change the world."

Interviewer: (*probe*) "How did that position live up to your expectations right out of school?"

Seymour: (*smiles and pauses*) "My boss was super. He gave me all kinds of leeway. I went in as the campaign manager for the capital fund campaign for the church's building project. I had never done anything like that before, but I researched what other churches had done and discovered lots of information. I designed my own campaign and involved many volunteers. There was so much energy and enthusiasm. My boss, the minister, helped me when necessary but mostly he left me alone. I couldn't have asked for a better first job."

Interviewer: (*paraphrase, reality test*) "So, without any experience in capital fund drives, you spearheaded one single-handedly?"

Seymour: (*laughs*) "Not exactly like superwoman. I had lots of help and support. The Methodist Church has consultants to help with these things and lots of how-to literature. I made use of everything I could. Also, the volunteers were great. We had professional people in our church whose jobs entailed development and fundraising. One man, in particular, helped me develop my plan. He took me through it step-by-step. I learned more from him than any of my college professors."

Interviewer: (*paraphrase*) "So, what you are saying then is you made use of all the information available to you and all the people you could to design the capital funds drive."

Seymour: "Absolutely. I've learned if you pretend to be an expert, people will watch you fail. But if you go in with an open mind, willing to listen to others, they'll join in and help. No campaign will succeed unless the organization buys into it. I've seen consultants come into organizations with plans and they try to shove them down the throats of the nonprofits. That only fails."

Interviewer: (*reflecting*) "You sound pretty confident in what you've learned in your work experience."

Seymour: "Perhaps I am confident about some things. I have learned a lot, but I'm sure there's a lot more to learn."

Interviewer: (*probe*) "You say you learned that people must buy into a campaign plan for it to work. How did you manage to get people on board?"

Seymour: (*crosses her legs and sits back*) "I set up committees. At the church they consisted of volunteers. When I worked for Telenet, the committees consisted of staff and some customers. But in both places the point was to get groups of people working with you on the project. Each committee had a task and all were linked."

Interviewer: (*probe*) "What did some of these committees do?"

Seymour: "I had a committee that identified and called donors; another committee was in charge of the publicity and communication; another worked on the budget."

Interviewer: (*paraphrase*) "So you had committees work on all the major campaign functions."

Seymour: "I did. I oversaw everything, but there was a committee chair who worked directly with me. We also had a steering committee. Members of that committee sat on all the other committees to maintain consistency."

Interviewer: (*self-disclosure and flip side*) "I've worked with volunteer committees before. It can be a very useful way to get work done, but it can also be frustrating. What frustrations did you encounter?"

Seymour: (*rolls her eyes*) "I won't say I didn't pull my hair out. Working with volunteers is quite a challenge. As you said, it can be useful and rewarding. But there are inherent problems. Some volunteers don't really get involved. They stay on the outside. They agree to do things and then never come through. But, what's equally difficult are the volunteers who get too involved and want to take over. They shut others out. I've had experiences with both."

Interviewer: (*probe*) "Give me an example of how you handled a situation where a volunteer overstepped the boundaries."

What has the interviewer learned so far about Sharon Seymour? First, she took initiative in her previous jobs, particularly her first job. We learned that although she never ran a capital fund drive, she taught herself how to do it by studying the literature available to her and by learning from experts. We've also begun to see how she works with people. She believes in involvement and ownership. She uses a system of committees, but organizes the committees into action. She doesn't attempt to "know it all," because she says that turns people off. As far as our goals are concerned we've covered her initiative, her people skills, and her leadership abilities. We don't yet know about her ability to manage budgets or her willingness to take risks or her creativity.

Seymour: (*sits up straight, looks upward, pauses*) "There have been several situations." (*another pause*) "The most obvious happened not long after I began working at the church. One man had spent two years surveying the church community about the possibility of a new building project. He was a volunteer, but he had spent hours on this issue. He was a great person, really committed to the church and the plan, but he wanted it done his way. He felt we needed to solicit donors immediately. He didn't want to spend any more time doing what I called market research. He had collected a lot of information, but it was from a small segment of the population. I knew for us to succeed, we needed a broader base. Convincing him to do more research wasn't easy."

Interviewer: "How did you manage to convince him?"

Seymour: "I'm not sure how it happened, but I think my naiveté helped. Others told me later that he had turned off lots of people because of his demanding, know-it-all personality. Since everything was new to me, I solicited his help. I innocently asked him questions he couldn't answer. When he realized I wasn't going to plunge ahead without more research and when he couldn't answer the questions I had, he gave in. It was interesting. At first, he told me what to do, by the time I left the church, we worked easily together."

Interviewer: (*reflect*) "Working with someone like that can zap all your energy. How did you manage not to lose your enthusiasm?"

Seymour: "I believe I did lose a little at first. I became disillusioned and frustrated. Rather than get on with a project I was really excited about, I spent hours smoothing out the feathers this man ruffled. He left a lot of broken people in his wake. But after a bit, people began to trust me. They wanted to see the project succeed. That helped."

Interviewer: (*combined paraphrase and probe*) "So, when people began to trust you, what happened to you?"

Seymour: "I started getting excited again. We basically diluted the power of this man. I won't say it was easy. I was consumed with it the first year I was at the church. But after that, he sort of disappeared. He remained active, but in the background."

Interviewer: "Dealing with this man sounds like a frustrating experience. I'm not sure I'd have the patience to keep going."

Seymour: "I did lose patience. There's no question about that. But my experience with him also threatened to break down my confidence. Looking back now, I see how much that experience taught me. I learned that we can't let others overstep boundaries, even when they're not volunteers. I learned that if we don't have clear boundaries, others will overstep. I finally managed to give this man a clear picture of my boundaries. He seemed to respect that. Others did, too. So, when I started the project at Telenet, that's one of the first things I did. I discovered my boundaries and helped others see theirs as well."

Interviewer: (*summarize and probe*) "If I'm hearing you, boundaries sound as if they're very important in your human interactions. How do you deal with situations when the boundaries aren't clear because the organization doesn't want boundaries?"

Seymour: "If you're talking about creative situations, I have some trouble there. I don't consider myself a real creative person. I also don't see myself as a risk-taker. I like to work within boundaries, and I can excel in that environment. A real loose organization without boundaries drives me nuts."

The interviewer understands a lot about how Sharon Seymour works and what she's looking for in a job. She's not rigid, but she requires parameters. She's not one to think beyond the box. If creativity is an important skill for this position, then the interviewer must reject Sharon. She sounds very good in all other aspects and she has an impressive résumé. But our strategic interview showed us she doesn't have the qualities needed to fit this job.

This example shows us how to use the INtentional listening skills to help us achieve our goals. Notice how each of the interviewer's responses fed off something Sharon said. Notice also how the interviewer varied the listening skills and periodically self-disclosed.

In the next chapter we will Test the interviewer's skills. We'll look at the T in the POINT process by examining how we performed as an interviewer. Did we give the candidate a solid strategic interview? Or did we allow our perceptions to guide us?

NOTES

1. Alessandra, *Charisma*, p. 14.
2. Pamela F. Butler, *Self-Assertion for Women* (San Francisco: Harper & Row Publishers, 1981), p. 104.
3. Butler, *Self-Assertion for Women*, p. 107.

13

Testing Yourself as Interviewer

To improve as an interviewer, you must add a third component to the test for success. Besides evaluating the fit and the candidate's skills (Chapter 5 and Chapter 9), you must test your skills as an interviewer. Think about the strategic goals you set out to accomplish. What did you learn in relation to those goals? How much time did you spend talking? A good interviewer allows the candidate to talk at least 75 percent of the time. Did you ask open questions? Were there places you could have followed up but didn't? How did your perceptions affect the interview?

In addition to your skills, what about the interview process? Some interviews fail because the process is at fault. How were candidates greeted? What did candidates see while in your organization? What experiences affected them? Recently I learned of a candidate who interviewed for a major company housed in the World Trade Center in New York City. Because of the bombing of that building, extreme security measures were in place. No one told the candidate about the security measures. He exited the elevator in a closed hallway with doors leading to places he couldn't enter without special cards. He stood there several moments before anyone rescued him. Imagine how that candidate felt and how that experience affected the remaining interview process.

This chapter will provide sample questions interviewers might ask at the conclusion of the interview to evaluate themselves and the interview process. We will also look at several interviews and evaluate them.

WHAT MAKES YOU A STRATEGIC INTERVIEWER?

Strategic interviewing takes more than good talking or even good listening. Although strong interpersonal skills (listening and talking) shape a quality interview, I learned early in my interviewing career that much more has to happen for an interviewer to succeed.

Interviewers must have a plan. They must stay focused and organized. The P in POINT plays a significant role in the success of an interview. Imagine a situation where an interviewer asks good, open-ended questions, listens with intentionality, and shares information about him or herself, but the questions drift from place to place without a specific plan. Afterwards the candidate may tell another person, "I really felt that interviewer listened to me. We developed a nice rapport." But what has the interviewer learned in relation to the vacant position? Can the interviewer answer the question, "Will this person fit this job?" Without a plan, without knowing where the interview is going, we cannot make that final judgment. Disorganized or haphazard interviews, even with good communication skills, aren't successful. For this reason many human resource managers turn to structure. They think structure will help them create the focus they need. We've learned in this book that structure can be as destructive to an interview as unstructured.

Let's look at an unstructured example where the interviewer demonstrated g)d communication skills:

Interviewer: (*probe*) "Tell me about your experience in the fraternity."

Candidate: "The University of Florida has a strong fraternity program. Almost everyone belongs to fraternities. It's a way to meet other people in a large university. I found it a rewarding and bonding experience."

Interviewer: (*paraphrase and disclose*) "So, you're saying most people belong to fraternities at Florida? In my school no one did. It was considered a little strange to be part of a fraternity."

Candidate: "Yeah, I know that's true in some places. But not Florida. Before I went there, I had heard that the Greeks were part of the culture. So, I expected I'd join one."

Interviewer: (*probe*) "How did you go about selecting which fraternity to join?"

Candidate: "Mostly I talked to people. I didn't want one that had a reputation for partying. I wanted a fraternity that had some purpose and did things in the community. I talked to other students and selected three I liked. One of those picked me, and that was it. I never looked back."

Interviewer: (*reality test*) "So you weren't interested in partying while in school?"

Candidate: "Hey, when I was eighteen, I was as interested in having a good time as the next guy, but some fraternities took that philosophy a little too far. They'd been in all kinds of trouble with the local police for making noise and other things. I didn't want any part of that."

Where is this interview going? The interviewer did a nice job probing, paraphrasing, disclosing, and even reality testing. But where was this interview going? What was the purpose? We've learned some important things about the candidate, but are they relevant to the particular skills you're searching for? Have we peeled away the superficial? Basically, the candidate told us he's a straight arrow. He belonged to a fraternity, but everyone did in that culture, and he picked the least "partying" one he could find.

Let's give this interview a purpose and some focus. Imagine the interviewer wants to find out more about the candidate's outside activities. Perhaps the interviewer probed about the job and his professional experiences and now wants to learn more about the overall person. What does the person like to do other than work? Let's follow that line of thinking and see how the same interview progresses:

Interviewer: (*probe*) "Tell me about your experience in the fraternity."

Candidate: "The University of Florida has a strong fraternity program. Almost everyone belongs to fraternities. It's a way to meet other people in a large university. I found it a rewarding and bonding experience."

Interviewer: (*probe*) "When you say rewarding and bonding experience, what do you mean?"

Candidate: "Well, in a large university, it's hard to meet people. Fraternities give you a smaller set of people to get to know. I met some guys I still stay in touch with. They'll be my friends for life."

Interviewer: (*Disclose and probe*) "I, too, went to a large university, but fraternities were pretty expensive. I couldn't afford to join one, but managed to meet people in the dorms. How do you see the fraternity life different from say, the dorm life?"

Candidate: "For me it meant really being there for the guys. I came from a small town and had close friendships with the kids I grew up with. I really missed that kind of friendship in the large university setting. Very quickly I knew I'd do anything for one of my 'brothers.' I don't think you get such strong bonding in the dorms."

Interviewer: (*paraphrase*) "You're right. I'm not sure I've ever had that kind of experience. So, you're saying that you were searching for strong personal friendships?"

Candidate: "It's something I tend to do. I don't like superficial relationships with people. I shy away from such friendships even though I know most relationships are superficial."

Interviewer: (*reflect*) "It sounds like superficial relationships annoy you."

Candidate: "Yeah, I see them as pointless."

Interviewer: (*probe for clarification*) "Help me understand what you might do in a strong personal friendship that you might not do in a superficial relationship."

Candidate: "My buddies and I hang out sometimes and do nothing. We just like being with each other. We talk about stuff, relationships and all. We talk about work and what goes on there. Other times we go places together. I go camping with a group about three times a year."

Interviewer: (*Close question to narrow the gap*) "These buddies are people you work with?"

Candidate: "Not usually. I find the people I work with aren't committed to strong personal relationships."

Interviewer: "And what kind of relationships do you like to have with people at work?"

Notice how this interviewer stayed with a line of questioning until he or she got to the meat of the issue. We learned what this person looks for in his leisure pursuits. He's not one to develop short-term friendships. He prefers lasting relationships in which meaningful give and take occurs. But how does that translate into work relationships? As the interview progresses, the interviewer corners the candidate to isolate his relations with people at work. We may find the candidate cannot tolerate superficial relationships or we may find the candidate tries to develop inappropriate relations at work or we may find a candidate who successfully separates his work and personal relationships. This information sheds some light on the candidate's fit with the job in question; otherwise the interviewer wouldn't have pursued it.

Interviewers must have good interpersonal skills. As we've seen throughout this book, interviewers must listen with intentionality; they must focus on what the candidate said in order to formulate their next response. Even if your plan is to transition to another area, you use what the candidate said in order to do that. Some interviewers have great plans, but their interpersonal skills hold them back. In my classes I run into interviewers who either don't listen or they ask closed questions.

Let's look at an example where an interviewer had a good strategic plan, but lacked interpersonal skills.

Interviewer: "Our goals today are to find out what you want to do with XYZ Company and to see if our job fits your needs. Do you have career goals?"

Candidate: "Oh yes, I want to learn all I can on the line, become a part of the team, and then move up to a supervisory position where I can help others learn what I've learned."

Interviewer: "What jobs have you had on the line?"

Candidate: "Actually, I worked for five years on the line at the Peter's Company. Then I was promoted to a team leader. That was a great experience. I enjoyed the opportunity to work with others and show them what I learned. I hoped to move into a supervisory position before the plant closed, but I didn't quite make it."

Interviewer: "Have you had other jobs that met your goals?"

Candidate: "Not really. I had a taste of what I wanted at Peter's, and that's what I'm pursuing now. I'm an ambitious person. I don't like feeling stuck, doing the same thing all the time and not growing. At Mark's Brothers I was in a routine job. I handled the clerical stuff, mainly filing and pulling records. To keep myself going, I took continuing education classes. I have to do something like that to maintain interest."

Interviewer: "Tell me about your job duties at the Sanders Company. I see you worked there for three years."

Let's examine this interview. Notice the interviewer had a goal which was stated at the outset: to learn the candidate's career objectives and determine if those objectives fit with the company. Not a bad goal and not a bad goal to suggest in the beginning. Did the interviewer accomplish that goal? What are the candidate's career objectives? All we learned is the candidate likes variety and looks for opportunities for self-improvement. Clearly these are things the candidate intended to share when he or she walked into the interview. We learned nothing beyond that. The interviewer asked closed questions and never once picked up on what the candidate said. Each response led to a different area rather than digging deeper into what the candidate said. Let's reinterview this candidate with the same goals in mind and see if we can demonstrate better interpersonal skills and learn more about the candidate's goals beyond what he or she wants us to learn.

Interviewer: (*Disclosure and probe*) "Our goals today are to find out what you want to do with XYZ Company and see if our job fits your needs. What are your career goals?"

Candidate: "I want to learn all I can on the line, become a part of the team, and then move up to a supervisory position where I can help others learn what I've learned."

Interviewer: (*probe*) "Share an example of a job when you've had a chance to learn on the line and become part of a team."

Candidate: "Actually, I worked for five years on the line at the Peter's Company. Then I was promoted to a team leader. That was a great experience. I enjoyed the opportunity to work with others and show them what I learned. I hoped to move into a supervisory position before the plant closed, but I didn't quite make it."

Interviewer: (*reflect*) "Sounds as if you were excited with the progress you were making before Peter's shut down."

Candidate: "Well, I was and I wasn't. Because the shutdown was apparent, they didn't hire new people. They allowed some of us more leeway to help with the final days. It turned out to be an opportunity for me, but it was frustrating because I haven't experienced that kind of freedom again."

Interviewer: (*summarize*) "So, you learned that freedom gives you a chance to do things you didn't have a chance to do before, and you liked that feeling. But you're now frustrated because you haven't had that experience since."

Candidate: "You got that right. That's exactly why I'm looking now."

Interviewer: (*probe*) "What exactly are you looking for now?"

Candidate: "I was the team leader, and the people on the team came to me for guidance and help. I had a chance to make decisions I wouldn't ordinarily make. I like to make decisions and to be in charge, especially if I feel I'm ready."

Interviewer: (*probe*) "When do you feel you're ready to make decisions?"

Candidate: "It's hard to say exactly. But when you've been doing a job for a period of time, you know the job best. You know what will work and what won't. So often supervisors don't give you any say or even ask your opinion. They just charge ahead. Meantime, you know something won't work, and you know what will make it work, but no one asks."

Interviewer: (*summarize*) "Let me see if I understand your goals. You like the freedom to make decisions when you've been in a job long enough. You also like to be asked your opinion about things."

Candidate: "That's part of it. I want a job where I can move up based on my abilities. I get tired of doing the same thing and being placed in a box—meaning the expectations are I can't do anything else. I like learning new things and being given chances to learn new things."

Interviewer: (*reflect and probe*) "It is frustrating to feel you're at the end of your career when it's really just starting. Tell me how you handled a situation where you didn't feel your job utilized your abilities."

In this instance, we see an interviewer with a clear agenda. We're trying to uncover the candidate's goals. The candidate's responses show the multifaceted goals. This candidate is looking for empowerment and respect in a new job, but the candidate is also looking for variety and opportunities to grow. The goals are lofty and our job may or may not meet the candidate's specific needs. We have learned that this candidate is clear on what he or she wants and won't be happy in a job that doesn't meet those needs. We must now discover by reality testing what this candidate does when a job doesn't quite meet those high expectations.

Notice the interviewer used several interpersonal skills to dig deeper. The interviewer probed, summarized, paraphrased, reflected, and if we let the interview go on, the interviewer will test reality.

The interviewer must not overtalk. Some interviewers have a definite plan, and they have good interpersonal communication skills, but they talk too much. Interviewers must talk only 20 to 25 percent of the time. The strategic interviewer wants to get the candidate talking. We want the candidate relaxed and sharing with us. We cannot accomplish that goal when we spend most of the interview talking.

An overly talkative interviewer usually represents a nervous interviewer and always represents a novice interviewer!

Interviewer: "Welcome to XYZ Company. We're delighted to have a chance to talk with you. Tell me about yourself."

Candidate: "I'm a very straightforward person. I tend to call the shots the way I see them. I've had many business experiences in my career, and I've learned that the best way to handle them is to be direct."

Interviewer: "Boy, are you right. I don't know how many times I've been frustrated with people who won't come to the point. Our company prides itself on quick, action-oriented decisions. We spend lots of money training our new managers on decision making. That's a value we constantly push. But so often people don't seem to understand how to make decisions. They talk themselves out of doing anything. We've got some managers who are so afraid to make a decision, they never get anything done. I think that's a symptom of problems at the top, don't you? When the upper managers support you, and you know they will, it's easier to make decisions. When you know you won't get fired if you make a mistake, it's easier to make decisions. Our company values decision making, but in recent years we've lacked that kind of support from the top. That's what we're looking for now."

Whew! This interviewer heard what the candidate said, but responded with a little too much information. What the interviewer shared might be of value, but we don't want to give it all away at once. The interviewer needs to slow down, sprinkle in bits of information as he or she goes through the interview and allow the candidate to talk. What have we learned about this candidate? Precious little. By the way, "Tell me about yourself" is not a strategic question. Strategic questions are probes you would ask this candidate and no one else. "Tell me about yourself" is too general. Avoid open-ended questions that might fit any person who walks through the door. Let's try to improve this interview with less talk, but still incorporate the information.

Interviewer: (*targeted icebreaker*) "Welcome to XYZ Company. We're delighted to have a chance to talk with you. I've been looking forward to this interview because you and I have something in common. We're both soccer fans."

Candidate: "Actually, I'm a soccer coach. On the weekends I coach a girls' soccer team at the Y. It's been great fun. It also keeps me in touch with young people now that my kids are grown."

Interviewer: (*self-disclosure*) "Young people can be quite a challenge. I've noticed generation changes, myself. Young people don't seem to value the kinds of things we did. They're more interested in themselves than the company. It's a hard transition for many of them to leave their adolescent world and enter the adult world."

Candidate: "No kidding. I'm very straightforward. I tend to call the shots the way I see them. I've had many business experiences in my career, and I've learned that the best way to handle them is to be direct. That works well with the young soccer players, too."

Interviewer: (*probe*) "How have the kids responded to your directness?"

Candidate: "Most kids appreciate it. They want to hear the straight scoop. What they don't like about adults is their inability to share. I've found that to be true at

work, too. If you're straight with people, they'll be straight with you. When someone screws up, I tell them they screwed up. No use beating around the bush. But,
I also let them know it's okay and what we can do to improve."

Interviewer: (*reality test*) "So you're saying you don't mind when people make
mistakes?"

Candidate: "Oh, I mind all right, but I don't blame. Back to my soccer coaching,
I hate to lose games, but I don't blame the kids. They know I hate to lose, and
they work hard with me to win. That's my philosophy at work. I'm driven and
will work harder than the next guy. If we lose, we'll all look at what happened
and how we can improve. If someone isn't pulling his weight, we try to discover
what's going on."

Interviewer: (*probe*) "I've noticed you keep saying 'we.' Who is the 'we'?

Candidate: "I'm a strong believer in teamwork to bring ownership to whatever
you're doing. Sure, as the boss I sometimes have to make decisions, but I rarely do
it alone. I involve others for input and then make the decision. If it's the wrong
decision, I take responsibility, but the others respect and appreciate that I involved
them as well. We go at it together."

Interviewer: (*paraphrase and probe*) "So, you tend to involve others in the decision making. How do you go about making fast decisions when you involve so
many people?"

Candidate: "The issue for me is quality, not speed. We're trying to make the best
possible decisions. Not all decisions take teamwork. People are empowered to
plunge forward when needed. But when a big issue comes up, we meet and hash
it out together. It takes more time, but it's worth the time in the long run."

Interviewer: (*disclosure and probe*) "At XYZ Company we've had trouble getting
people to feel comfortable making decisions. How have you managed to make it
safe for people to take risks and make decisions?"

Candidate: "I never blame people for failures. We accept failure together. I reward people for their independent thinking. The rewards must be tangible, that is,
things people really want. I try to model the behaviors I expect of others."

Interviewer: (*summarize*) "Let me see if I'm clear on what you're saying. You
allow people to make certain decisions on their own. They know they've been
empowered to do that. But when big, tough issues come up, a team looks at it and
makes the decision together. If failures happen, you don't blame but search for a
solution. And you reward people for making their own decisions."

Candidate: "I also said I model the behaviors. Sometimes that's the hardest part.
But I believe leaders need to practice what they preach."

Interviewer: "Give me an example of a situation where the decision soured and
your response to that decision."

Notice how the interviewer enabled the candidate to talk, rather than
the reverse, and by so doing led the candidate to share his or her philosophy
on decision making and leadership. We didn't have to tell the candidate
everything at the outset. The interviewer sprinkled in a little information

at the end, but much had already been disclosed. The last question leads us into areas the candidate probably wishes to leave hidden. As we probe, however, we will uncover those areas to determine if and how this candidate models the behaviors he or she is talking about.

Interviewers must stay sensitive to the nonverbal cues. We've seen in previous chapters the importance of the nonverbal message. We've learned that both the interviewer and the candidate communicate nonverbally throughout the interview. A good interviewer stays aware of these cues and uses them to his/her advantage.

What nonverbal messages might an interviewer use?

- Lean back in the chair but maintain eye contact. Message: "I'm listening."
- Lean back in the chair and break eye contact. Message: "I'm no longer interested."
- Sit up straight and lean toward the candidate. Message: "You just said something important."
- Gather up the papers on the desk. Message: "The interview is about to end."
- Jot down a note. Message: "You said something important or I need time to think."
- Look away when the candidate speaks. Message: "You just said something I don't understand."
- Use a hand gesture that cuts the air. Message: "I've made an important point."
- Cross a leg in front of the table. Message: "I need a barrier between you and me."
- Place a hand on the table in front of the candidate who is speaking. Message: "I've got something to say."
- Rise from your seat. Message: "This interview is over."

Practice Exercise

Read the following interview and rate the interviewer's effectiveness:

Interviewer: *"Thank you for coming to XYZ Company. I have several questions for you before you see Mr. Jones. Please take a seat." (candidate sits down)*

Interviewer: *"I noticed on your résumé that you worked for five years with the Staples Company, but I see no other work experience. Was that your only job?"*

Candidate: *"It was my only real job. I worked at Kentucky Fried Chicken and Publix for the summers in between school."*

Interviewer: *"I see. Tell me about the work you're doing with Staples."*

Candidate: *"I'm in charge of their advertising program. I sell ads for their magazine and write ads from the copy." (responds with brisk, short responses)*

Interviewer: *"So, you run the advertising for the company?"*

Candidate: *"Yes, I am in charge of the program, but it's not very large. It's just me and one secretary. They keep threatening to expand but that never will happen. It's all just talk." (rolls his eyes upward)*

Interviewer: *(sits forward)* "You sound frustrated with the future of your department."

Candidate: *"You could put it that way. I've seen no support in the five years I've been there. They talk a good game but that's about it."*

Interviewer: "When you say support, what do you think the company should do to boost the advertising department?"

Candidate: *(sits up and gives the interviewer direct eye contact)* "For one thing we need to hire more staff. I can't do the job all by myself. I'm on the road five days a week and trying to prepare the ads when I'm not in my car. It's nuts. They also need to branch out beyond the regular customers. They're stuck in a rut."

Interviewer: "Have you communicated these problems upward?"

Candidate: *(sits back in his seat and breaks the eye contact)* "Of course I have. But it was a waste of time."

Interviewer: "What happened when you communicated upward?"

Candidate: *(shakes his head)* "I got the run around. They said they needed to talk to someone else and would be back in touch. I never heard anything else."

Interviewer: "Are you saying you spoke to someone about expanding the program and they agreed but never took action?"

Candidate: "Basically, yes. I don't really think they did anything. I never heard another peep."

Interviewer: "Did you try to contact that person again or maybe go around that person?"

We're going to use the following questions to evaluate this interview.

1. *What was the interviewer's plan?* The interviewer began with an open question that was too general. "Tell me about your job at Staples." But since the interviewer didn't use an icebreaker, this general question might be okay. As the interview progressed it became clear the interviewer wanted to learn how successfully the candidate communicates upward.

2. *How much time did the interviewer talk versus listen?* The interviewer talked less than 20 percent of the time and listened more than 80 percent of the time.

3. *Did the interviewer probe with open questions?* Most of the probes were open, but toward the end of the interview, the interviewer threw in two closed questions: "Did you try to communicate these problems upward" and "Have you tried to contact that person again or go around that person?" Both of these questions are "solution-laden questions"—they give the candidate information about what he or she should or should not do. They are not probes and should be reworded as probes, i.e., "What did you do to let others know about these problems?" and "What happened after you contacted that person?" The closed questions at the end suggest the interviewer is no longer interested in the candidate. Perhaps the interviewer has made up his or her mind, but we don't want to make that decision so obvious.

4. *What strategic reasons did the interviewer have for asking closed questions?* The two closed questions above have no strategic purpose and should have been open questions. The interviewer paraphrased once using a closed question, "Are you saying . . ." When the interviewer asked in the beginning, "Was that your only job?", strategically the interviewer was trying to get specific information and focus the candidate on other employment experiences.

5. *Did the interviewer use other INtentional listening skills* (paraphrase, reflect, summarize, reality test, flip sides)? The interviewer paraphrased once, reflected once, and summarized once.

6. *Did the interviewer "react" to what the candidate said to formulate his or her next question, or did the interviewer ask something unrelated to what the candidate said?* Although this interviewer didn't phrase the probes well, the interviewer did react to what the candidate said in each instance.

7. *How did the interviewer react to the candidate's nonverbal cues?* Most of the time the interviewer didn't seem to notice the nonverbal cues. On one instance, when the candidate rolled his or her eyes, the interviewer reacted by sitting forward and reflecting. That response seemed to indicate a sensitivity to the candidate's nonverbal cue.

8. *Did the interviewer self-disclose during the interview?* We saw no instances when the interviewer self-disclosed.

9. *Did the interviewer share information about the job?* We saw no instances when the interviewer shared information about the job.

10. *What could this interviewer do to improve?* The interviewer could have self-disclosed and shared information about the job. We suspect the candidate shared only what he or she intended to share. This interviewer needed a clearer strategic plan.

11. *If you had to grade this interviewer, what grade would you give?*   C.

TESTING THE INTERVIEW PROCESS

The following questions will help test your interview process:

1. Who are the people most affected by this vacant position? Are these people part of your interview team?

2. Did your team study the résumés and applications separately or together?

3. Did your team examine the position and identify the organizational culture?

4. Did your team identify the qualities needed to successfully perform the functions of this position?

5. How many people within your organization need to interview this candidate? If more than eight, did your team organize and plan team interviews?

6. What visual messages about your organization do you want to send? How did you set up ways for the candidate to experience those messages?

7. Did someone in your organization make contact with the candidate to give him or her directions and make arrangements for the visit?

8. Did your team avoid asking similar questions by focusing on particular areas and by tagging each other at the end of interviews to help build consistency from one interview to the next?

9. Did team members refrain from sharing their impressions as they escorted the candidate from one interviewer to the next?

10. Did you avoid interviewing the candidate during meals?

11. Did the candidate have a chance to visit with people he or she might supervise?

12. Did the candidate have a chance to visit with peers?

13. Were the interviews conducted in a timely fashion?

14. At the conclusion of the process, did the interview team meet together to share the results of their interviews?

14

Handling the Most Challenging Interviews

Throughout this book we've looked at ways to improve our interviewing skills and ways to become more strategic in our approach. By strategic we mean developing a plan and probing until we've satisfied that plan. The examples we've looked at represent typical interview situations.

In this chapter we will examine the most challenging kind of interviews—interview nightmares and interviewing for lesser skilled positions.

The examples in this book were for professional or semiprofessional positions. Believe it or not, these are the easiest positions for most human resource managers to interview. Why? The people applying for these jobs look most like us. We can relate to them. Furthermore the résumé gives us lots of potential topics to discuss: education, work, career. Less educated people applying for line positions give us more trouble. Most human resource managers, who are themselves college graduates at some level, find it difficult to relate to the needs of these candidates. Similarly, the application form gives us less to work with. Nonetheless we put our most inexperienced interviewers in positions to hire for these jobs. Organizations do this because there is less cost to the company when hiring mistakes occur. Replacing and training a line worker costs less in time and money than replacing and training a vice president or department head. Even so, hiring mistakes at this level are costly. Those who experience constant turnover will tell you, it's a very frustrating place to be. We must, therefore, improve our interviewing skills for a diversity of people, not just the ones who look like us.

Every once in awhile an interviewer comes face to face with an interview nightmare. Of course, you need not hire a person who presents a nightmare during the interview, but how do you gracefully get through the interview? Most new interviewers expect they will face an interview nightmare all the time. Nightmares are their greatest fears. Seasoned interviewers know these instances are rare, but they do require skill.

In this chapter we will explore ways to improve our interviewing skills for the most challenging kinds of interviews: nightmares and semiskilled labor.

WHAT IS AN INTERVIEW NIGHTMARE?

The most obvious interview nightmares occur when candidates do something we don't expect. The responses surprise us, take us off our guard, leave us frustrated and ready to terminate the interview. Let's look at some examples.

Candidates Who Refuse to Talk

Interviewer: "I'm a great baseball fan as I see you are from your résumé. How far do you think the Mets will go this year?"

Candidate: "It's hard to say."

Long pause over ten seconds

Interviewer: "Well, that's certainly true given the past. (*Pause*) I'm going to visit with you for a short while and then Mac Smith, our director, will talk with you. I'm interested in the work you did with Allied. As project manager, what were your specific duties?"

Candidate: "The usual—reports, supervision, some training."

Interviewer: "So you supervised other managers?"

Candidate: (*Head nod*)

Interviewer: "How many people did you supervise?"

Candidate: "It varied."

Interviewer: "Of the duties you named, which did you find the most rewarding?"

Candidate: "I liked them all."

Interviewer: "So, you're saying you liked all your duties and none stood out."

Candidate: "Unhuh."

Interviewer: "Tell me about the training you did."

Candidate: "I taught new people to do the job."

Interviewer: "So, you were actually more like a coach than a trainer?"

Candidate: "I suppose so."

This kind of interview is painful. The interviewer asked open questions and tried to probe deeper by following up on what little the candidate said.

The interviewer paraphrased, tested reality, and still got little information. At this stage of the interview, most interviewers want to say, "Thank you very much," and exit. The candidate appears uninterested in the job. Let's take the interview a little further and see if we can't break this candidate's shell.

Interviewer: "I'm not getting very much information from you, Mr. Lewis. I am assuming you are interested in the position we have open?"

Candidate: "I do have some questions about it."

Interviewer: "What are those questions?"

Candidate: "I heard you had already made up your minds and my interview was just to satisfy EEOC regulations."

Interviewer: "We've got three excellent candidates interviewing for this job. After all the interviews are completed, a team of people in the company will select the finalist. You are the second candidate we've seen. I can assure you we have not made up our minds. What other questions or concerns do you have?"

Candidate: "I was told you only hired from the inside for your upper management positions. That even if I was offered a job, it wouldn't be for the Senior Vice President position but for something lower than that, and then at some later point in my career I might be promoted."

Interviewer: "We strive to promote when we can. But like any other organization, we can't always find the skills internally. In fact, some jobs require a fresh look. The three candidates we're interviewing for this job all come to us from the outside. I hope that answers your concerns."

Candidate: "It does. Thank you for your candor."

Interviewer: "Tell me, Mr. Lewis, what interests you about our company?"

This interviewer will continue the interview until its conclusion. When the interviewer **said what was going on**—*"I'm not getting very much information from you,"* the candidate opened up. Many times that is all it takes. You stop dancing around the issue and face it. This interviewer tired of pulling information from a reluctant candidate. When the candidate asked his questions, the tone seemed defensive. The interviewer responded without getting defensive. If this person was a minority candidate, the interviewer would need to be especially sensitive. Minority candidates face discrimination more often than majority candidates, and the discrimination translates into defensiveness. We should respond with sensitivity and not be angered by the defensiveness. As this interview progresses and the candidate relaxes, the interviewer may discover a quality candidate.

Candidates Who Respond Inappropriately

Interviewer: "Thank you for coming this afternoon, Ms. Stanley. I'm going to talk with you for a little while first and then Mac Smith, our director, will talk to you. I noticed on your résumé that you play classical guitar. I love classical music. How did you get into playing classical guitar?"

Candidate: (*smiles, direct eye contact*) "I love anything beautiful. Classical music is both beautiful and seductive. Being a passionate person myself, I can't resist the combination."

Interviewer: "I enjoy other kinds of guitar music, like jazz and rock. What other types of music do you play?"

Candidate: "Why waste my time on something so plebeian when I can strum the chords of Mozart? Why read trashy novels when you can read poetry? (Smiles) The sound of those notes while my fingers caress the instrument takes me to new heights of pleasure. Have you ever known such joy?" (*Her voice is soft, almost like a whisper.*)

Interviewer: "Perhaps I haven't. (Pause) I'm interested in the marketing program you ran for XYZ Company. How did you develop that program?"

Candidate: "We were having such fun talking about music, why divert ourselves into such trivial matters as marketing? To me music is life. It's everything beautiful, everything worth living for. I feel myself soar beyond the clouds when the music enters my soul. Surely you've had a similar, transcending experience?"

Interviewer: "If music is so important to you, how do you manage to put it aside to do your work?"

Candidate: "I never put music aside. It plays in my head and my heart all the time. It is a part of me. I think it could be a part of you as well if you give it a chance. Let me help you. (*The candidate closes her eyes and begins humming a tune and swaying in her seat.*)

Again, we have a situation where the interviewer wishes to end the interview quickly and exit. How can the interviewer get away from the candidate's obsession with music to learn about her skills in marketing? Perhaps you say, why doesn't the interviewer stop the interview now rather than go on? As a professional interviewer, we want to give the candidate every chance. There's still more this interviewer can do to get on track. Even so, I doubt this interviewer will recommend offering this candidate the job.

The new goal for the interviewer is to get through the interview as professionally as possible.

You might wonder about icebreakers when you see how badly this icebreaker went for the interviewer. Remember these instances rarely happen. The goal of the icebreaker is to get the candidate to relax and open up. This candidate turned out a little too relaxed to begin with. From the responses, the interviewer might wonder if the candidate might be on some sort of medication.

Interviewer: "Ms. Stanley, perhaps this isn't a good time for you?"

Candidate: (*Opens her eyes. Sits up straighter.*) "Good time for what?"

Interviewer: "To proceed with the interview?"

Candidate: "I thought we were proceeding with the interview. I got caught up with the music in my soul. That happens to me sometimes."

Interviewer: "I have a good sense of how important music is to you. In order for this interview to proceed, I need to learn more about how you developed the marketing program with XYZ Company. What kinds of things did you do to launch that program?"

This interviewer found himself in an uncomfortable situation. The candidate seemed to check out. How can we get people back on track? What the interviewer did was *name the candidate*. Calling the candidate's name got her attention. The interviewer also showed sensitivity to the candidate by saying, "perhaps this isn't a good time for you." He gave the candidate a chance to end the interview. Had the candidate been unwell, ending the interview would be the best solution. This candidate perked up and seemed willing to continue the interview. The interviewer didn't ignore or discount the importance of music, but shared his need to move on. Again, the goal now is to get through the interview successfully, not to recommend this candidate for hire.

Candidates Who Take Over the Interview

Interviewer: "I'm curious about how you handled difficult customers when you worked for the Jewelry Store."

Candidate: "Oh, my, that was definitely a challenge. Difficult people came in all the time. My boss taught me how to handle them. He was my mentor. But what I really liked about working there was the buying. We got so many catalogues with the most beautiful jewels, all colors and sizes. Some designed by the best artists in the world. After I'd only been working there for a year, I started doing some of the ordering. You had to really know the customers to order correctly. Otherwise you'd buy something that would just sit on the shelf and never move. That wasn't good for business—"

Interviewer: "Sorry to interrupt, but you said your boss taught you how to handle difficult customers. What did he teach you?"

Candidate: "Let me see. Basically, you know, the customer is always right. That's my philosophy, too. You can't argue with a customer. I tried to sell a ring to a customer once, and she really should have bought it. I knew she wanted it. I could tell. You can see it in their eyes. I was so close to selling it. Just as she was about to say 'yes,' she stopped herself. 'Maybe I shouldn't,' she said. That ring even fit her. We wouldn't have to size it. The color was perfect, and she loved it, but she felt buying it would be too indulgent. I knew she had money so that wasn't the issue. I tried to tell her she was worth it. But I'm sure she wanted her husband to buy the ring for her—"

Interviewer: "When you say the customer is always right, what do you mean?"

Candidate: "Well, I don't mean in this instance because this customer wasn't right. She should've bought the ring. I knew it, and she knew it. She would have cherished it for the rest of her life. It's so hard sometimes to help people do what they want to do. We all feel so guilty."

The interviewer is trying to determine how the candidate handles difficult customers. Instead the candidate wants to share her experiences as a buyer for the store and how she knows what's right for the customers. The candidate overtalks in order to keep control of the interview. The interview continues to probe but hasn't had a chance to use other communication skills. The goal of the interviewer is to get the candidate talking about what the interviewer is interested in rather than what the candidate wants to talk about. How can the interviewer maneuver the interview according to the strategic plan? Let's take the interview a little further.

Interviewer: "So you're saying when customers don't want to buy something you think they should, they're wrong?"

Candidate: "Not exactly wrong. I just knew this customer wanted the ring. I had to come up with a way for her to see what I saw so clearly. That's the rub."

Interviewer: "How is it you can see something so clearly and the customer cannot?"

Candidate: "I can't always see that clearly. But I can tell when someone really wants to buy something but they don't."

Interviewer: "In what situations do you find yourself not being able to see that clearly?"

Candidate: "I suppose when people get upset. I'm baffled by some customers' distress with our products. We sell the best jewelry in town at the most affordable prices. Why would anyone complain?"

Interviewer: "So, situations where customers purchase something and then come back disappointed baffle you?"

Candidate: "Absolutely."

Interviewer: "I suppose I'd be baffled, too, if someone returned something I thought was really special. Give me an example of a situation like that."

The interviewer took control by quickly paraphrasing and probing around what the candidate was talking about. The interviewer didn't give the candidate time to elaborate or detour into another area. Some candidates will still detour into other areas. If they do and you've done all you can to pull them back, the only recourse is to allow the candidate to go off on his or her own tangent, complete the interview, and then hire someone else.

A Candidate Is Disabled

Some candidates prefer not to tell the interviewer of their disability. Because employers often make quick judgments about a person's capability to do a job, they will often not interview a person with a disability—assuming that person incapable. Seasoned human resource managers know this is a false assumption. People with disabilities prove themselves much more driven and capable than many of us with all our "abilities." I stand in amazement and watch the feats of handicapped athletes. Making quick decisions about a person's ability can result in losing a very capable, loyal, and dedicated employee.

The real world, however, is often cruel. The competitive nature of hiring forces disabled candidates to do all they can to get their foot in the door. One thing they often do is neglect to tell you they're in a wheelchair or they're legally blind. Let's look at an example when an interviewer is taken by surprise by a disability.

The interviewer is seated behind his desk, studying the résumé, and thinking about his strategic plan. A young woman in a wheelchair rolls up to the door and knocks. The interviewer looks up, gives a startled expression, and rises to help the candidate enter. The woman rolls inside and places her wheelchair next to the chair in front of the desk. She reaches out her hand and gives the interviewer a firm handshake.

Candidate: "Good afternoon, Mr. Harris. I hope I didn't get here too early."

Interviewer: (*settling himself behind his desk*) "Of course not. Did you have any trouble getting in?"

Candidate: "No, your facility is very handicap friendly. I must apologize for not telling you about my disability. I hope you'll forgive me."

Interviewer: "No problem. Although you did take me by surprise."

Candidate: (*laughs*) "You're not the first."

Interviewer: "I suppose you know the position we're trying to fill is for a floor supervisor. Our plant covers quite a distance. How might you handle such a position?"

Candidate: "This wheelchair is motorized. I can move more swiftly than the average Olympic runner. What other duties are involved in the position?"

Interviewer: "Before we delve into the specific duties, tell me about your role in the development of the financial plan with ABC Company."

What we see here is a candidate with enough confidence to help the interviewer get over the initial shock. Some candidates might not be so kind. Some disabled candidates feel defensive about other people's assumptions about their skills. In this instance the candidate showed sensitivity to the interviewer and helped the interviewer recover. The last question showed us the interviewer got his wits about him and returned to the strategic interview. Let's look at a similar situation where the candidate is less kind and what the interviewer can do to recover.

The interviewer is seated behind his desk, studying the résumé, and thinking about his strategic plan. A young woman in a wheelchair rolls up to the door and knocks. The interviewer looks up, gives a startled expression, then rises to help the candidate enter. The woman rolls inside and places her wheelchair next to the chair in front of the desk. She reaches out her hand and gives the interviewer a firm handshake.

Interviewer: "Hello." (pause) "You're Ms. Marshall?"

Candidate: "Yes, I'm here to interview for the floor manager position."

Interviewer: "Forgive me. I didn't realize you were wheelchair bound."

Candidate: "I hope that doesn't make a difference. I can still interview for the job."

Interviewer: "Of course you can still interview for the job. Never having experienced a disability myself, you'll need to help me understand if this is a job you'd want."

Candidate: "You mean if this is a job I can do."

Interviewer: "I can well imagine your defensiveness. But, our company has hired a number of handicapped persons who are some of our most reliable and capable employees. I see you in that light. The floor manager position requires some movement, but I doubt that movement will challenge you. Let's talk about your job with the XYZ Company. I see you developed the financial plan there. Tell me what you did."

Here the interviewer was taken off guard, but the candidate offered no help toward his recovery. He began by openly and honestly sharing his surprise. The candidate responded defensively. The interviewer continued to be open with the candidate expressing his need for her help. She once again responded defensively. That's when the interviewer reflected her feelings ("I can well imagine your defensiveness.") and answered her concerns. If the candidate continues to remain defensive, there's no law requiring you to hire her. My guess is this interview will proceed more smoothly from here.

These examples illustrate for us that interviewing nightmares need not be so scary. There are communication skills available to all strategic interviewers that you can use. These are the skills we saw used in the examples above:

• *Say what's going on.* Don't beat around the bush or dance around the obvious. Both you and the candidate know what's going on. If you say it you can both deal with it.

• *Call out the candidate's name.* When you call someone's name, you get that person's attention. Remember, as your mind thinks four times faster than the average person can speak, so does theirs. Sometimes they drift off, and we must call them back.

• *Stay focused.* When candidates try to detour you, stay focused on your goal.

Don't allow them to take you somewhere else. One way to do that is to repeat your goal over and over. "We're talking about difficult customers . . . We're talking about difficult customers." The broken record routine will eventually wear down a stubborn candidate.

- *Be open and honest.* When you share your feelings it turns you into a person and not an "interviewer." By sharing your feelings, you enable candidates to share theirs and to break down whatever barriers they've erected.
- When all else fails *detach yourself from the interview plan* and use your intentional listening skills to keep the candidate talking. Probe, paraphrase, reflect, reality test, summarize, flip sides. At this stage, you no longer need to continue the strategic plan, you merely need to get through the interview professionally.

INTERVIEWING FOR SEMISKILLED LABOR

One of the problems interviewers have when interviewing for semiskilled jobs is they believe they need no preparation. This is the first myth. As with any other interview, the interviewer must plan strategically. That means determining what skills and qualifications are needed to perform successfully in the job and to examine the candidate's application to see what is there and what is missing. In fact interviewers must go through the POINT process from the beginning to the end to design a successful interviewing program for semiskilled labor.

Another problem interviewers have with hiring those with fewer skills is the belief that people applying for lower paying jobs are unable to respond to the questions. This is the second myth. Interviewers tend not to treat these candidates with the same respect they do professional hires. In other words, we go through the interview, one, two, three, and make fast hiring decisions without really knowing anything about the candidates, their skills, or interests. Then we wonder why our turnover is so high!

This is how most interviews go for production or line workers:

Interviewer: "Hello, Mr. Jones. So, you're interested in working in our plant. When can you start to work?"

Candidate: "Anytime."

Interviewer: "Have you ever worked for our company before?"

Candidate: "No."

Interviewer: "What makes you want to work here?"

Candidate: "I heard you had good benefits."

Interviewer: "Do you have adequate transportation to get to work?"

Candidate: "I have a car."

Interviewer: "I see on your application you say you can work shifts. Can you start on the third shift?"

Candidate: "Sure."

Interviewer: "We'll have to give you a physical and a drug test. Then you can start to work. I can arrange that for Monday. Can you come in Monday for those tests and begin work afterwards?"

Candidate: "No problem."

Interviewer: "Do you have any questions?"

Candidate: "What is the pay?"

What have we learned about this candidate? What was the interviewer's strategy? Would you be surprised if Mr. Jones didn't come in on Monday? Perhaps your typical interview with a production or line worker might not be this bad, but I suspect it's similar. Let's take note of the problems:

- All the questions were closed. Here we have candidates who notoriously don't talk much, and we ask mainly closed questions which exacerbates the non-talking status of the interview.
- None of the questions led from anything the candidate said. Each question addressed some other area as if the interviewer was checking off a list of questions. Actually most companies have prepared lists of questions for interviewing for the semiskilled positions. We've learned such practices are "structured" and do not afford the candidate the latitude of a strategic interview. Human resource managers, who prepare such questions, limit the effectiveness of the interview rather than increase it. We'd be better off training those who interview with solid communication and listening skills and with the tools to help them interview strategically.
- The interviewer learned nothing about the candidate.

Let's look at a strategic interview with a semiskilled candidate. The position the candidate is applying for is a line worker in a manufacturing plant. It pays just over minimum wage. One of the issues the interviewer sets out to ascertain is if the nature of the work is something the candidate wants to do. This is an important question to answer because most semiskilled jobs require a high level of motivation to perform. In other words, people **could** do the job **if they wanted to**. The **if they want to** gets in the way of performance.

Interviewer: "Hello, Mr. Jones. Thanks for coming in and applying for the machine operator position with our company. I see from your application you've lived in Littletown all your life. I've been here five years and really like living here."

Candidate: "I wouldn't know how to live anywhere else. All my folks still live in Littletown."

Interviewer: "So you've never lived anywhere else?"

Candidate: "No. My brother moved away to Nevada, but the rest of us stuck around here."

Interviewer: "I see you've worked with many companies in this area over the years. What kinds of things have you done?"

Candidate: "Spinning in the textile mill. I did that for nearly five years. Then I did some work on engines at the Ford place. Usually I just do odds and ends—handiwork."

Interviewer: "What sorts of handiwork do you like?"

Candidate: "I like doing stuff with my hands. Working on the engines or fixing things or painting. The spinning work wasn't so great."

Interviewer: "So you like more mechanical things?"

Candidate: "Yeah. I'm one to get my hands dirty. I like to fix stuff."

Interviewer: "What sorts of things have you fixed?"

Candidate: "Usually old cars or lawn mowers; mainly I work with motors.

Interviewer: "Our job is working on a machine that does have a motor. But it's not exactly fixing anything. It's more like running the machine. How does that sound to you?"

Candidate: "Fine."

Interviewer: "What about the running of the machine sounds fine?"

Candidate: "I suppose any work with a machine I would like."

Interviewer: "Tell me about the other jobs you've had where you had to run machines or were involved with heavy machinery."

Notice the difference in the two interviews. The interviewer asked mainly open questions. The interviewer shared information about the job late in the interview, only after the candidate said what he liked to do. The interviewer attempted to "piggyback" the candidate's responses for his or her next questions. Also, the interviewer began with a short icebreaker.

Usually the people who interview for lower-level jobs come in with a closed Johari Window—even closed tighter than those interviewing for professional positions—particularly when they face you, the human resources manager or the manager of production. The candidate knows you are better educated; you dress neater; you look different—they enter intimidated. A strategic interviewer knows this, attempts to put the candidate at ease as much as possible, but understands candidates rarely feel completely at ease.

The less educated candidate is also less verbal. They may talk more with a peer, but not with you. So, even when you ask open questions and paraphrase, don't expect a lot of conversation.

Part of the interview process, particularly with lower-level hires, should include interviews with peers. Candidates open their Johari Windows much more readily with their peers. To develop rapport, we look for similarities. When you design a hiring system for production or line workers, you should include interviews with peers who have been trained to interview strategically.

In this chapter we looked at the kinds of interviews that present a challenge to the interviewer—interview-nightmares and hiring for semiskilled labor.

The next chapter will focus on legal do's and don'ts and the ways legal issues affect the strategic interview.

15

Keeping the Interview Legal

The strategic interview and the POINT process build on the notion of stripping away the superficial to get to the real person. Throughout this book we've discussed ways to do that in both the planning for the interview and the actual interview itself. We recognized the importance of reacting to what the candidate says—taking whatever is said, doing something with it, and either giving feedback or bridging to another area. This process forms the foundation of the strategic interview. When dealing with legal issues, however, things change. For example:

Interviewer: "I see you live in Birmingham. How do you like living in Alabama?"

Candidate: "We've had some trouble adjusting. My kids don't like the neighborhood. I've got two kids, both toddlers."

Interviewer: (*paraphrase*) "So, you have children?"

Candidate: "Yes, they are the center of my life. My husband and I divorced two years ago. My children are very important to me. I don't know what I'd do without them."

Interviewer: (*reflect*) "It sounds as though your divorce distressed you, and the children mean a lot to you."

What we have in this example is an interviewer using good, solid communication skills. The paraphrase and reflection encourage the candidate to continue talking and sharing. The problem we face in this example is that probing deeper into someone's marital status and family relationships violates the law. It's an area that interviewers must avoid. Furthermore, you might ask yourself what this line of questioning tells you about the candidate's ability to do the job. Even though the interviewer used good communication skills, the P in POINT appears missing.

In this chapter we will look at the laws that define the legal do's and dont's. We will also examine sensitive legal areas and determine how to handle sensitive legal situations when they arise in an interview.

THE REALITIES

In years past fewer sensitive legal areas existed. Today the list grows exponentially. Why? Part of the reason is the diversity of family life, the diversity of the workplace, and our shortcomings of the past.

Diversity of Family Life

More and more families are nontraditional. Families that haven't experienced divorce or the death of a spouse seem unusual nowadays. More and more single individuals raise children. This may startle us, but as we observe our own families, we acknowledge its truth. In years past not only did wives stay home to take care of the kids and other household duties, but grandparents, aunts, and uncles lived nearby. Today more and more people live miles from their extended families. Even after divorce, single parents face raising the children without the support of family members. Furthermore, as parents become aged they migrate to their children's homes for care. Many families are raising their children and also giving care to aged parents.

Diversity of the Workplace

With more single parents working, the workplace had to change. The workplace today is more responsive to the needs of working mothers and fathers. Today's workplace provides child care options, insurance options that allow for day care, family planning options, lenient maternity and paternity leaves, flexible hours, and at-home work options. The list goes on. In other words, the workplace responded to the changing social needs of our families. This trend promises to continue in the next century. With all these changes and the impact the changes make on the worker, why can't employers explore the familial needs of its work force? Unfortunately our past behavior negates that.

Sins of Our Past

Employers of the past asked certain questions of some people and not of others, considered certain issues important with some, and not others.

For example, who received the bulk of questions related to families and child care? Females. Employers assumed the women took responsibility for the family. They assumed if a child were sick, the woman would stay home. Employers assumed the reliability of women in the workplace would be less stable than that of men.

The same holds true for other sensitive issues. We asked questions related to a person's age and didn't hire people we assumed would retire in a few years. We asked questions about a person's national origin and didn't hire people we assumed would return to their foreign home. As we fuss and complain about the litigiousness of our society, we must also take some responsibility for our past sins.

Meanwhile, the workplace becomes more and more diverse. Employers of the past primarily hired white men to fill their managerial jobs. Today's employers hire females, males, persons of color, citizens of other countries, and persons with disabilities. The generation following the baby boomers is smaller. Fewer births produced a shrinking population that will translate into lower and lower unemployment rates as each year passes. Employers will have to look outside their usual resources for hiring. I spoke to a human resources manager who was searching for quality people to fill his production positions. The unemployment rate is 1.7 percent. He's desperate for people. He's courting the Mexican immigrants hoping to attract them to his jobs. But the immigrants must have proper papers to work. Many do, but they still fear deportation. This manager is working to help these people overcome their fears, help his current workers accept the largely Spanish-speaking workers and fill his jobs with a reliable workforce. More and more managers will face similar situations and will find themselves searching for ways to attract workers. We're seeing the beginning of new trends in hiring.

Finding quality people in a shrinking population will be the employment challenge of the new century.

Looking realistically at the legal do's and don'ts, however, we must put potential lawsuits into perspective. Some of the participants in my classes and some of the books you'll find on the shelves seem almost paranoid about legal issues—fearful that any question they ask will land them in court. This paranoia is unrealistic. Think about the purpose of an interview.

Candidates come to you not in search of a legal experience but in search of a job.

What is the likelihood you'll hire a candidate who sues you for asking the wrong question in an interview or one who has sued someone else? What is the likelihood of that candidate winning the lawsuit? In most instances it's your word against the other person's. If you've had no other legal violations, your word should stand firm. Usually you bring a truckload of attorneys to represent your company. The candidate often has fewer resources. In addition, the time it takes to go to court, conduct a trial, and reach a verdict discourages many potential suits. So, interviewers need not needlessly worry about being sued. But interviewers must take heed and learn what is and is not legally appropriate. Even if a candidate chooses not to sue you in the event you ask illegal questions, you put your company at risk and you jeopardize your company's reputation. Candidates talk to one another. You don't want to establish your company as one that lacks professionalism by asking clearly illegal questions during the interview process.

HOW DO YOU KNOW WHAT NOT TO ASK?

The Laws

According to the United States Equal Employment Opportunity Commission, the following laws currently shape what we can and cannot ask in an interview:[1]

- The Equal Pay Act, 1963
- Title VII Civil Rights Act, 1964
- The Immigration Reform and Control Act, 1986
- Age Discrimination in Employment Act
- Vocational Rehabilitation Act
- Vietnam Era Veteran's Readjustment Assistant Act
- The Privacy Act, 1974
- The Fair Credit and Reporting Act, 1970
- The Family Education Rights and Privacy Act and Buckley Amendment, 1974
- The Freedom of Information Act, 1966
- American Disabilities Act

Each of the above laws and those coming out every day affect what we can and cannot ask in interviews. The Civil Rights Act protects people from discrimination due to race and national origin; the Age Discrimination Act protects people against discrimination because of age; the American Disabilities Act protects people from discrimination based on handicaps. Human resource managers face a daily barrage of new laws affecting the interview process whenever they open their mail.

The Litmus Test for Interview Questions

With daily changes in the laws and the litigious nature of our society, how can interviewers protect themselves against lawsuits? We've learned in this book that the strategic interviewer probes deeply and encourages candidates to express themselves openly. Yet, we must weigh this technique against the legal issues.

One test to determine legal fitness is "job relatedness." Is the question job related? In other words, *do I need to know this information to determine if the person can do the job?* If the answer is yes, the question can be justified. That doesn't mean someone won't sue you for asking that question (people can sue you anytime they wish, regardless of the justification of their suit), but it does mean you can show purpose and nondiscrimination in your questioning. If the answer is no and the question is legally suspect, don't ask it. Job relatedness is the bottom line for all interviewers.

According to Olson in *Managing the Interview,* the term used to determine job relatedness is BOQ or bona fide qualification for the occupation. Olson says there are two kinds of BOQ—"that which may be *useful* and that which is absolutely *necessary* to perform the job."[2] For example, if an employer says previous fund-raising experience is necessary for the job, but he's hired others in the past who don't have fund-raising experience, an inexperienced candidate might file a complaint, and the EEOC could find fund-raising experience *useful* but not absolutely *necessary.*

Mary Ann Wersch, in *Interview Guide for Supervisors* (1998), writes, "Ask questions only for information that will serve as a basis for the hiring decision, know how information will be used to make the decision, and do not ask for information that will not or should not be used in hiring decisions."[3] With this guidance in mind, employers must apply the standards for a job across the board. Part of the purpose of the strategic interview is to develop those standards at the outset rather than making them up as you go along. Employers who use the POINT process will be better equipped to justify their actions should they face a lawsuit.

To avoid lawsuits, interviewers must:

- Stay abreast of the changing laws and how they affect the interview.
- As part of your strategy, ask yourself, is this question absolutely necessary to do the job?
- As part of your strategy, determine which questions aren't absolutely necessary but useful to do the job.
- Plan for the job, citing the absolute necessary qualifications before you see the first candidate.

Consistency in the strategic interview is assured due to the qualifications needed to do the job. You and your team established those skills and qualities before the first candidate walked through the front door. Then you screened the résumés to determine which candidates fit your needs.

In your planning phase, you must determine what is absolutely necessary for the job. In other words, you establish the essentials and if a candidate doesn't meet those essentials, you do not hire that candidate.

We discussed in Chapter 4 the possibility of taking the time to train someone who lacks needed skills, but we make that decision only when none of the candidates interviewed have the skills we're searching for. If, for example, one of the candidates you've interviewed has the skills to do the job, but another does not have the skills, and you choose to hire the lesser skilled candidate and train that individual, you put your decision in legal jeopardy. You would be better off starting the interview process over than hiring the lesser skilled candidate.

By setting the standards of absolutes for the job before you examine résumés and interview candidates, you reduce the chance for bias.

Practice Exercise

Determine what is right and what is wrong (possibly illegal) with the following interview.

Interviewer: *"I appreciate your taking the time to visit with me today. My name is Janice Walker. I'm the human resources manager for XYZ Company. I'm intrigued by your job history. You've worked in both manufacturing and the service environment. What prompted you to move from one to the other so frequently?"*

Candidate: *"My husband works for a large company that has divisions all over the country. We've moved seven times in ten years. The only way for him to move up is to transfer to new divisions. I found different jobs in each community where we've lived, and I've loved all the experiences I've had."*

Interviewer: *"So, you've postponed your career until your husband's stabilizes?"*

Candidate: *"You could say that. Because I'm good in sales, I tend to have little trouble getting jobs. Sales associates usually don't last a long time in most companies anyway. Those are the burnout jobs."*

Interviewer: *"When you say sales positions are burnout jobs, what do you mean?"*

Candidate: *"I've seen young people come into the job all excited and ready to run. But after a few weeks on the road, they give out. I'm no longer young. At forty-five, I've been doing sales jobs for nearly ten years, and I still love it."*

Interviewer: *"So at forty-five, the traveling doesn't bother you?"*

Candidate: *"Now I wouldn't go that far. It's hard living in hotel rooms, eating alone each night. I don't enjoy that. But I love the work. I love meeting new people everywhere I go and the thrill of making a sale still sends me. The travel is exhausting."*

Interviewer: *"How do you handle the exhaustion?"*

Candidate: *"I tend to be a positive thinker. I try to see the bright side of things. My Jewish father helped me with this. He said even though the Jews were persecuted throughout history, God is on our side. We have to believe that."*

Interviewer: *"What other things did your Jewish father teach you to help you cope with the exhaustion of traveling?"*

Candidate: *"There's much in the Jewish tradition that teaches positive thinking. I read the Torah regularly and teach my children the lessons there. I believe strong faith can help people overcome all kinds of situations. Don't you agree?"*

Interviewer: *"I, too, am a firm believer in faith. It's gotten me far in my career and my life. What other things do you do to help you overcome exhaustion?"*

1. List the things the interviewer did right in this interview.
2. List the things you believe might be illegal in this interview or could be contested.
3. What angles might you have taken with this interview?

This interviewer started out fine. Although she totally skipped the ice-breaker and went directly into a probing question, the question she asked had no legal implications. We notice, however, the candidate told us about her husband's work history. We didn't ask for that, and we shouldn't. We cannot probe a spouse's, boyfriend's, or fiancée's intentions. But, as we saw in this instance, the candidate chose to tell us things, and there's no law against listening. There are laws, however, against probing. When the interviewer paraphrased, *"So, you've postponed your career until your husband's stabilizes?"*, she moved into dangerous territory. Had the interviewer merely said, "Sounds as if you've postponed your career?", that would have been sufficient for a response.

The probing question about burnout jobs is fine, nothing illegal there. But when the candidate shared her age, and the interviewer picked up on the age and exhaustion factor, here again, the interviewer treads on dangerous ground. This candidate will probably leave the interview thinking the interviewer felt she was too old for the job.

Looking at the exhaustion issue in this case was a poor choice on the interviewer's part. The interviewer reality tested about traveling, which was fine. But exhaustion came up only once. The interviewer picked up on that rather than some of the other issues: What does this candidate love about sales? What does this candidate see as important for making sales? How has selling so many different products affected her sales ability?

Nonetheless the interviewer traveled in dangerous territory and that led to more dangerous territory with the discussion of what the Jewish father taught the candidate. Again, there's nothing wrong with listening. After the candidate said, *"I tend to be a positive thinker. I try to see the bright side of things. My Jewish father helped me with this . . . ,"* the interviewer might have asked, "Give me a specific example of how you've used positive thinking." In other words, the interviewer must ignore everything that is related to the candidate's Jewish heritage.

The following table gives you an idea about what you can and cannot ask and where the sensitive areas lie. Bear in mind, according to the law, there are times when many of these questions are possible, so long as job relatedness is absolute. Also note that this table serves merely as a guide. States differ considerably in what is lawful and what isn't. It's best to check the practices in your particular state.

Sensitive Areas	Lawful Inquiries	Unlawful Inquiries
Name	"Have you worked for this company before using a different name?"	Inquiries about a candidate's lineage, ancestry, or national origin.
Marital and Family Status	Whether a candidate can meet specific work schedules.	Any inquiry about whether a candidate is married, single, divorced, or number of children.
Pregnancy	When the workplace might endanger a fetus (chemical exposure).	Never ask about a candidate's family plans or availability.
Age	Minors must show proof of age and appropriate work permits.	Never discuss age with older candidates. Don't ask for proof of age by birth certificate until after hired.
Handicaps	Whether candidate has handicaps or health problems that might affect specific job performance or which should be considered before making job placement.	General inquiries, "Do you have any handicaps or health problems?" that do not relate to performance on the job.
Sex	Only when sex of the candidate affects performance in the job.	Never when related to sexual preference. Never assume a certain sex can or cannot perform a job (heavy lifting, etc.).
Race	Never lawful.	Never ask questions that deal with a person's race.
Birthplace	Okay after employment.	Never ask for birthplace of candidate or candidate's family that might suggest national origin.
Military Record	Type of education or experience while in service.	Type of discharge.
Photo	Okay after hiring.	Request candidate to submit a photo or affix one to a résumé.

Sensitive Areas	Lawful Inquiries	Unlawful Inquiries
Citizenship	"Are you a citizen of the U.S.?" or "Are you allowed legally to work in the U.S. and, if so, for what length of time?" Told if hired they will need to present proof of citizenship.	"Of what country are you a citizen?" "When did you become a U.S. citizen?" "Are your parents U.S. citizens?" Other questions that probe the country of citizenship, the nature of citizenship, or the nature of the parent's citizenship.
Ancestry or National Origin	Languages candidate reads, speaks, or writes.	Inquiries into candidate's lineage or mother tongue. National origin of parents or spouse.
Education	Candidate's academic, vocational, or professional schools attended.	Asking about specific national, racial, or religious affiliation of a school.
Experience	Candidate's work history. Other countries visited.	
Conviction, Arrest, Court Record	Inquiries into actual convictions that relate to fitness for a job. Convictions are public record.	Inquiries about any arrests. Ask the court to check a person's arrest record or court appearances.
Relatives	Names of candidate's relatives employed by the company. Names of parents or guardians of minors.	Name or address of any relative of an adult candidate.
Organizations	Inquiry into organizations in which candidate is a member so long as the organization doesn't have any racial, religion, or ancestry membership. What offices held.	Request a list of all organizations, clubs, or societies to which a person belongs. No questions related to past or present union affiliation.
Religion	Questions related to ability to work certain days of the week and holidays.	Questions related to religious affiliation.
Credit Rating	Ask only if related to jobs handling money or trust funds.	Never ask about credit rating, garnishments, or charge accounts.

Nepotism comes up in many of my workshops. Many organizations make it a practice not to hire relatives. It is legal, however, to hire relatives in an organization so long as the relative has no supervisory or managerial status above his or her relative. Nepotism happens when relatives promote one another or give raises to each other above other employees. Employees who are relatives, and work side by side or in very different parts of an organization without supervisory control over one another, may legally work in the same organization. Companies that husbands and wives jointly own do not violate the laws of nepotism.

High Risk Areas

Testing presents one of the highest legal risks. As pointed out in Chapter 9, many organizations use different tests to determine a candidate's abilities. The problem with all tests is their cultural bias. Recently I learned that the Scholastic Aptitude Tests (SATs) for college entrance tend to screen out Hispanic youth. Hispanics who achieve straight A's in school and often work nearly full time, score 1200 or less on the tests, with particularly low scores on the verbal portions. With just a little thought, we can see why. Hispanic youth are meeting difficult verbal challenges in a foreign language. Even though they're proficient with English, it's not their native language. Should they receive lower scores and fewer opportunities to get into the best colleges because of this problem? This is the reason tests alone cannot determine a person's skill level. This is why employers must use the interview to balance whatever scores a test might reveal. If employers put too much weight on tests and the test proves biased, the employer puts his company at risk for legal action and could lose a number of very good candidates. My recommendation is to avoid testing. Testing adds structure to interviews and structure destroys the strategic interview process. Not only is testing legally sensitive but it is also costly. Note, however, that many tried and true skills tests do not cause legal problems. One example is the typing test.

Balancing the interview with non-job specific activities. In Chapter 7 we talked about the interviewers' need to know the entire person. Focusing on job experiences or professional activities shows us only one side of a person. Strategically we want to see more than one side. Many times we've set standards that include such qualities as flexibility, risk taking, team building, and leadership. Often these qualities come out in a person's leisure pursuits. Even so, interviewers must understand that questions delving into a candidate's leisure pursuits are more risky. That doesn't mean we ignore those areas; it only means we're careful and alert. Again, finding out about a person's ability to handle conflict from that person's experience on a basketball team gives the interviewer as much or more information than perhaps the person's experience as a computer operator.

Conducting interviews in informal environments. When we take candidates out to dinner, breakfast, lunch, or for a round of golf, we risk letting our interviewer-guard down. During those informal interactions it is often easy to throw in a question like, "Do you have any kids?" or "Does your spouse work?" These are the kinds of questions we'd ask someone we just met. They're the kinds of questions that enable us to develop a rapport with a new person. But in the interviewing world, they're illegal whether you ask the question over a beer or whether you ask them behind your desk at the office. Interviewers must remember they wear their "interviewer" hat at all times. Human resource managers struggle with this problem. They ask other managers to entertain candidates but worry the other managers don't understand their roles as interviewers. Until a prospective candidate is hired, you and your interview team are interviewers. Anything you say or do could be legally suspect. Again, we're not saying don't entertain the candidate, we're saying be careful. It isn't appropriate to strategically probe candidates during those informal exchanges, but at the same time, you are always the "interviewer" and must maintain that detached professionalism. One thing to bear in mind—many organizations ask the least experienced interviewer to entertain the candidates. Since the informal environment presents such a tempting place to loosen our ties and casually ask illegal questions, either we must give our "least experienced" interviewers a lot more training or we should ask only the seasoned interviewers to entertain candidates.

The following example illustrates an interview where certain sensitive issues came up and how the interviewer handled those situations.

Interviewer: "I appreciate your coming in to interview for the executive director of our company. My name is Henry Lee. I'm the director of human resources. I noticed on your résumé that you wrote a monograph on funding for nonprofits. We've had quite a time getting grant support. I submitted a grant last quarter for the first time. What an ordeal!"

Candidate: "My experience with nonprofits led me to write the monograph. So often we depend on outside funds, both public and private, but no one teaches us about how to go about asking for money."

Interviewer: "I had a difficult time asking for money. I hated it. But I noticed your monograph tells us to think of our cause. If we don't believe in our cause, we can't succeed in finding funds."

Candidate: "I see you studied my monograph carefully. I also talked about lobbying. Staying in close contact with the local politicians helps."

Interviewer: "So you've had experience in both fund-raising and lobbying in your career. What other areas interest you?"

Candidate: "I'm a progressive person. It took me a long time to adjust to this culture. I came to the U.S. with my parents when I was fifteen. We lived off the beaten path for Puerto Ricans—that is, we didn't live in New York City. We lived in Atlanta. There weren't many Hispanics in Atlanta at that time. I had to find my way on my own."

Interviewer: "So you're saying being progressive keeps your interest in the jobs you've had?"

Candidate: "My early experiences taught me that I like to plunge forward. I hate organizations that aren't going anywhere. When I worked for the XY nonprofit, I felt we were at a total standstill. I joined with others to change the focus of the group and to push ahead."

Interviewer: "If an organization reaches a standstill, what do you do?"

Candidate: "I look for other options. If I can't find them, I leave. It's hard for me to remain committed to anything static."

Interviewer: "When you look for other options, what do you do when the organization resists?"

Candidate: "I'm a great believer in compassion. I show the people what they can be with a little effort. I help them see a brighter, more secure future. I've worked for the Peace Corps in some of the worst parts of the world. My experience taught me people will respect you if you show them compassion. I don't try to fight resistance, I try to break it down."

Interviewer: "I'm not sure I understand what you mean by break it down."

Candidate: "I was raised a Catholic with all the tradition and ritual. I went to mass with my mother and brothers every Sunday. I went to confession and was absolved. I did it without thinking. One day I opened my eyes. I saw money being poured into the churches all over South America while the people lived in abject poverty. Something was wrong with that picture. But who is going to move the Catholic Church? Talk about a stuck nonprofit. I took little bits at a time. I worked with a priest in Atlanta who helped me gain entry to a priest in Mexico. Before long, new charities formed. Little by little the church is giving back to the people."

Interviewer: "That sounds like a very rewarding experience for you. I know you were proud of the work you did."

Candidate: "I was proud and overwhelmed at what more needed doing. That was the beginning of my commitment to working with nonprofits to help them be all they can to the people they serve. I've spent my career trying to accomplish that goal."

Interviewer: "How do you handle situations where your values and those of the nonprofit don't jive?"

We see in this example two potentially risky situations. The first occurred when the candidate discussed ethnicity. Notice, the interviewer picked up on what the candidate said without dwelling on the ethnic background. The interviewer's response, **"So you're saying being progressive keeps you interested in the jobs you've had?"**, led to a question of what the candidate looks for in jobs rather than ethnicity.

The second situation occurred when the candidate talked about having a Roman Catholic upbringing. Again the interviewer sidestepped the religious issue by focusing on the candidate's accomplishments. The interviewer reflected, "That sounds like a rewarding experience for you. I know you were proud of the work you did." Here the interviewer's reflection focused on work.

There will be instances throughout the interview when candidates will share intimate things about themselves that we cannot probe. If we conduct the strategic interview effectively, those instances will happen. The strategic interviewer expects those instances and moves the interview away from the sensitive areas.

In this chapter we saw how legal do's and don'ts crop up throughout the interview. We examined the changes in the workforce and the workplace and how those changes affect the legality of certain questions. Every day the courts rule on certain behaviors that influence what we can or cannot do or say in an interview. Testing candidates and the inherent biases of tests create particularly sensitive legal issues. Our informal entertainment of candidates puts us on precarious ground as does our interest in the leisure pursuits of candidates.

So, what's an interviewer to do? Strategically we know what we can and cannot ask. We shift interviews away from sensitive areas, we ask questions that are job-related, and we stay alert to potential problems when we delve into leisure activities or when we entertain candidates. The strategic interviewer belongs to professional organizations that keep him or her abreast of the changing legal environment. Using the POINT process, planning ahead, and applying the same standards to all candidates will help protect you against the likelihood of lawsuits.

NOTES

1. United States Equal Employment Opportunity Commission, August 1981.
2. Olson, *Managing the Interview*, p. 115.
3. Mary Ann Wersch, *Interview Guide for Supervisors* (Washington, DC: College and University Personnel Association, 1998), p. 4.

Appendix 1: A Trainer's Guide for Human Resource Managers

This appendix contains sample materials and a suggested agenda for training people to interview strategically. All the reference material for the content of short lectures, sample forms, and practice exercises are found in the body of the text.

Human resource managers encounter people within their organizations who lack the skills to interview effectively. This book provides the basis for learning the tactics of strategic interviewing. It is a practical guide, complete with exercises, explanations, and concrete examples. Human resource managers may also wish to design an in-house training experience. The following guide will help create such an experience.

ONE HALF-DAY CLASS (The basics)

Suggested Agenda: 4 hours
Goals:

- Define Strategic Interviewing and Communication Skills
- Identify Corporate Culture
- Define the POINT process
- Practice Résumé Screening
- Practice INtentional Listening Skills
- Discuss Legal Do's and Don'ts

Introduction and Orientation (Chapter 1)

Define Strategic Interviewing vs. Structured Interviewing (Chapter 1)

Define Communication: Visual, Vocal, and Verbal (Chapter 1)

Practice Using the POINT Process (Chapter 1)

*P*lan
*O*pen
*IN*tentional Listening
*T*est

Determine Your Company Culture

In small groups (no more than seven per group), practice Planning by responding to questions on determining your company culture (Chapter 2).

1. Over the past five years, what is the rate of growth (human and profit)?
2. List the behaviors that reap rewards. (Examine the people that have been promoted. What qualities do they possess?)
3. What do others say are the qualities that make your company successful?
4. How do people respond to errors?
5. How often do conflicts arise?
6. What happens during a conflict?
7. How do people dress?
8. What amount of time do people spend communicating?
9. How much meeting time is spent looking at past history versus creating new policies and procedures?
10. How do people feel about the future of the organization and their job security?

Résumé Screening

In the same groups, review a sample résumé, either one from your supply or one from Appendix 2. Give each group a different résumé. Use the following steps to determine if the résumé meets the needs of the culture and the job (Chapter 6).

1. List the candidate's knowledge and experiences in relation to the skills you're looking for.
2. What knowledge or experiences are missing in relation to the skills you're looking for?
3. How does it appear the candidate interacts with others?
4. Would you recommend this person for an interview? If yes,

    a. What would you use as an icebreaker in this interview?

b. What would you want to explore with this candidate?

c. Develop two questions that would help you extract the type of information you need to help you reach a decision.

Afterwards, ask each group to report its responses.

Practice INtentional Listening

- Examine when to strategically ask open vs. closed questions (Chapter 7)
- Discuss what the INtentional Listening Skills are (Chapter 8)
- Practice INtentionally listening in pairs. Write responses to the following exercises. Share those responses with the entire group.

Write a *probe* for each of the following candidate responses:

Interviewer: "What is the most important aspect of the job you're seeking?
Candidate: "It has to be challenging."
Your response:

Interviewer: "What makes you want to work for XYZ Company?
Candidate: "I want to work for a progressive company."
Your response:

Interviewer: "Describe some of your professional successes."
Candidate: "I was elected spokesperson for the team."
Your response:

Interviewer: "I noticed on your résumé that you held two jobs last year, one for a short time. Tell me what happened in that job."
Candidate: "My boss was real hard to work for. I worked hard but we just couldn't get along. So I got another job."
Your response:

Write a *paraphrase* for each response below:

Candidate: "In my last job I had lots of freedom."
Your response:

Candidate: "I really enjoy working with people rather than sitting in front of a computer all day."
Your response:

Candidate: "My hobbies include reading and skiing. I usually go to Denver once a year for a week-long skiing trip. It's become a family tradition."
Your response:

Write a *summary* response:

Interviewer: "Looking over your career, tell me what prompted you to move from sales to training."

Candidate: "I suppose it was a number of things rather than just one event. I had worked in direct sales from the time I sold magazines in high school. It seemed no matter what career options I pursued, I fell into sales. I suppose that meant I was good at it. Anyway, after working for six years with XYZ Company, selling the product, traveling from pillar to post, I became restless. I wanted to challenge myself to do something else. I began teaching people how to better use the product. I was interested in selling it, but I became more interested in product retention by teaching others how to better use it. This was a new idea at the time and created lots of interest among the management team. One thing led to another and before long, I was teaching the sales force about product retention and creating new ideas for usage."

Your response:

Write *reality tests* for the following series of responses.

Candidate: "Even though I've never worked on teams, I love people and a job that enables me to interact with others is exactly what I am looking for."

Your reality test:

Candidate: "When it comes to hard work, I'm the one. I'm the kind of person who never gets tired. I could work eighty hours a week and you'd never know it."

Your reality test:

Write a *flip side* response to the following:

Interviewer: "Tell me about your experiences on the Excel project with the management team."

Candidate: "I led a group of sixteen people. We met twice a week for the first six months of the project. Then we cut down to once a week. The experience taught me a lot about how to manage a group, especially one that large and that diverse. I enjoyed the sharing and the amount of experience in the room. Often I'd leave a meeting overwhelmed with how much the people knew in our company. The project was a great success. Afterwards we celebrated as a team. It was hard to break up when the project ended."

Interviewer: "Team work can be a rewarding experience, especially when groups work so well together."

Candidate: "I had no idea when I began the project I would enjoy the experience so much. At first I was daunted by the challenge. But now I have to say that it was one of the most valuable experiences in my career."

Your flip side response:

Write a *reflecting response* to each of the following. Rephrase the feeling, not the content, in the following candidate responses.

Candidate: "I really don't like doing the same thing over and over."

Your response:

Candidate: "Working the night shift was too much work."

Your response:

Candidate: "Between my scholarship and my part-time jobs, I managed to pay for my entire college education."

Your response:

Lecturette: Legal Do's and Don'ts (Chapter 15)

Ask the group as a whole to list what they believe the illegal questions are. Once you have all the responses on a flip chart, go through the list and discuss whether the question is a *Don't* and under what conditions it might be permissible to ask it.

In small groups, no more than seven, examine the case in Chapter 15 to determine what was right or wrong with the following interview.

Interviewer: "I appreciate your taking the time to visit with me today. My name is Janice Walker. I'm the human resources manager for XYZ Company. I'm intrigued by your job history. You've worked in both manufacturing and the service environment. What prompted you to move from one to the other so frequently?"

Candidate: "My husband works for a large company that has divisions all over the country. We've moved seven times in ten years. The only way for him to move up is to transfer to new divisions. I found different jobs in each community where we've lived, and I've loved all the experiences I've had."

Interviewer: "So, you've postponed your career until your husband's stabilizes?"

Candidate: "You could say that. Because I'm good in sales, I tend to have little trouble getting jobs. Sales associates usually don't last a long time in most companies anyway. Those are the burnout jobs."

Interviewer: "When you say sales positions are burnout jobs, what do you mean?"

Candidate: "I've seen young people come into the job all excited and ready to run. But after a few weeks on the road, they give out. I'm no longer young. At forty-five, I've been doing sales jobs for nearly ten years, and I still love it."

Interviewer: "So at forty-five, the traveling doesn't bother you?"

Candidate: "Now I wouldn't go that far. It's hard living in hotel rooms, eating alone each night. I don't enjoy that. But I love the work. I love meeting new people everywhere I go and the thrill of making a sale still sends me. The travel is exhausting."

Interviewer: "How do you handle the exhaustion?"

Candidate: "I tend to be a positive thinker. I try to see the bright side of things. My Jewish father helped me with this. He said even though the Jews were persecuted throughout history, God is on our side. We have to believe that."

Interviewer: "What other things did your Jewish father teach you to help you cope with the exhaustion of traveling?"

Candidate: "There's much in the Jewish tradition that teaches positive thinking. I read the Torah regularly and teach my children the lessons there. I believe strong faith can help people overcome all kinds of situations. Don't you agree?"

Interviewer: "I, too, am a firm believer in faith. It's gotten me far in my career and my life. What other things do you do to help you overcome exhaustion?"

1. List the things the interviewer did right in this interview.
2. List the things you believe might be illegal in this interview or could be contested.
3. What angles might you have taken with this interview?

Afterwards, ask each group to report its findings.

FULL DAY CLASS (Beyond the basics)

Suggested Agenda: 6–8 hours
If videotaping is used for the practice role-plays, limit the class size to six.
    Goals:

• Define Strategic Interviewing and Communication Skills
• Define the POINT Process
• Perception Identification
• Learn What Interviews Can and Cannot Do
• Identify Corporate Culture
• Practice Résumé Screening
• Practice INtentional Listening Skills
• Examine the Legal Do's and Don'ts
• Practice Interviewing in Role-Plays

Introduction and Orientation (Chapter 1)

• Define Strategic Interviewing vs. Structured Interviewing (Chapter 1)
• Define Communication: Visual, Vocal, and Verbal (Chapter 1)

To demonstrate the power of vocal communication, ask a participant to read each sentence below emphasizing the underlined word:

I didn't say he <u>killed</u> the bird.
I didn't <u>say</u> he killed the bird.
I didn't say <u>he</u> killed the bird.

I didn't say he killed the <u>bird</u>.
<u>I</u> didn't say he killed the bird.

Practice the POINT Process

Plan

Open

INtentional Listening

Test

Lecturette: Define Perceptions and Groupthink (Chapter 4)

Practice understanding the effects of Inference vs. Observation (Chapter 1). Read the following story two times. Ask the group to answer the questions. Afterwards give the group the correct answers based on whether we inferred or observed something.

Story: Mark and Mary Wilson turned out the lights in their living room when they heard a crash from the den. Mark went into the den and saw a man climbing out the window. The dog had the man's leg in his mouth. A scuffle ensued and the man escaped. Mary Wilson called a member of the police force.

Answer the questions as follows: True = The story states this fact. False = The story states a contrary fact. Inference = This cannot be determined from the story.

1. Mr. and Mrs. Wilson turned out the lights in their living room.   T F I
2. Someone broke a lamp in the den.   T F I
3. Mark and Mary Wilson didn't hear any noise from the den.   T F I
4. The dog barked at the man.   T F I
5. Mrs. Wilson screamed when she saw the intruder.   T F I
6. A man was climbing out of a window in the den.   T F I
7. The neighbors called the police.   T F I
8. The man escaped before the police arrived.   T F I
9. Mary Wilson went to the den when she heard the crash.   T F I
10. The dog didn't bite anyone.   T F I

Let's look at the correct responses to these ten statements in terms of inference and observation.

1. I—You don't know if Mark and Mary are married. They could be son and mother or brother and sister.
2. I—Perhaps. We don't know.
3. F—They heard a crash.

4. I—We don't know if the dog barked or not. The only sound they heard was a crash.

5. I—Maybe there is a Mrs. Smith and she screamed. We don't know.

6. T—That's what the story says.

7. I—Maybe they called the police, too. We don't know.

8. I—We're not even sure the man got out of the window. We know he escaped, but maybe from the scuffle or from the dog.

9. I—We don't know where Mary Wilson went.

10. F—The dog bit the man's leg.

What an Interview Can and Cannot Do

Have each person read the list below and check those factors they feel they can easily determine during an interview.

1. _____ The candidate's philosophy and objectives

2. _____ Reason for choosing your organization

3. _____ General career aspirations

4. _____ Background

5. _____ Interests and hobbies

6. _____ Attitude

7. _____ Enthusiasm

8. _____ Willingness to accept criticism

9. _____ Loyalty

10. _____ Ability to solve problems

11. _____ The candidate's job performance

Determine Your Company Culture

In small groups (three per group), practice Planning by responding to questions on determining your company culture (Chapter 2).

1. Over the past five years, what is the rate of growth (human and profit)?

2. List the behaviors that reap rewards. (Examine the people that have been promoted. What qualities do they possess?)

3. What do others say are the qualities that make your company successful?

4. How do people respond to errors?

5. How often do conflicts arise?

6. What happens during a conflict?

7. How do people dress?

8. What amount of time do people spend communicating?

9. How much meeting time is spent looking at past history versus creating new policies and procedures?

10. How do people feel about the future of the organization and their job security?

Résumé Screening

In the same groups, review a sample résumé, either one from your supply or one from Appendix 2. Give each group a different résumé. Use the following steps to determine if the résumé meets the needs of the culture and the job. (Chapter 6).

1. List the candidate's knowledge and experiences in relation to the skills you're looking for.

2. What knowledge or experiences are missing in relation to the skills you're looking for?

3. How does it appear the candidate interacts with others?

4. Would you recommend this person for an interview? If yes,

    a. What would you use as an icebreaker in this interview?

    b. What would you want to explore with this candidate?

    c. Develop two questions that would help you extract the type of information you need to help you reach a decision.

Afterwards, ask each group to report its findings.

Practice INtentional Listening (Chapter 4)

- Hear what the candidate said
- React
- Give feedback
- Examine when to strategically ask open vs. closed questions (Chapter 7)
- Discuss what the INtentional Listening Skills are (Chapter 8)
- Practice INtentionally listening in pairs. Write responses to the following exercises. Share those responses with the entire group.

Write a *probe* for each of the following candidate responses:

Interviewer: "What is the most important aspect of the job you're seeking?"
Candidate: "It has to be challenging."
Your response:
Interviewer: "What makes you want to work for XYZ Company?"

Candidate: "I want to work for a progressive company."

Your response:

Interviewer: "Describe some of your professional successes."

Candidate: "I was elected spokesperson for the team."

Your response:

Interviewer: "I noticed on your résumé that you held two jobs last year, one for a short time. Tell me what happened in that job."

Candidate: "My boss was real hard to work for. I worked hard but we just couldn't get along. So I got another job."

Your response:

Write a *paraphrase* for each response below:

Candidate: "In my last job I had lots of freedom."

Your response:

Candidate: "I really enjoy working with people rather than sitting in front of a computer all day."

Your response:

Candidate: "My hobbies include reading and skiing. I usually go to Denver once a year for a week-long skiing trip. It's become a family tradition."

Your response:

Write a *summary* response:

Interviewer: "Looking over your career, tell me what prompted you to move from sales to training."

Candidate: "I suppose it was a number of things rather than just one event. I had worked in direct sales from the time I sold magazines in high school. It seemed no matter what career options I pursued, I fell into sales. I suppose that meant I was good at it. Anyway, after working for six years with XYZ Company, selling the product, traveling from pillar to post, I became restless. I wanted to challenge myself to do something else. I began teaching people how to better use the product. I was interested in selling it, but I became more interested in product retention by teaching others how to better use it. This was a new idea at the time and created lots of interest among the management team. One thing led to another and before long, I was teaching the sales force about product retention and creating new ideas for usage."

Your response:

Write *reality tests* for the following series of responses:

Candidate: "Even though I've never worked on teams, I love people and a job that enables me to interact with others is exactly what I am looking for."

Your reality test:

Candidate: "When it comes to hard work, I'm the one. I'm the kind of person who never gets tired. I could work eighty hours a week and you'd never know it."

Your reality test:

Write a *flip side* response to the following:

Interviewer: "Tell me about your experiences on the Excel project with the management team."

Candidate: "I led a group of sixteen people. We met twice a week for the first six months of the project. Then we cut down to once a week. The experience taught me a lot about how to manage a group, especially one that large and that diverse. I enjoyed the sharing and the amount of experience in the room. Often I'd leave a meeting overwhelmed with how much the people knew in our company. The project was a great success. Afterwards we celebrated as a team. It was hard to break up when the project ended."

Interviewer: "Team work can be a rewarding experience, especially when groups work so well together."

Candidate: "I had no idea when I began the project I would enjoy the experience so much. At first I was daunted by the challenge. But now I have to say that it was one of the most valuable experiences in my career."

Your flip side response:

Write a *reflecting response* to each of the following. Rephrase the feeling, not the content, in the following candidate responses.

Candidate: "I really don't like doing the same thing over and over."

Your response:

Candidate: "Working the night shift was too much work."

Your response:

Candidate: "Between my scholarship and my part-time jobs, I managed to pay for my entire college education."

Your response:

Lecturette: Legal Do's and Don'ts (Chapter 15)

Ask the group as a whole to list what they believe the illegal questions are. Once you have all the responses on a flip chart, go through the list and discuss whether the question is a *Don't* and under what conditions it might be permissible to ask it.

In two small groups (or in pairs for a group of six), examine the case in Chapter 15 to determine what was right or wrong with the interview:

Interviewer: "I appreciate your taking the time to visit with me today. My name is Janice Walker. I'm the human resources manager for XYZ Company. I'm intrigued by your job history. You've worked in both manufacturing and the service environment. What prompted you to move from one to the other so frequently?"

Candidate: "My husband works for a large company that has divisions all over the country. We've moved seven times in ten years. The only way for him to move up is to transfer to new divisions. I found different jobs in each community where we've lived, and I've loved all the experiences I've had."

Interviewer: "So, you've postponed your career until your husband's stabilizes?"

Candidate: "You could say that. Because I'm good in sales, I tend to have little trouble getting jobs. Sales associates usually don't last a long time in most companies anyway. Those are the burnout jobs."

Interviewer: "When you say sales positions are burnout jobs, what do you mean?"

Candidate: "I've seen young people come into the job all excited and ready to run. But after a few weeks on the road, they give out. I'm no longer young. At forty-five, I've been doing sales jobs for nearly ten years, and I still love it."

Interviewer: "So at forty-five, the traveling doesn't bother you?"

Candidate: "Now I wouldn't go that far. It's hard living in hotel rooms, eating alone each night. I don't enjoy that. But I love the work. I love meeting new people everywhere I go and the thrill of making a sale still sends me. The travel is exhausting."

Interviewer: "How do you handle the exhaustion?"

Candidate: "I tend to be a positive thinker. I try to see the bright side of things. My Jewish father helped me with this. He said even though the Jews were persecuted throughout history, God is on our side. We have to believe that."

Interviewer: "What other things did your Jewish father teach you to help you cope with the exhaustion of traveling?"

Candidate: "There's much in the Jewish tradition that teaches positive thinking. I read the Torah regularly and teach my children the lessons there. I believe strong faith can help people overcome all kinds of situations. Don't you agree?"

Interviewer: "I, too, am a firm believer in faith. It's gotten me far in my career and my life. What other things do you do to help you overcome exhaustion?"

1. List the things the interviewer did right in this interview.
2. List the things you believe might be illegal in this interview or could be contested.
3. What angles might you have taken with this interview?

Afterwards, ask each group to report its findings.

Practice Role-Plays

Give each person in the group two résumés: One will be a person they will interview; the other will be a person they will role-play. Make sure each participant-interviewer is a person in the class who will role-play the candidate. Allow fifteen to twenty minutes to plan for a five-minute role-play. Advise the group to use the Interviewer's Guide (Appendix 4) if needed.

Videotape each role-play. After all the interviews are completed, the instructor and the class give the interviewer feedback using the Testing the Interviewer's Effectiveness form (Chapter 13).

1. What was the interviewer's plan?
2. How much time did the interviewer talk vs. listen?
3. Did the interviewer probe with open questions?
4. What strategic reasons did the interviewer have for using closed questions?
5. Did the interviewer use other INtentional listening skills (paraphrase, reflect, summarize, reality test, flip sides)?
6. Did the interviewer "react" to what the candidate said to formulate his or her next question, or did the interviewer ask something unrelated to what the candidate said?
7. Did the interviewer react to the candidate's nonverbal cues?
8. Did the interviewer self-disclose during the interview?
9. Did the interviewer share information about the job?
10. What could this interviewer do to improve?

OTHER TOPICS TO EXPLORE, GIVEN THE NEEDS OF THE PARTICIPANTS

- Evaluating the Interview and Hiring Process (Chapter 4, 10, 13)
- Handling the Most Challenging Interviews (Chapter 14)
- Focusing on Unskilled or Semiskilled Interviews (Chapter 14)
- Conducting and Practicing Team Interviews (Chapter 10)

Appendix 2: Sample Résumés

The following sample résumés may be used to help teach people how to apply the skills in this book. They may be adapted in any way you wish. It is advisable to use résumés that closely approximate the kind of positions you will actually see during the interview process. I've included several different kinds, but if you have your own supply, you'd be advised to adapt them instead.

RÉSUMÉ 1

MARY MORGAN

CURRENT ADDRESS   PERMANENT ADDRESS
477 10th St. NW   11 Narrow Corner
Charlottesville, VA 22903   Greenwood, SC 29646
(804) 977–3215   (803) 223–2189

OBJECTIVE   To secure a position relating to the field of business

EDUCATION   **MacIntire School of Commerce, University of Virginia**
                 Candidate for Bachelor of Science in Commerce, May 1996
                 Minor in biology
                 Cumulative GPA: 3.28   Major GPA 3.58

EXPERIENCE

Ultimate in Food Catering (Dec. 1996–present)
Manager. Met with clients to plan menus and decorations and design floor plans for various events; monitored inventory levels and placed weekly orders from food distributors; designed and co-authored a bimonthly newsletter; initiated a computerized mailing list; light accounting work; prepared and served food.

Greenwood Country Club (Dec. 1995–August 1996)
Waitress. Established strong interpersonal skills; gained efficiency in working in a demanding, fast-paced setting, contributed significantly to the team atmosphere in order to ensure customer satisfaction.

Wishful Jewels (June 1994–August 1995)
Sales Associate. Patiently assisted customers in jewelry purchases and personal jewelry design; gemstone appraisals, developed in-store promotions and newspaper advertisements; designed counter and window displays.

ACTIVITIES

Jefferson House Volunteer, Big Sibling
Planned activities both recreational and educational for under-privileged children in the Charlottesville community.

Inter-Sorority Council, Rho-Chi
Competitively selected to educate and counsel first-year women on the Greek system; Rush process liaison between my sorority and the Inter-Sorority Council.

Delta Delta Sorority, Vice President
Presided over chapter meetings in the president's absence; educated all members on national policies and regulations; leader of Officer's Training Committee; acted as a link between the chapter and nationals; compiled chapter calendar.

RÉSUMÉ 2

JIM MICHALS

University Commons #121   342 Chesterfield Rd.
Wilmington, Delaware   Wilmington, Delaware
(609) 920–6232   (609) 345–5423

CAREER OBJECTIVE   To obtain an entry-level management or management
                    trainee position which allows me to make use of my degree
                    in business and psychology

EDUCATION   UNIVERSITY OF DELAWARE
                    HONORS COLLEGE

                    BA, May 2000
                    GPA 3.7/4.0 Major in Psychology; Minor in Business
                    Administration

HONORS   Dean's List 1997–2000
                    President's List 1995
                    Golden Key National Honor Society 1998–1999
                    Current candidate, Who's Who Among Students in
                    American Colleges and Universities

ACTIVITIES   Treasurer, Psi Chi (Psychology Honor Society) 1997–present
                    Gamma Beta Phi Honor Fraternity (Academic/Service) 1997–
                    present
                    Chapin Recreational League Boys Basketball Coach 1997–
                    1999
                    Intramural Football and Basketball 1997–present

WORK EXPERIENCE

        • DELAWARE STATE SENATE
        Page, 1997 to present (part-time and summers)

        • MERRILL LYNCH, PIERCE, FENNER, & SMITH
        Intern, Summer 1997

        • WILSON, STEWART AND JONES LAW FIRM
        Runner, Summer 1996

PERSONAL DATA   Born in Wilmington, Delaware
                    Interests: literature, local and national politics, sports
                    Willing to relocate and travel

REFERENCES   Available upon request

RÉSUMÉ 3

KERRY PHILLIPS
497 West 123 Street
Brooklyn, NY 10372
(718) 549–2315

SUMMARY: Experience in commercial credit analysis

EXPERIENCE:

Nelson Lewis, Inc.   **7/92–present**

Credit Analyst
- Approve orders and coordinate shipments of materials to over 1200 corporate clients
- Maintain seasonal credit lines totaling over 5 million dollars in sales volume
- Control collection of revenue for more than 100 commercial accounts
- Support sales department in efforts to establish new customers

Smith & Jones, Inc.   **12/90–7/92**

Credit Analyst
- Determined credit and collection policies for major manufacturers and retail chain outlets
- Developed, analyzed, and interpreted financial information obtained from financial institutions and trade references.
- Monitored orders and shipments for over 40 accounts
- Conducted in-field customer visits and meetings to determine credit policy
- Reviewed and approved letters of credit.

Aries Financial, Inc.   **11/87–12/90**

Credit Analyst
- Interacted with manufacturing clients and retailers to ensure proper flow of credit
- Prepared credit reviews on major customers for presentation to credit committee
- Determined credit lines through analysis of financial information
- Coordinated credit investigators in the collection of data
- Supervised the collection of funds and follow-up work necessary

EDUCATION: Manhattan College
                          BS Marketing

REFERENCES: Furnished upon request

RÉSUMÉ 4

Diane Brooks

14332 Addison Street #11, Sherman Oaks, CA 91423
Home Phone (818) 990–1889

Employment: **Account Manager**
Milstone Envelope Corporation, Los Angeles, CA
9/97–Present
- Manage and increase sales in existing accounts
- Solicit new accounts through customer relations and sales presentations
- Prepare quotes and contracts for new and existing clients
- Consult clients on envelope design and postal regulations
- Increased sales within current accounts by 20% in the first quarter
- New clients include: U.S.C., Nabisco, Seaboard, Coca-Cola and J. Paul Getty

Sales Director
Forward Thinking Financial Services, San Diego, CA
7/90–8/97
- Managed and coordinated marketing/sales on a daily basis
- Responsible for training and developing 10 sales representatives
- Qualified, developed, and sold new and current clients
- Prepared seminar presentations on delinquent accounts
- Increased sales territory throughout California (120% to objective)
- Expanded business in states of WA, OR, AZ, NV (New business sales 125% to objective, renewal sales 130% to objective)
- Prepared budget proposals, negotiated contracts, and determined cost analysis of products
- Sales representative of the year 1991 and 1992. Promoted to sales director in 1993

Sales/Marketing Manager
Total Education Company, Los Angeles, CA
9/87–4/90
Responsibilities included: Marketing, advertising, sales and client relations, implemented programs with management personnel and corporations.

Marketing Analyst
Southern California Gas Company, Los Angeles, CA
9/78–6/87
Responsibilities included: Marketing and sales of new products for
residential and commercial customers; consulting customers on
productive methods of using natural gas in a cost effective
manner

Education: B.A. Business Administration, California State University, Los
Angeles, 1984

RÉSUMÉ 5

Teresa Lynn Cason
4321 West Astor Dr.
Raleigh, NC 27604
Phone Number—919-981-4318

Education

North Carolina State University's
Masters of Science in Management
Technical option - Management Information Systems;
Minor - Statistics G.P.A. 3.13/4.00. December 1998

8/84–12/89

Bachelor of Science degree in Information Systems
Management conferred from the **University of Maryland**
Baltimore County December of 1996 (G.P.A. 3.11/4.00)

Software/Hardware

Operating Systems		**Hardware**
Vax/Vms		IBM personal computer
DOS 3.1		Amdahl
Unix		Vax

Programming Languages

Fortran 77	Pascal	Cobol I
Cobol II	IDEAL	Basic
TDMS	ACMS	FDU
Dbase III	Dbase IV	Clipper
VG-LIMS	ZPL	HTML
	C++	

Software Packages	**Query Languages**	
Wordperfect 5.1	RDO	Dbase III
Lotus 123	SQL	Dbase IV
Professional Write	IDEAL	
Microsoft Word 6.0		
Microsoft Excel		
PowerPoint		

Professional
Experience
1/99–present

North Carolina State University
Raleigh, North Carolina
Graduate Assistant

Duties included grading papers and developing
management reports via Excel, Word and PowerPoint

1/90–3/94   **Dow Chemical Company**
                   Rochester, New York
                   Systems Analyst

                   Duties included but were not limited to:
                   • analyzing systems for computerized implementation,
                   • designing systems for computerized implementation,
                   • writing session narratives for end-users,
                   • holding meetings to finalize session narratives with end-
                     users,
                   • participating in peer reviews of system's program/
                     programs and documentation,
                   • testing program/programs in the test environment,
                   • finalizing program/programs for the production
                     environment (shop-floor usage),
                   • writing end-user documentation for training,
                   • answering all questions pertaining to the usage and
                     implementation of the system installed.

                   Project Leader

                   Duties included but were not limited to:
                   • self-instruction of VG-LIMS software and concepts,
                   • analyzing laboratory operations for computerized
                     implementation,
                   • designing laboratory system for computerized
                     implementation,
                   • writing session narratives for end-users,
                   • holding meetings to finalize session narratives with end-
                     users,
                   • writing program/programs as specified by end-users
                     session narratives,
                   • participating in peer reviews of system's program/
                     programs and documentation,
                   • testing program/programs in the test environment,
                   • finalizing program/programs for the production
                     environment (shop-floor usage),
                   • writing end-user documentation for system,
                   • teaching a two-day course on the usage of the system in
                     the laboratory.

Qualities   Ambitious, Determined, and Dependable

Interests   Writing, Walking, Traveling, Reading, and Volunteering
                   (presently working for Habitat for Humanity)

References   Excellent references available upon request

RÉSUMÉ 6

JACK STEPHENS
PO Box 221
Auburn, AL
(205) 321–9932

OBJECTIVE   Interested in an Electrical Engineering position in a stimulating work environment

PROFILE

- **Problem solver, team player with proven leadership qualities**
- **Management experience**
- **Excellent written, oral, and interpersonal communication skills**
- **Works well with fellow employees, flexible and dependable**

EDUCATION

Auburn University, Auburn, AL
BEE, Electrical Engineering, December 1996

EXPERIENCE

12/97–present   **WIRELINE & TESTING, Casper, WY**
Field Engineer
- Perform daily field engineer operations
- Utilize Maxis 500 system to acquire geological data for clients
- Supervise daily operations of a three man crew
- Administer district safety and radiation program

03/96–12/97   **ALABAMA AGRICULTURAL EXPERIMENT STATION RESEARCH INSTRUMENTATION, Auburn, AL**
Instrumentation Assistant part-time
- Perform work on agricultural research projects
- Trouble shoot and repair equipment

06–95–09–95   **LOCKHEED MARTIN ENERGY SYSTEMS, Oak Ridge, TN**
Engineer Cooperative Education (Q Clearance)
- Install software and hardware for assay stations
- Assist in program management for the development of leak test stations
- Program Allen-Bradley controllers for test ovens

COMPUTER SKILLS

Hardware: Macintosh, IBM PC's, Sun Workstations, Scanners, Vax/VMS
Language: Assembly, Fortran, Quick Basic

HONORS

Who's Who Among Students in American Universities & Colleges
John C. Tucker Scholar
Alpha Phi Alpha/Omicron Kappa Chapter Leadership Award 1995

ACTIVITIES

President Alpha Phi Alpha Fraternity, Inc., Omicron Kappa Chapter;
President National PanHellenic Council; Mentor, Alpha Phi Alpha, Auburn
Junior High Mentor Program; Career Awareness Committee Chair, National
Society of Engineers.

RÉSUMÉ 7

PAUL STUGS
313 Callie Street, Suite W
Orangeburg, South Carolina 29115
(803) 535–7765

CAREER OBJECTIVE: To utilize expertise in mathematics while broadening knowledge of statistical research and analysis.

QUALIFICATIONS: Excellent college training and a solid mathematics background. Good analyst and problem solver. Very disciplined with a great desire to learn.

EDUCATION: **SOUTH CAROLINA STATE UNIVERSITY**
Orangeburg, SC
Bachelor of Science Degree, Mathematics, May 1999
GPA 2.9

WORK HISTORY: **WALMART INCORPORATED**
Orangeburg, SC   3/97–present
Garden Center Sales Associate: Advise customers on healthy and attractive lawns and gardens. Maintain a beautiful array of plants, flowers and other outdoor accessories.

BLACKS INCORPORATED
Klinko's
Orangeburg, SC   9/97–1/98
Cashier: Provided outstanding service, attention, and satisfaction to customers by addressing their needs.

SOUTH CAROLINA STATE UNIVERSITY
Bass Residence Hall
Orangeburg, SC   8/95–5/96
Dormitory Counselor/Resident Advisor: Maintained reasonable level of order throughout the residence hall. Addressed concerns of residents, parents, and university personnel. Made responsible decisions in a myriad of situations while always keeping the best interests of all parties involved.

BI-LO INCORPORATED
Statesboro, GA   6/94–8/95

Courtesy Clerk: Packaged customer's goods, and kept store in sanitary condition.
Produce Attendant: Inspected produce for freshness, maintained clean department, and created vivid fruit and vegetable dishes.
Cashier: Understood customer's concerns and desires. Maintained composure while responding patiently and professionally to customer's needs.

AFFILIATIONS: Omega Psi Phi Fraternity, Inc.
Student Government Association

RÉSUMÉ 8

RICHARD M. GREEN

Current Address
4321 Wabash Ave, Box 621
Terre Haute, IN 47803

e-mail: greenr@nextwork.rose.hulman.edu

Objective:	Employment in a field utilizing my chemical engineering education and interpersonal skills.
Education:	Rose-Hulman Institute of Technology, Terre Haute, IN **BS Chemical Engineering**, May 1998 GPA: 3.1/4.0 Current Status: Senior
Relevant Courses:	Chemical Engineering Statistics, Air Pollution Control
Skills:	Statistical Analysis Program: Minitab Spreadsheets: Excel, Quattro Pro Symbolic Math Programs: Mathematics, Maple V
Experience:	Rose-Hulman Institute of Technology, Terre Haute, IN **Resident Assistant** August 1997–Present – Manage a residence hall of 76 students – Provide academic and personal counseling – Organize hall and campus wide programs **Learning Center Office Manager/Tutor** September 1996–Present – Report to professors on individual students' tutoring progress – Payroll, keep record of tutors' hours and wages **Operation Catapult Counselor** Summer 1996, 1997 – Advised high school seniors on technical aspects of engineering projects – Organized team activities for groups of 10–90 students – Participate in recruitment process; presented information on Rose-Hulman to students and provided feedback to admissions staff on individual students
Honors:	Elks National Scholarship, Tri Kappa Scholarship, 10 year 4-H member, Dean's List three times (twice in Junior year)
Activities:	National Society of Engineers: Vice President American Institute of Chemical Engineers Rose-Hulman Pep Band 1997 Career Fair Organization Team

Appendix 3: Sample Forms

The following sample forms appear throughout the text. I've included them in an appendix so you may copy them to use in developing your strategic interviewing process.

DETERMINE YOUR CORPORATE CULTURE

To determine your company's phase of development, answer the following questions:

1. Over the past five years, what has been the rate of growth (human and profit)?
2. List the behaviors that reap rewards. (Examine the people that are promoted. What qualities do they possess?)
3. What do others say are the qualities that make your company successful?
4. How do people respond to errors?
5. How often do conflicts arise?
6. What happens during a conflict?
7. How do people dress?
8. What amount of time do people spend communicating?
9. How much meeting time is spent looking at past history versus creating new policies and procedures?
10. How do people feel about the future of the organization and their job security?

RÉSUMÉ SCREENING

From the résumé do the following:

1. List the candidate's knowledge and experiences in relation to the skills you're looking for.

2. What knowledge or experiences are missing in relation to the skills you're looking for?

3. How does it appear the candidate interacts with others?

4. Would you recommend this person for an interview? If yes,

   a. What would you use as an icebreaker in this interview?

   b. What probe points do you want to explore with this candidate?

   c. Develop two questions that would help you extract the type of information you need to help you reach a decision.

CANDIDATE EVALUATION

Rate the candidate with a number on each of the six attributes below.
1–5 Scale: 1 = Highest, 5 = Lowest

1. Communication:	Expressive/ listens	True empathy	Confident in speech	_____
2. Organization:	Plans well	Takes initiative	Systematic	_____
3. Leadership:	Directs	Takes an active role	Inspires	_____
4. Decision Making:	Decisive	Gets results	Implements ideas	_____
5. Responsibility/ Maturity:	Self-confident	Dependable	Sets priorities	_____
6. Assertiveness:	Fair but firm	Takes action	Shows empathy	_____

Using the scale above, how would the candidate fit in the organization?
_____

EVALUATE THE INTERVIEWER

1. What was the interviewer's plan?
2. How much time did the interviewer talk versus listen?
3. Did the interviewer probe with open questions?
4. What strategic reasons did the interviewer have for asking closed questions?
5. Did the interviewer use other INtentional listening skills (paraphrase, reflect, summarize, reality test, flip sides)?
6. Did the interviewer "react" to what the candidate said to formulate his or her next question, or did the interviewer ask something unrelated to what the candidate said?
7. How did the interviewer react to the candidate's nonverbal cues?
8. Did the interviewer self-disclose during the interview?
9. Did the interviewer share information about the job?
10. What could this interviewer do to improve?
11. If you had to grade this interviewer, what grade would you give?

TEST THE INTERVIEW PROCESS

1. Who are the people most affected by this vacant position? Are these people part of your interview team?

2. Did your team study the résumés and applications separately or together?

3. Did your team examine the position and identify the organizational culture?

4. Did your team identify the qualities needed to successfully perform the functions of this position?

5. How many people within your organization need to interview this candidate? If more than eight, did your team organize and plan team interviews?

6. What visual messages about your organization do you want to send? How did you set up ways for the candidate to experience those messages?

7. Did someone in your organization make contact with the candidate to give him or her directions and make arrangements for the visit?

8. Did your team avoid asking similar questions by focusing on particular areas and by tagging each other at the end of interviews to help build consistency from one interview to the next?

9. Did team members refrain from sharing their impressions as they escorted the candidate from one interviewer to the next?

10. Did you avoid interviewing the candidate during meals?

11. Did the candidate have a chance to visit with people he or she might supervise?

12. Did the candidate have a chance to visit with peers?

13. Were the interviews conducted in a timely fashion?

14. At the conclusion of the process, did the interview team meet together to share the results of their interviews?

Appendix 4:
The Interviewer's Guide

This format is only one model for carrying on an interview. The important thing to remember is to ask questions which are relevant to the job or which elicit information which is relevant to the job.

Prior to carrying out any interviews, make sure you identify the specific skills, education, and character you are looking for in the successful candidate.

No single strategic interview would address all the areas listed in this guide.

TRANSITION AND PUTTING THE CANDIDATE AT EASE

- *How did you happen to become interested in our company, organization?*
- *What do you know about our organization?*

Begin by reviewing the pieces of information on the resume, i.e., confirm current permanent address and telephone numbers. "We will have a chance to discuss your work and school experiences in more detail later in the interview."

OVERVIEW

Before we get started, let me give you some idea of what I'd like to cover today. I want to review your background and experience so that we can decide whether our company has the opportunity suited for your talents and interests. I'd like to hear about your jobs, education, interests, outside activities, and anything else you want to tell.

ICEBREAKER

I noticed on your application that you play hockey. I'm a great hockey fan, but there aren't many of us around . . .

WORK EXPERIENCE

I'm interested in your work experience and the jobs you've held: your likes, dislikes, responsibilities, and what you've learned from them. Let's start with your most recent job experience. (Cover all jobs including part-time or temporary, military assignments, and volunteer work.)

Potential Probe Areas

- Things liked best
- Things liked least
- Major accomplishments
- What was learned from job
- Difficult problems faced
- Ways most effective with people
- Skill level with systems
- Ways least effective with people
- Types of challenges
- Reasons for changing jobs
- Preferred job environment
- Expectations for job
- Dealing with troublesome people

EDUCATION (particularly for people just finishing school)

You've given me a good review of your work experience. Now let's talk about your education. I'm interested in the subjects you preferred, your grades, outside activities, and anything else of importance.

Potential Probe Points

- Subject liked best
- Subject liked least
- Reaction to teachers
- Choosing major

- Specialized training
- Toughest courses
- Major achievements
- Extracurricular activities
- Relation of education and career
- Future educational plans

LEADERSHIP

You've belonged to several professional organizations. What leadership positions did you have?

Potential Probe Points

- Offices held in civic, volunteer, church organizations
- Coaching sports teams for adults or children
- Supervision of workers
- Informal group leader at work or outside

ACTIVITIES AND INTERESTS

I'd like to hear about your interests and activities outside work and school. (Discuss interests, hobbies, civic and community involvement, geographical preferences, and any personal limitations which may prevent them from meeting any of the job requirements.)

Potential Probe Points

- Spare time activities
- Hobbies and interests
- Community involvement
- Learning from activities
- Reaction to specific job requirements such as:
    - Travel
    - Relocation
    - Overtime
    - Weekend work
    - Shift work

SELF-ASSESSMENT

Assets: *Now let's try to summarize our conversation. Thinking about what we've covered today, what would you say are some of your strengths? What would you say are some of the qualities, both personal and professional, that make you a good prospective employee for our company?*

Potential Probe Points

- Contributions made
- Talents
- Abilities
- Best qualities seen by others
- Assets in working with others

Development Needs: *You've given me some real assets and now I'd like to hear about areas you would like to develop further. All of us have qualities we'd like to change or improve on. What are some of yours?*

Potential Probe Points

- Areas for improvement
- Qualities to develop
- Further training or experience
- Recent performance review
- Advice received from others

TRANSITION QUESTION TO INFORMATION-GIVING PHASE*

You've given me a good review of your background and experience and I have enjoyed talking with you. Before we turn to my review of our organization and the job is there anything else about your background you'd like to cover?

PRESENTING INFORMATION AND ANSWERING QUESTIONS*

What specific questions or concerns do you have before I give you some information?

Potential Probe Points

- What concerns do you have?
- What questions do you have about our company?
- What interests you most about the job?

- What interests you most about our company?

TELL ABOUT*

- Career opportunities
- Stability
- Educational opportunities
- Challenges
- Salary
- Benefits

CLOSING

What other questions do you have about our company, the job, or anything else?
Let me review the next steps . . .
(End of interview) *I want to thank you for coming today.*

NOTE

*These items should be covered throughout the interview rather than saved for the end.

Selected Readings

Alessandra, Tony. *Charisma: Seven Keys to Developing Magnetism that Leads to Success*. New York: Time Warner Books, 1998.

Brewer, James H., Ainsworth, J. Michael, and Wynne, George W. *Power Management: A Three-Step Program for Successful Leadership*. Englewood Cliffs, NJ: Prentice-Hall, Inc., 1984.

Butler, Pamela F. *Self Assertion for Women*. San Francisco: Harper & Row Publishers, 1981.

Hacker, Carol A. *The Costs of Bad Hiring Decisions and How to Avoid Them*. Delray Beach, FL: St. Lucie Press, 1996.

Luft, Joseph. *Group Processes: An Introduction to Group Dynamics Third Edition*. San Francisco: Mayfield Publishing Company, 1984.

Olson, Richard, F. *Managing the Interview*. New York: John Wiley & Sons, Inc., 1980.

Raines, Claire. *Beyond Generation X: A Practical Guide for Managers*. Menlo Park, CA: Crisp Publications, 1997.

Schultz, William C. "The Interpersonal Underworld." *Harvard Business Review* 36 (1958): 123–135.

Smalley, Larry. *Interviewing and Selecting High Performers*. Irvine, CA: Richard Chang Associates, Inc., 1997.

Wersch, Mary Ann. *Interviewer Guide for Supervisors*. Washington, DC: College and University Personnel Association, 1998.

Yate, Martin John. *Hiring the Best: A Manager's Guide to Effective Interviewing*. Boston: Bob Adams, Inc., 1987.

Index

About the Author

JOAN C. CURTIS manages her own consulting firm, Executive Expertise, in Athens, Georgia. She is a specialist in developing and presenting communication and motivation seminars throughout the country, and has held various positions in training and development capacities, including Director of Management Development at the University of Georgia. She also spends a great deal of time facilitating team building and goal setting retreats for elected, appointed, and volunteer boards as well as upper management teams.